Distributed Objects

Distributed Objects
Methodologies for Customizing Systems Software

Nayeem Islam

IEEE Computer Society Press
Los Alamitos, California
Washington • Brussels • Tokyo

Library of Congress Cataloging-in-Publication Data

Islam, Nayeem.
Distributed objects: methodologies for customizing systems software / Nayeem Islam.
p. cm.
Includes bibliographical references.
ISBN 0-8186-7193-9
1. Operating systems (Computers) 2. Object-oriented programming (Computer science) 3. Application software. I. Title.
QA76.76.O63I75 1996
005.4′2–dc20

95-36600
CIP

IEEE Computer Society Press
10662 Los Vaqueros Circle
P.O. Box 3014
Los Alamitos, CA 90720-1264

IEEE Computer Society Press Order Number BP07193
Library of Congress Number 95-36600
ISBN 0-8186-7193-9

Additional copies may be ordered from:

IEEE Computer Society Press
Customer Service Center
10662 Los Vaqueros Circle
P.O. Box 3014
Los Alamitos, CA 90720-1264
Tel: +1-714-821-8380
Fax: +1-714-821-4641
Email: cs.books@computer.org

IEEE Service Center
445 Hoes Lane
P.O. Box 1331
Piscataway, NJ 08855-1331
Tel: +1-908-981-1393
Fax: +1-908-981-9667
mis.custserv@computer.org

IEEE Computer Society
13, Avenue de l'Aquilon
B-1200 Brussels
BELGIUM
Tel: +32-2-770-2198
Fax: +32-2-770-8505
euro.ofc@computer.org

IEEE Computer Society
Ooshima Building
2-19-1 Minami-Aoyama
Minato-ku, Tokyo 107
JAPAN
Tel: +81-3-3408-3118
Fax: +81-3-3408-3553
tokyo.ofc@computer.org

Assistant Publisher: Matt Loeb
Editor-in-Chief: Mohamed E. Fayad
Acquisitions Assistant: Cheryl Smith
Advertising/Promotions: Tom Fink
Cover Artist: Alex Torres

Printed in the United States of America by BookCrafters, Inc.

The Institute of Electrical and Electronics Engineers, Inc

Contents

Foreword

The computer industry is rallying around two major goals: distributed applications and mass customization. In recent years, the move toward distributed computing has been very strong. The number of enterprises that use distributed applications to run their core business functions grows at a staggering rate. Standards such as OpenDoc/CORBA and OLE/COM, and technologies such as Sun Microsystem's Java, are making it possible to fulfill the vision that the network is the computer. Concepts such as autonomous, intelligent agents that roam networks in search of resources are no longer theoretical research projects.

The two forces driving the move toward mass customization are customer demand and development cost. Customer demand for customizable systems has become so common as to be unnoticed. The days of fixed-function terminals with hard-wired, menu-driven applications are over. All the great "killer apps," such as Lotus 1-2-3 and object-oriented user interfaces, have a major similarity: they empower their users. Customers are willing to pay for software that puts them in control.

The other force driving the industry toward mass customization is development cost. As the complexity of software systems increases, it has become almost impossible for developers to create the ideal mix of user interface, infrastructure and performance in the first version. The ever increasing gap between the concept and the solution has outstripped our ability to perform requirements analysis. In many cases, we simply cannot know what the customer will want when we are done. The only viable response is therefore to build changeability into the fabric of our systems. The software must be able to adapt to requirements changes made late in the life cycle. Our software must be soft.

Object-oriented design patterns and object-oriented frameworks have been successfully applied to these problems; however, the combination of high-performance distributed applications with mass customization is still an art form. The industry needs resources to help navigate these relatively uncharted waters. The book you hold in your hands is such a resource. It describes how high-performance distributed systems that exhibit a large degree of mass customization can be designed and constructed using object-oriented design patterns. For example, traditional attempts to achieve mass customization have caused performance degradation; this book shows how to exploit mass customization as a means of *improving* performance.

The advice provided in this book makes a valuable contribution to the literature. It distills the state of the art into the state of practice. I trust the industry will benefit from the author's combination of distributed computing, mass customization, and object-oriented technology as much as I did.

Marshall P. Cline, Ph.D., President
Paradigm Shift, Inc.

Despite dramatic increases in the performance of networks and computers, designing and implementing software for distributed and parallel operating systems remains enormously complex. Substantial investments of time, effort, and expense are typically necessary to develop these types of systems. Moreover, due to the growing diversity of hardware and software, it is hard to directly reuse existing algorithms, designs, interfaces, or implementations in these systems. Thus, all too often, large-scale parallel and distributed operating systems fail to meet their performance, functionality, and cost requirements.

Much of the complexity of building distributed and parallel operating systems stems from the need for the system software to be highly flexible and highly efficient. Flexibility is needed to respond rapidly to the changing requirements of next-generation applications that span an ever-growing range of multimedia services. Efficiency is needed to support the quality of service demands of performance-sensitive applications—such as interactive teleconferencing, scientific visualization, and medical imaging—that possess stringent throughput and delay requirements.

Traditional methods for building operating systems are increasingly inadequate, since they utilize monolithic designs and implementations. Monolithic systems try to integrate every conceivable type of service into a single inflexible interface. This procrustean approach yields complex operating systems that are hard to implement correctly, difficult to port and extend without considerable effort and expense, and incapable of efficiently supporting new services (such as voice, video, and image processing).

In this book, Nayeem Islam presents a more flexible methodology for developing next-generation operating systems and thoroughly illustrates the benefits of these methods with extensive examples and empirical studies. Nayeem makes two important contributions to the study and practice of distributed and parallel operating systems. First, he precisely describes how object-oriented programmers can customize operating systems with strategies that utilize application attributes (such as communication patterns, reliability requirements, or concurrency constraints) to optimize system performance. Second, he presents in-depth coverage of the strategies and tactics used in an industrial-strength C++ framework that orchestrates these customize strategies to facilitate flexible implementation choices.

The benefits of software customization have long been applied successfully in application domains such as graphical user interfaces. However, Nayeem's book is the first to demonstrate how customization can be applied successfully in the systems software domain, which has traditionally emphasized raw performance over flexibility and extensibility. What impresses me most is Nayeem's sophisticated understanding and use of object-oriented frameworks. These frameworks capture the common structural and behavioral abstractions of the operating system domain, while allowing programmers the flexibility to reconfigure and extend the system dynamically. Most importantly, the astute principles and patterns presented by Nayeem can be reused to construct reliable, modular, extensible, and efficient object-oriented frameworks for many other systems software domains such as embedded systems, telecommunication systems, and transaction processing systems.

Expert object-oriented systems developers rarely take time off from building systems to write such an outstanding book. We are fortunate that a pioneering book about customizable distributed and parallel object-oriented operating systems has been written by an expert in the field. If you want concise and comprehensive coverage of the object-oriented development methods and techniques that will shape next-generation systems software, read this book. I've learned much from it, and I am confident that you will too.

Douglas C. Schmidt
Washington University

Preface

Message-passing systems allow architecture-independent parallel and distributed programming. On particular hardware architectures, however, performance is an important issue for parallel and distributed applications. Restructuring parallel message-passing applications using better parallel decompositions can improve their performance [KGGK94]. Even after such restructuring has been performed, however, and the most appropriate parallel decomposition performed by an application programmer, for communication-intensive applications a significant amount of the application's execution time may still be spent in the message-passing system.

An inadequacy of many current message-passing systems is that they do not take a global view of using application communication patterns to increase performance. For example, for parallel applications running on a local area network there are numerous ways to guarantee reliable message delivery since local area networks can lose messages. The popular message-passing library Parallel Virtual Machine (PVM) [Sun90] employs an alternative that generates an acknowledgment message for each application-level message. This is efficient for an application that uses a single asynchronous message transmission, but it is inefficient for request-response [Che88a] and more complex communication styles [BPG+94]. A global view of the communication patterns in an application can generate fewer overall network messages by piggybacking acknowledgments on regular communications or by using a single acknowledgment for a group of messages. Such optimizations can improve the performance of applications on distributed systems.

Experiments demonstrate that these message-passing system optimizations are highly application dependent; that is, communication patterns vary from application to application. A single message-passing implementation therefore cannot perform well for all applications. This suggests the need for customized message-passing systems: An optimized message-passing system is custom built for each application. To maximize application performance, the subsystems of an operating system, such as its message-passing system, must be tailored to the needs of the application.

The optimization problem for message-passing applications is not limited to distributed systems; it appears in other architectures. The performance of message-passing applications on a bus-based, shared-memory multiprocessor is also dependent on application communication patterns. For example, there are a variety of ways to implement multicast on a shared-memory multiprocessor, but a naive implementation using shared variables will be slower than one using explicit data copying because it suffers from contention for the multicast buffer.

Similarly, application-specific scheduling improves the performance of applications on both distributed and shared-memory multiprocessor systems. In particular, gang scheduling is generalized for parallel applications on both types of systems. Distributed gang scheduling reduces the variability of execution times in parallel applications and allows the easy transition of distributed systems from special purpose to general purpose.

To generate application-specific optimizations, a set of characterizing attributes of applications is presented in this book. These attributes are determined by examining a representative class of parallel and distributed applications, and the usefulness of each attribute is determined experimentally. Each attribute guides the minimization of operating system overhead. For example, communication pattern is an application attribute that reveals how to generate message-passing systems on unreliable networks to minimize the number of acknowledgment messages, thus reducing operating system overhead.

A sample tool kit of implementations is also presented to exploit the set of application attributes. When an optimized message-passing system is required for a new application, the attributes of the application dictate how best to use the tool kit to minimize overhead. For example, given a multicast communication pattern in a distributed-system application, the attributes select an implementation that minimizes the number of acknowledgment messages. The tool kit is extensible, and new optimizations can be incorporated.

Optimization results are presented for both parallel and distributed applications. The parallel applications studied include Simplex and adaptive quadrature. The distributed applications are client-server programs used in distributed system services including name servers and distributed schedulers. Although only a small number of attributes characterize the applications studied, the combinations of these attributes lead to many possible implementations.

Since there is a large number of different optimizations, they are organized using an extensible object-oriented framework. An alternative would be to embed the optimizations in a compiler; however, compilers customarily do not generate message-passing system implementations for the programs they compile. Message-passing libraries such as PVM [Sun90] and Express [Cor88] and the message-passing primitives of operating systems such as V [Che88a], Mach [Lop91], and Amoeba [TvRvS+90] are difficult to extend with multiple optimizations because there is no methodology for incrementally adding new algorithms and techniques. Object-oriented frameworks directly support incremental, per-application specializations. They also allow easy porting of the message-passing and scheduling system to new hardware architectures.

The object paradigm supports an implementation technology that directly captures the structure of objects in an application domain, making the transition from design to implementation easier than in other approaches. Object-oriented programming techniques have been used extensively for application programs and some popular object-oriented application frameworks exist, but there is a dearth of such frameworks for systems software. Traditionally, operating systems designers have been reluctant to use object-oriented frameworks because the languages used to implement them performed poorly. With the availability of efficient compilers for object-oriented languages such as C++, however, it is possible to build efficient object-oriented operating systems.

The object-oriented framework approach classifies the components used in customized schemes into a few of basic components that can be represented by classes. These classes are organized into class hierarchies. The class hierarchies include components for a variety of message-passing and scheduling primitives and implementations of those primitives. For any application, the message-passing and scheduling system support is customized by selecting a combination of components based on application attributes. Two types of subclassing are presented: one for functionality, which is common in object-oriented systems; and the other for performance, which is less common in most system designs. This book presents the use of objects in system software, an area in which software engineers have traditionally shied away from using objects. But objects are a natural way of implementing an operating system that is designed to be customizable.

Since C++ has certain deficiencies for designing large-scale systems, library support is included to help in the construction of large-scale C++ programs. This support includes first-class classes, dynamic code loading, and first-class frameworks. A system shell design is presented that allows one to view the design of the operating system at runtime.

The notion of customized implementations for operating systems is not new. Haberman et al. [HFC72] recognized the need for systems with multiple implementations and introduced the concept of a family of operating systems. Each family member is designed for a set of applications with similar attributes. This book takes Haberman's notion one step further by advocating the use of an operating system customized for each application.

The customized operating approach grew out of the author's work on the object-oriented operating system Choices. Readers interested in the Choices operating system will find more information in the reference list [CI93a, CIM92, CIMR93].

This book discusses research in the design of operating systems, parallel programming techniques, and software engineering. Five main topics are discussed in this book.

1. New message-passing optimizations for applications running on a distributed system of unreliable networks.
2. New message-passing optimizations for applications running on a bus-based, shared-memory multiprocessor.
3. Optimized scheduling for applications on both a distributed system and a shared-memory multiprocessor.
4. The characterization of a set of parallel and distributed applications to determine the attributes relevant to the construction of optimized message-passing and scheduling systems.
5. A software architecture that uses object-oriented frameworks to manage the multiple message-passing and scheduling systems and organize them for selection. The frameworks allow easy porting of the message-passing and scheduling systems to new architectures.

OUTLINE OF THE BOOK

Because of this book describes a methodology for building customized system software using object-oriented frameworks, it will appeal to practicing software engineers who build large software systems that must be customized to suit the specific needs of a customer or an environment. For those building embedded systems, the book demonstrates how generic objects can be systematically specialized to solve specific problems. Since the customization methodology has been used in an area in which customization is not normally used (that is, operating systems and system software) it has been stress tested. While traditional customization has been used to provide appropriate functionality, this book demonstrates how one might customize objects for performance. The book also presents detailed performance experiments to show that the customization approach presented does not adversely affect application performance.

The book will be of value to graduate students studying operating systems, parallel programming, and object-oriented programming. Of particular interest to the graduate student is the way in which the three areas of computer science are integrated. The book also includes a discussion chapter that will be useful to anyone who wants an introduction to the area of customized system software.

The approach advocated in this book is not limited to operating systems per se. A general customization methodology is presented that can be used in a variety of applications and middleware domains, including real-time software, client-server software, and embedded systems. Increasingly, customers are demanding customized solutions; hence, the techniques discussed in this book will be useful to practitioners in those areas as well. In particular, the methodology closely ties code to customer requirements. This link is missing from many methodologies and was chosen because it allows code to be developed quickly.

A road map of the material covered in this book is shown in Figure P.1. Chapter 1 describes the optimization methodology; it discusses the types of applications and system customizations covered in this book. This chapter describes the steps that a programmer must follow in order to create a customized system for an application. Chapter 2 describes the software engineering methodology that is used in coding the system customization. It describes object-oriented frameworks, and techniques for creating customized software in C++. This chapter contains many useful programming tips for engineering large systems in C++. This chapter will be of interest to object-oriented programmers.

Chapter 3 presents the attributes of parallel and distributed applications that are used to design and implement optimized message-passing and scheduling systems on a bus-based, shared-memory multiprocessor and a distributed system. This chapter will be of interest to parallel programmers.

Chapter 4 describes how to select optimizations in the message-passing system framework using the application attributes described in Chapter 3. Chapter 5 describes the major abstractions in the message-passing framework and demonstrates the use of the techniques described in Chapter 2. These two chapters will be of interest to researchers in object-oriented design and programming, and to those designing and implementing communication systems for an operating system.

The optimizations for message passing on distributed systems appear in Chapters 6 and 7. Chapter 6 discusses the general methodology for generating message-passing optimizations on distributed systems and how to use the various optimizations. Chapter 7 presents parallel application performance results on a distributed system and the performance of distributed system services. Chapters 8 and 9 discuss optimized message passing on a bus-based, shared-memory multiprocessor. Chapter 8 describes details of optimization selection on a bus-based, shared-memory multiprocessor, and Chapter 9 presents application performance.

Chapter 10 describes the design and implementation of optimized scheduling systems. This chapter discusses a generalization of gang scheduling on a distributed system and a bus-based, shared-memory multiprocessor. Chapter 11 presents a detailed discussion of related approaches to customizations of systems software. Chapter 12 draws conclusions from the work presented in this book and identifies avenues for future research.

Appendix A describes the hardware architectures of the distributed system and the bus-based, shared-memory multiprocessor on which the experiments discussed in this book were conducted. Appendix B lists the programming interfaces used for parallel applications. The glossary lists terms relating to object-oriented programming, parallel systems, and operating system the are used in the book.

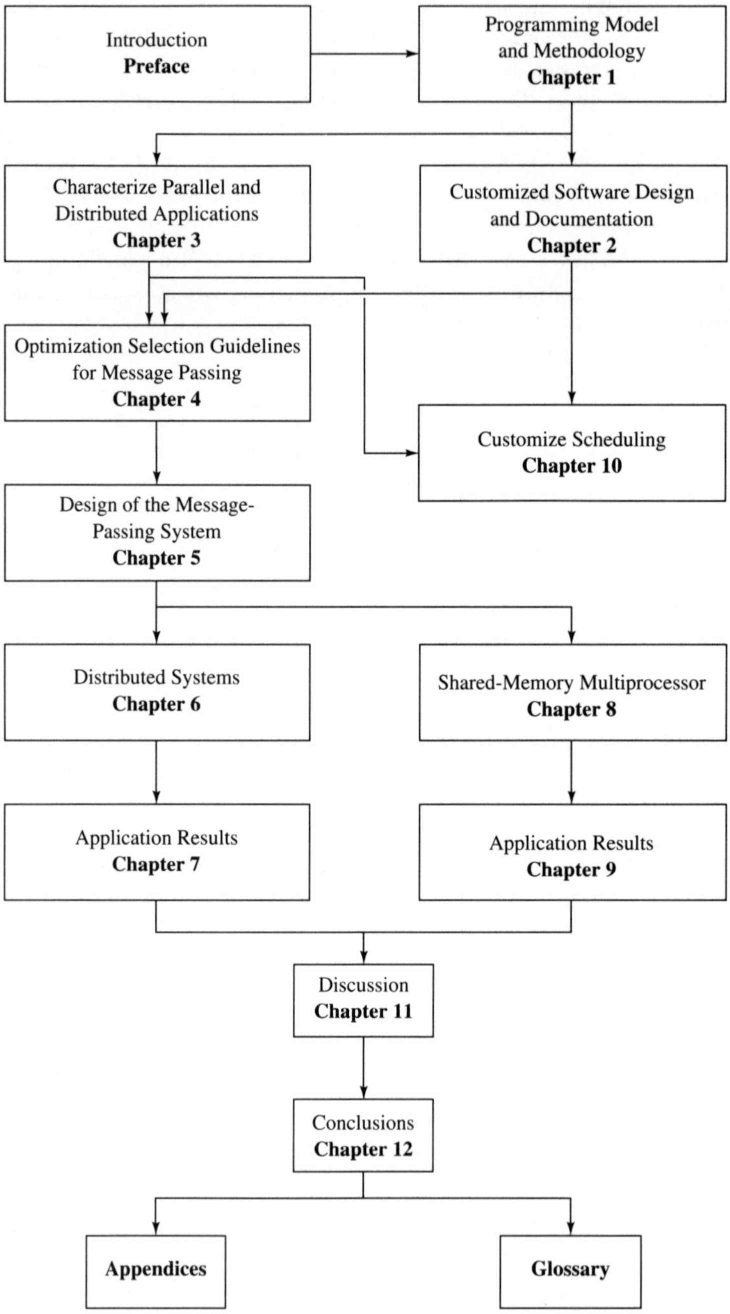

FIGURE P.1 A guide to the book.

Chapters of Particular Interest to Operating Systems Programmers. Chapters 6 and 7 will be of particular interest to distributed operating systems designers and implementers. Chapters 8 and 9 will be of particular interest to operating systems designers of shared-memory parallel systems.

Chapters of Particular Interest to Parallel Systems Programmers. Chapters 3, 6, 7, 8, 9, and Section 4.2 contain material of interest to parallel application writers and parallel system designers. Those interested in the performance issues of the message-passing system are referred to Chapters 6, 7, 8, and 9.

Chapters of Particular Interest to Object-Oriented Programmers. Those interested in object-oriented design issues are referred to Chapters 2, 5, and 10.

ACKNOWLEDGMENTS

It is impossible to list all of the people who have influenced this book in some way and there are many contributors to this book, both direct and indirect. Much of the research and work presented in this book is an outgrowth of my Ph.D. thesis at the University of Illinois. My advisor, Roy Campbell, gave me the freedom to take my own path. He was always receptive to my ideas no matter how wild and wacky they were. He read many early drafts of this book and provided extremely valuable comments. Daniel Reed provided me with a lot of technical advice on parallel computing and performance analysis. He always urged me to be precise in my writing. Gul Agha always provided me with very useful advice about how to make my book more appropriate for a larger audience. Andrew Chien provided many insightful ideas on how to implement message passing on funky hardware. Many professors at the Univerisity of Illinois had an effect on this work, including Simon Kaplan, Duncan Lawrie, and Ralph Johnson. Don Batory at the University of Texas at Austin took a keen interest in my work on framework design and documentation.

Mohamed Fayad showed a keen interest in my work when I was a graduate student and helped enormously in the many details involved in publishing. His guidance and support have made this book better.

Many people have helped me improve the technical clarity and readability of this book. Peter Madany read various versions of my manuscript and provided valuable advice. I have appreciated his candid evaluations. Many algorithms and ideas were perfected working with Amitabh Dave. The sharp mind of Theron Tock has taken a stab at proving many an optimization incorrect. I now know that a system works when it has been scrutinized by Peter, Amitabh, and Theron.

Rajendra Panwar helped with the parallel algorithms, and Svend Frolund provided advice on types and object-oriented programming. Dan Sturman read parts of this work in a variety of forms and always provided great advice on how to present my ideas. Panayotis Kougiouris was a helpful office mate during my first year at the University of Illinois. Many other students at the university helped me, including Vince Russo (now at Purdue University), Aamod Sane, David Dykstra, and Lee-lup Yuen. Many others provided support and help, including Anda Harney, Mark Simon, Helge Zieler, and Jeff Warwick.

I want to express my deepest gratitude to my parents, Rowshan Ara Islam and Dr. Nurul Islam, for their encouragement and support throughout my Ph.D. work and when I was writing this book. My sister, Dr. Roumeen Islam, provided endless advice on how to cope with the ups and downs that are part of earning a Ph.D. It was always a joy to play with my niece, Yasmin. During the final stages of writing this book I met Anisa, who is now my wife. I thank her for her patience, understanding, and support.

I want to thank IBM for allowing me to complete this book. In particular, I would like to thank Brent Hailpern for being very supportive of my work on object-oriented programming, operating systems, and this project. I want to thank Ajei Gopal for giving me the time and freedom to work on a variety of projects. Many ideas were crystalized after my discussions with him. I would like to thank Ambuj Goyal, director of server systems, for providing me with the necessary hardware to continue my work.

Finally, I would like to thank the entire crew at the IEEE Computer Society Press for helping with this book.

CHAPTER 1

Programming Model and Customization Methodology

The goal of this chapter is to describe the approach to system software optimization used in this book. This chapter describes the types of applications for which system-level optimizations can be generated, and briefly outlines the process of optimization from the perspective of an application programmer. The chapter introduces the two subsystems that will be studied and optimized in this book: message passing and scheduling. It describes abstractly how these subsystems will be customized to increase application performance.

The processes of parallel and distributed applications can communicate through either message passing or shared variables. This book focuses on applications that are written in the message-passing style. A variety of interfaces and implementations of message passing exist, and given a particular interface, there are many ways of implementing message passing on the hardware architecture. Depending on how the message-passing system is used by the application, a number of implementations can improve performance. Similarly, various types of scheduling algorithms may be used by different classes of applications.

For any given interface for a subsystem, such as message passing or scheduling, there are potentially many implementations. Thus, a software structure that is easily extensible to new optimizations is required. Object-oriented frameworks provide such an organization.

1.1 PARALLEL AND DISTRIBUTED APPLICATION MODEL

One of the main purposes of writing a parallel program is to reduce the execution time of an application [HQ91, CG90]. Parallel programs have been used to solve many scientific problems [FJL$^+$88] and commercial applications.

Most parallel applications are structured as distinct parallel processes that communicate to collectively solve a problem. Thus, there is a strong connection among the processes of a parallel application. This connection manifests itself through frequent communication between the processes. For example, in a parallel version of the adaptive quadrature algorithm, different processes compute the integral below the function for different subranges. A central process sums all the values submitted by the various processes and terminates the computation when the integral has been computed.

Distributed applications, on the other hand, are often written for fault tolerance, availability, and resource sharing. Typically, the various processes of the application are loosely coupled; that is, they communicate infrequently. For example, a file service manages files (on a remote disk) for a group of users. A variety of clients could be using this file service for their files. When users need access to their files they contact the file service, which retrieves the data from the disk. The file server is a shared resource.

Each application uses the communication interface differently. The different uses can be exploited to improve the underlying message-passing implementation. The user of the interface may provide hints on how the interface will be used. These hints can be used by the programmer or system to select the appropriate implementation. One approach is that hints are provided as user annotations.

Whether parallel or distributed applications are being considered, the processes of the applications must be scheduled on physical processors. The scheduling may be customized based on how often the processes communicate. Thus, the scheduling system can also be customized. The purpose of this book is to describe the construction of a software framework that can be configured to satisfy the needs of an application; that is, an application-specific instance of the operating system may be instantiated through this software framework.

An abstract view of the system environment is shown in Figure 1.1. It shows that parallel and distributed applications are supported by an operating system, which in turn is supported by a hardware architecture. The operating system implements the message-passing and scheduling primitives and must support the different communication paradigms of the applications. It is possible, however, to build most of the more complex communication primitives from simple send-and-receive primitives. In most operating systems, the underlying network protocols are generic or are typically suited for a single style of interaction. If, however, multiple network protocols exist or a methodology exists for extending the network protocols, the application could perform better. One approach is to explicitly require that the programmer rewrite the application to use newer, more optimized primitives. For example, many operating systems and message-passing libraries provide a set

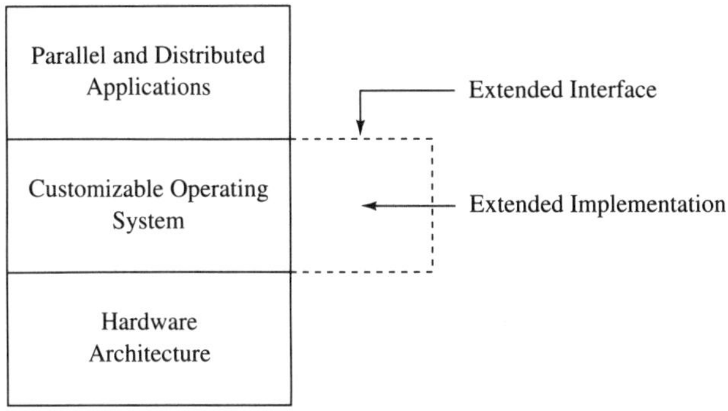

FIGURE 1.1 The system environment.

of routines that are optimized for collective communication [BPG+94, Com89]. If the library interface changes, the application program must change as well. In the second implicit approach, the application program does not have to be rewritten. Thus, message-passing optimizations and application development proceed independently. The communication pattern and other application attributes can be used to design optimized message-passing systems. This second approach is the most important advocated in this book. Sometimes the interface of a subsystem must be extended; such extensions will also be addressed.

The next section discusses some design alternatives for message-passing systems. Some of the common interfaces for message passing and scheduling are included, and a high-level view of the optimization process is presented.

1.1.1 Message Passing

Parallel and distributed applications are structured as concurrent processes that communicate using message passing. The message-passing model includes both asynchronous [Agh86] and synchronous message passing. In the message-passing model, processes communicate by sending messages to endpoints of communication, such as ports or channels.

The channels [And91b] or ports [Ras86] are often named in message-passing systems. When two processes communicate, one process invokes the `send` operation on a channel or port, and the other process invokes a `receive` operation on the same channel or port. Messages that are sent but not yet received are placed in the message queue associated with that port or channel.

Figure 1.2 shows an example of two processes communicating through message passing using ports. It shows process 1 sending a message1 to port2. Process 2 then invokes the receive operation on port2 and reads the message into its own local buffer, message2. Process 2 then send a message to port1, and process 1 invokes the receive operation on port1 and reads the message into its local buffer, message4. Processes 1 and 2 are concurrent. If process 2 has not executed its

Process 1	Process 2
send(message1,port2)	.
.	receive(message2,port2)
.	send(message3,port1)
receive(message4,port1)	.

FIGURE 1.2 Processes communicating through message passing.

`receive` operation, then messages are buffered for it until it retrieves them from the system using a `receive` call.

Several popular programming interfaces are variants of the interface shown in Figure 1.2. For example, the NX/2 operating system includes a set of message-passing primitives for asynchronous and synchronous communication [Pie86]. Two calls implement synchronous message passing.

1. `csend(type,buffer,length,node,pid)`
2. `crecv(typesel,buffer,length)`

The `csend` call does not return until the message has been put on the network and the buffer specified by the application is free to be used again. A `csend` call does not necessarily wait for a corresponding `crecv` to occur at the destination process. The `crecv` call selects an incoming message by type and receives it in a buffer. This call is blocking, and it does not return until the message is in its buffer. Similarly, calls are supported by the PVM [Sun90]; both procedural and object-oriented interfaces are supported. Procedural interfaces are supported to enable the porting of a large number of existing applications. The object-oriented message-passing interface is given in Chapter 5 and Appendix B.

The message-passing interfaces required for distributed applications may be different from those required by parallel applications. For example, many distributed systems require request-response style message passing, whereas parallel applications often exploit asynchronous message passing. Request-response style message passing is often used to support the language-level mechanism known as remote procedure call (RPC) [BN84]. Other types of interfaces exist, including those that support "generative" and "rendezvous" style communication [And91b].

Many message-passing systems support special primitives for group or collective communication. An example of group communication is a broadcast, where one process sends a message to all other processes in the system. Some message-passing systems provide special implementations for collective communication such as broadcast.

The `send` and `receive` calls are implemented by a message-passing system. To move a message between processes, a protocol must be obeyed between the sending and the receiving processes. The job of the message-passing system is to implement this protocol on behalf of application processes. Message-passing protocols can be implemented on a distributed system built from unreliable networks or on a shared-memory multiprocessor.

On distributed systems, the implementation of a message-passing protocol requires the use of connection management and error handling because the underlying network hardware is unreliable. How such protocols are implemented affects the performance of parallel and distributed applications running on them. There are two important types of connection management: timer based (such as that used in the VMTP protocol) and handshake based (such as that used in the TCP protocol). On distributed systems, message-passing protocols must recover from lost, corrupted, and disordered messages. Message-passing protocols employ error-handling mechanisms that wait for certain events to occur and take corrective action when these events do not occur. Many protocols generate explicit acknowledgments for each message sent, which helps in the detection of lost messages.

For example, there are a variety of ways to implement the pattern implicit in Figure 1.2 on a distributed system. On unreliable networks, acknowledgments are generated to detect lost messages. Naive implementations that generate too many acknowledgments suffer from poor performance.

In an implementation of the message-passing system, the send from process 2 to process 1 can be used as an acknowledgment of the original message from process 1 to process 2. If the pattern repeats in a loop, the send from process 1 to process 2 could be used as an acknowledgment of a send from process 2 in the previous iteration. A naive implementation would generate a separate acknowledgment packet for each message. By knowing how the application uses the primitives, it is possible to generate half as many network messages.

In another example, application-level message types are used to order system-level multicast messages. There are three types of ordering constraints for multicast messages [MS91].

1. Single-source ordering. If two messages originate at the same site and they are addressed to the same multicast group, all destinations get them in the same relative order.
2. Multiple-source ordering. If two messages originate at two different sources, all destinations get the messages in the same relative order.
3. Multiple-group ordering. If two messages are delivered to two processes, they are delivered in the same relative order even if the processes belong to two different but overlapping multicast groups and the messages originate from two different sites.

Parallel applications discussed in this book require static groups with single- and multiple-source ordering. To permit the porting of applications between shared-memory and distributed systems, message-passing systems are implemented on shared-memory multiprocessors. A message-passing protocol on a shared-memory multiprocessor employs control and data transfer mechanisms between the sending and the receiving processes. On such architectures there are a variety of methods for passing data between address spaces, including by value and by reference. The performance of these data-transfer mechanisms depends on the memory architecture. The shared data structures of the various message-passing structures may use any of a variety of locking algorithms.

1.1.2 Scheduling

In uniprocessors, scheduling is deciding which process to run and when to run it on the processor. In multiprocessors, multicomputers, and distributed systems, scheduling has another dimension: One must decide which process must run, when it must run, and where it can run. When parallel applications (that is, those with more than one process) are run on systems with more than one processor, gang scheduling can be used to increase the throughput of the system, and decrease the response time for the application. The term *gang scheduling* refers to giving more than one processor to an application at once, and making sure that the processes of the application run on the group of processors at approximately the same time. Gang scheduling may be preemptive or non-preemptive.

The scheduling system may also be customized to the needs of a workstation owner or to those of an application. When gang scheduling is implemented on a distributed system, it can be customized in a variety of ways. For example, application-specific resources can be monitored in a system. The rate at which such a resource is monitored can be specified for different applications. One application may require that each of its processes run on a dedicated workstation; another may require its nodes to be multiprogrammed. A typical operating system or system library call to schedule the processes of an application on `NUMNODES` processors is shown below.

```
schedule(program name, NUMNODES);
```

The underlying system will implement `schedule` to suit the needs of the application. An object-oriented interface is shown in Chapter 10 and Appendix B.

1.1.3 Object-Oriented Frameworks

Clearly, there are many possible optimizations for message-passing systems and scheduling systems. Object-oriented frameworks are used for designing customizable operating systems. Object-oriented frameworks define sets of classes and their interactions. A framework comes with guidelines on how instances of classes are used together and how they may be subclassed to address the needs of the user. Object-oriented frameworks have been used to design and implement applications, but their use in system software development is new.

1.2 THE OPTIMIZATION APPROACH

In order to optimize system software, three questions must be answered.

1. What part of the system software can be optimized?
2. What application attributes can be exploited to generate optimizations?
3. What system software structure will allow optimizations to be easily created and organized for selection based on the application attributes?

This book provides answers to these three questions. In particular, the optimization of the message-passing and scheduling subsystem of an operating system is considered in detail.

The approach advocated in this book is that application attributes can be used to select or create optimized implementations of system services for individual applications, as well as for classes of applications that can be similarly characterized. When a programmer wants to develop an application and use optimized operating system services for that application, the following strategy is employed. First, the application is written by the programmer. Although the applications considered in this book were written in C and C++ they could have been written in any language. Next, the application is characterized by the programmer using a predetermined set of attributes. In order to determine the attributes, the program may be run on an instrumented version of the operating system. Once determined, these attributes are used to select the appropriate system-level customized objects. A selection tool helps in this process. The customization profile that describes the system objects is then passed to the operating system through the system shell. A special system call, `inform`, is used to implement this functionality.

```
inform ( framework name, concrete class name list )
```

The operating system then instantiates the appropriate framework, and the application is run on the optimized operating system. This is the typical model of application execution.

If the application programmer wishes to use special optimizations rather than those chosen with the selection tool, he or she can code his or her own optimizations. Such optimizations are performed by extending an existing object-oriented framework that implements a particular subsystem. For example, to generate a new instance of a message-passing system, the object-oriented framework representing the message-passing system is customized. Extensions can be created only in C++ since the object-oriented frameworks were designed in C++. If the customizations must run in protected or kernel mode, then these optimizations are dynamically loaded into the operating system.

The selection tool is invoked, and the inform method is invoked as shown. The application is then run on the customized operating system. As the number of optimizations increases and stabilizes, fewer new optimizations will be performed.

The extension technique described is general and can be used on any application domain. The optimizations provided by one application programmer should not adversely affect other applications. Therefore, two levels of applications developers are defined: system level and user level. A system-level application developer can perform customizations that reside in the kernel or in user-level libraries. A user-level application developer can only perform optimizations at the user level. The scheduler customizations presented are meant for system-level developers. Much of the message-passing optimizations discussed, however, can be performed either at user-level or system-level.

In summary, once the optimization coding is complete, there are three steps in the optimization process for an application (see also Figure 1.3).

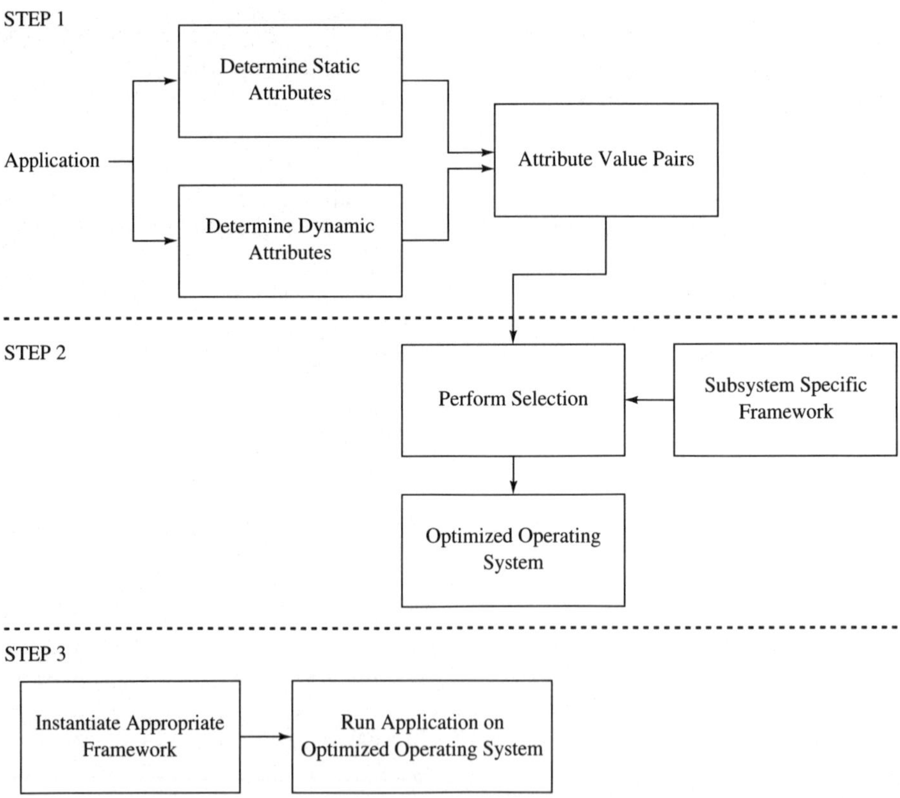

FIGURE 1.3 The process of creating an optimized implementation of a system service tailored to an application.

1. Characterize the application using predefined attributes. This may involve running the application on an instrumented version of the operating system.
2. Using these attributes, select the system class that is best suited to the application. If no appropriate match is found, perform the appropriate coding to create a new optimization.
3. Configure the operating system to run the application with requested system objects. The operating system may be monitored and the information used to make optimization selections for the next run of the application.

These techniques for the message-passing system are described in Chapter 4; for the scheduling system they are described in Chapter 10.

1.3 SUMMARY

Parallel and distributed applications are written as concurrent processes that communicate through message passing. The message passing may be asynchronous or synchronous. Message-passing systems provide implementations for explicit data movement primitives, such as `send` and `receive`. A variety of ways exist to implement message-passing primitives on various architectures, including distributed systems and bus-based, shared-memory multiprocessors. Distributed systems consist of unreliable network hardware, and the message-passing system must guarantee reliable message delivery. The performance of the message-passing system on distributed systems is sensitive to the error-handling mechanisms implemented to manage message loss. On shared-memory multiprocessors, the design and performance of the message-passing system is sensitive to the memory architecture.

Optimizations of a message-passing system can be created by using application-specific information. These optimizations can then be configured into the operating system to create a customized operating system for the application. Parallel applications benefit from specialized scheduling disciplines such as gang scheduling. Finally, object-oriented frameworks are a valuable technique for organizing customizable message-passing and scheduling systems.

CHAPTER 2

Customized Software Design and Documentation

Libraries for message passing, such as PVM and Express, and operating systems such as Mach and V, were not designed with extensibility in mind. Since the message-passing and scheduling systems presented in this book will be customized to the needs of applications, they were designed to be extensible. In order to design extensible software, frameworks [Deu89] are used. The instances of the framework form a tool kit of implementations much like those used for building graphical user interfaces [Isl90]. In this chapter, four important aspects of frameworks are covered. First, the notion of subframeworks is introduced. Second, two new techniques for documenting subframeworks—entity relationship diagrams and control flow graphs—are introduced. Third, subframework composition and refinement to generate application-specific optimizations is discussed. Finally, the use of frameworks to design portable software is described.

Frameworks are a composition of subframeworks. Each subframework consists of a strongly connected set of classes. The relationship between these classes in a subframework may be specified using entity relationship diagrams and control flow graphs.

This section presents object-oriented frameworks in three new ways.

1. The frameworks are constructed to allow easy, per-application customizations.
2. Framework customizations are performed to increase performance as well as enhance the funcationality of applications.

3. Object-oriented frameworks are applied specifically to operating systems and, in particular, to the message-passing and scheduling subsystems of an operating system.

This section presents some software tools built on top of C++ that support framework construction and debugging. These include first-class classes and first-class frameworks, and dynamic code loading.

2.1 CUSTOMIZATION METHODOLOGY

The experiments described in this book use object-oriented frameworks to facilitate the building of customized software systems that support parallel and distributed programming. The following programming techniques are used to create object-oriented frameworks: (1) data encapsulation; (2) data abstraction; (3) polymorphism; and (4) interface and code sharing. Since most of the software discussed in this book is built using C++, many of the concepts are explained in terms of facilities provided in the C++ language. This book is not meant to be a tutorial on C++, although solutions are suggested to handle some of its shortcomings. Several good books exist on the subject of C++ [Str91, Mey92].

2.1.1 Data Encapsulation, Data Abstraction, and Polymorphism

An object consists of state data and a set of operations on those data [Weg87]. Data encapsulation has two requirements: (1) state changes on objects must occur through the invocation of operations only, and (2) systems must be decomposed into objects insulated from other objects [Nie89].

In C++ [Str91], invoking an operation on an object is equivalent to calling a member function (or method) on that object. Public member functions define an object's interface protocol. A class is a template for building similar objects [Nie89]; it specifies the instance variables and operations common to all objects belonging to that class. Data abstraction is supported by classes since they describe the structure and behavior of a set of objects [GR83, Str91]. Classes allow programmers to extend the set of built-in types provided by the programming language. Classes differ from traditional user-defined type mechanisms in that they support the notion of subtypes [Nie89]. A class is a subtype of a second class if instances of the first class can be used where instances of the second class are expected.

Polymorphic base-class interfaces allow objects to be manipulated uniformly, although they can be instances of either the base class or any other class [Jor90]. In object-oriented languages, dynamic binding mechanisms support polymorphism. In C++, the virtual function mechanism [Str91] supports dynamic binding of methods and hence supports polymorphism. The actual method invoked depends on the instance of the derived class that is being used. New derived classes can be defined and easily incorporated into a system, as existing software expects the interface of the base class.

2.1.2 Interface and Code Sharing

Classes can belong to a class hierarchy and share structural and behavioral descriptions through inheritance. Within a hierarchy, a subclass or derived class can inherit methods and data from one or more base classes or superclasses. If subclasses have more than one superclass, the hierarchy uses multiple inheritance; otherwise, it uses single inheritance.

Some classes only specify an interface and are not meant to be instantiated. These classes are called *abstract* classes. By subclassing an abstract class one can achieve interface sharing. Subclasses of abstract classes that implement the operations specified by a superclass are called *concrete* classes. By subclassing a concrete class one can achieve both interface and code sharing. In practice, many classes both specify an interface for subclasses and provide an implementation of that interface. A concrete class must have an implementation for all methods, either through inheritance or its own implementation (overloading). In C++ the virtual functions of a parent class are overloaded. An example of overloading of methods is shown in Figure 2.1. The abstract class Buffer has two methods: put and get. The figure shows two implementations of message buffers, LIFO (last in, first out) and FIFO (first in, first out). Both classes have the same interface: put and get. The semantics of get, however, are different. The get method on a FIFO class returns the message that has been in the queue for the longest amount of time. The LIFO get method returns the message that was most recently deposited in the buffer. This technique is called *overloading* and is used extensively in designing object-oriented frameworks.

In this book, class hierarchies consist of abstract classes, often at the root of the hierarchy, and concrete subclasses, often at the leaves. In class hierarchies, illustrated in the figures, abstract classes are shown in italics, whereas concrete classes are shown in bold. In the text of the book, all class names appear in a sans serif font and all method names appear in a `monospace` font.

To ensure full substitutability, subtype programming is enforced in the system design by making all inheritance public. In particular, all the methods available in a superclass are part of the interface in the subclass. An example is shown in Figure 2.2. In this figure, subclass RRMessage inherits the methods of its parent class, preserving the subtyping relationship. RRMessage may be used wherever Message is expected.

Experience has shown that inheritance for code reuse is good for rapid prototyping and completing applications quickly. Interface reuse, however, is more important for creating frameworks that are easy to extend. Interface reuse is chosen over code reuse throughout this book.

In this example, class RRMessage is a public subclass of the Message class and inherits its public methods. To further illustrate code and interface reuse in

```
class Buffer {
public:
        void put(Message*)=0;
        Message* get()=0;
};

class FIFO : public Buffer {
public:
        void put(Message*) { /* put into linked list */}
        Message * get() { /* find message which was put
                                in buffer before all other messages */
                               return OldestMessage;}
};

class LIFO : public Buffer {
public:
        void put(Message*) { /* put into linked list */}
        Message * get() { /* find message most recently added to buffer */
                               return LatestMessage;}
};
```

FIGURE 2.1 An example of overloading methods. The get and put methods have the same interface but different semantics.

TABLE 2.1 Interpreting Symbols in Interface Protocol Tables

Method Types	
=0	Pure virtual
•	First implemented
▽	Inherited
△	Overloaded or refined
-	Undefined

complex hierarchies, interface protocol tables are used. Each abstract and concrete class has a set of methods that it exports as its interface protocol. An interface protocol table lists all the public methods of a class and shows how subclasses inherit them. The interface protocol tables use the symbols defined in Table 2.1. A pure virtual function is used to specify a prototype for a class method; the class in which it appears will not have an implementation for it. Sometimes method names are abbreviated in the interface protocol tables. C++ class definitions are used to describe the public member functions of individual classes in more detail.

```
class Message {
public:
  Message(char* initData,int initSize,int delData=1); /* default is to delete related
data */
  Message(int delData=1); /* default is to delete related data */
  ~Message();

  void setReceiveContainer(MessageContainer *);/* set receiver container */
  void setDestination(ContainerRepresentative *);/* set destination field */
  void setSize(unsigned int size);/* set size field of message */
  void setData(char *data); /* set pointer to data area */
 ContainerRepresentative* destination(); /* destination of MessageContainer */
  MessageContainer* receiverContainer(); /* destination of MessageContainer */
  long size(); /* size of message */
  char* data(); /* pointer to data area of msg */
  void send(); /* send the message */
  void receive(); /* send the message */
};

class RRMessage : public Message {
public:
  RRMessage(char* initData,int initSize,int delData=1); /* default is to delete
related data */
        RRMessage();
        void rr(); // client calls this function

        void reply(); // server calls this function


        void rrReceive(); // server calls this function

        void setReplyContainer(MessageContainer*); // to set reply container

        MessageContainer* getReplyContainer(); // to set reply container


};
```

FIGURE 2.2 The public subclassing illustrating how subtypes may be obtained in C++.

2.2 OBJECT-ORIENTED FRAMEWORKS

Object-oriented frameworks add another dimension to the design of object-oriented software by describing how classes and objects interact. An object-oriented framework is an architectural design for object-oriented systems [Deu89]. This book describes experiments accomplished using customized software for parallel and distributed applications organized within frameworks. By allowing easy porting to new architectures, the frameworks also allow experiments on a shared-memory multiprocessor and a distributed system. A framework consists of a set of interconnected subframeworks. These subframeworks are refined and then brought together to form a framework for a subsystem of the operating system. Subframework documentation, building, refinement, and composition are now discussed in detail.

2.2.1 Techniques for Documenting and Building Subframeworks

To document the design of an object-oriented subframework, conventional software engineering design documentation is coupled with an object-oriented approach. In this chapter, two new techniques for describing subframeworks are introduced: entity relationship diagrams and control flow graphs. Other framework documentation techniques are discussed in [CI92, CI93b]. Information about subframeworks is presented at the abstract-class level. In any complete description of the system, concrete classes will replace abstract classes. Each subframework has a set of class hierarchies that defines the abstract and concrete classes in the system.

Control flow graphs are often used for intermediate program representations [ASU87]. A control flow graph is a directed graph: CFG $= < N_{CFG}, E_{CFG},$ **entry**, **exit** $>$. In traditional representations, the set of nodes, N_{CFG}, represents basic blocks of a program. The two additional nodes, **entry** and **exit**, represent points of transfer into and out of the control flow graph, respectively. The edges, E_{CFG}, represent transfers of control (jumps) between the basic blocks. The edge to any basic block is labeled with an **entry** node, and the edge from any basic block is labeled with an **exit** node. The edges are numbered showing the order of flow through the system from **entry** to **exit**. The base of an arrow depicts the caller, and the point of the arrow is the callee of a method.

Control flow graphs depict the runtime behavior of the system. For an object-oriented system, such a graph represents an ordering on method invocations.* Each subframework has a control flow graph that describes the important control flows through it. Abstract control flow graphs represent an abstraction of the control flow

*The major flow of control through each of the subframeworks is captured by the notation in this section. The decomposition into subframeworks makes the flow of control through the different subframeworks much simpler.

through the instances of classes in the subframework. As abstractions, these control flows may only pass through classes that are abstract. In any implementation of the operating system, there will be a concrete control flow, representing the control flow through a series of objects that are instances of concrete classes. A concrete control flow is a refinement of an abstract control flow. To describe abstract control flow graphs, the following convention is used: Method `m` is invoked on an instance of class A even though class A may be abstract. In an implementation, some concrete subclass of A will have its `m` method invoked on it as part of a concrete control flow that is a refinement of the abstract control flow.

Figure 2.3 shows this control flow relationship between three abstract classes. The graph is entered when method `m` is invoked on AbstractClassA. The point of entry is denoted by the dashed rectangle labeled **Entry**. The control flows through the graph in the following sequence.

1. Method `m` is invoked on AbstractClassA.
2. Method `n` is invoked on AbstractClassB.
3. Method `o` is invoked on AbstractClassC.
4. The control flow then leaves the system through the node labeled **Exit**.

Abstract entity relationship diagrams are similar to abstract control flow graphs, in that they can be used to express the relationships between abstract classes in the system. Abstract entity relationship diagrams are referred to as abstract class relationship diagrams. Pressman's [Pre87] entity-relationship and instance-connection notation is used to describe abstract class relationships. An abstract class may have an instance name attached to it, which is necessary when the class appears in a diagram more than once. These names represent instances in an implementation that are instantiations of a concrete subclass of the abstract class. In Figure 2.4, a single bar denotes a one-to-one relationship, and a three-pronged fork indicates a one-to-many relationship. These relationships may be mandatory (denoted by an

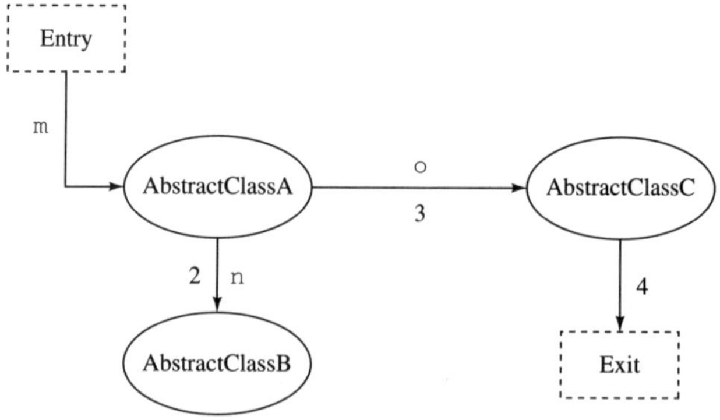

FIGURE 2.3 Abstract flow of control between three abstract classes A, B, and C.

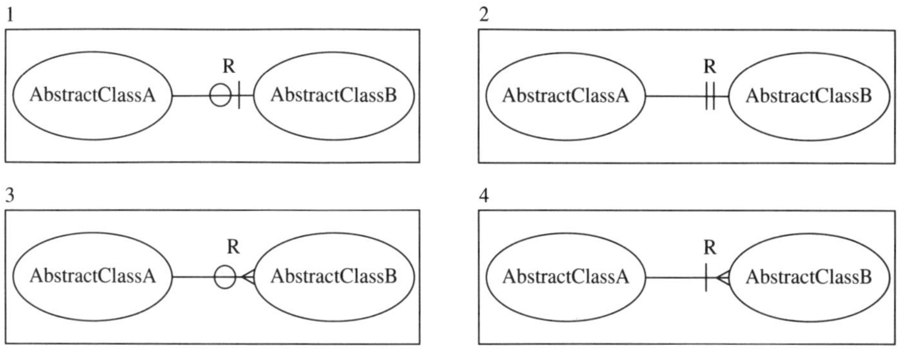

FIGURE 2.4 Entity relationship links between abstract classes.

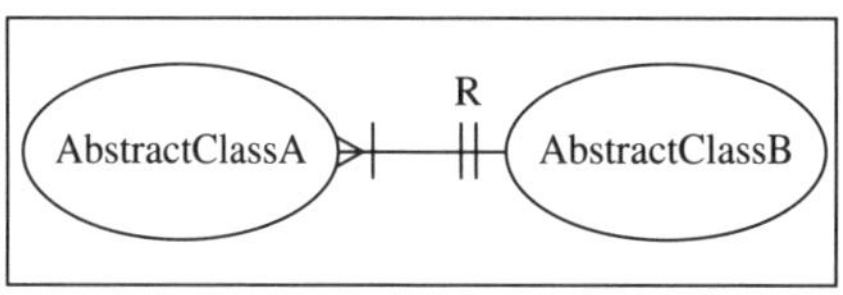

FIGURE 2.5 Relationships between instances of classes.

additional line) or optional (denoted by an additional small circle). Figure 2.4 depicts the possible entity relationships between two abstract classes. In Figure 2.4, diagram 1 shows a one-to-one optional connection; diagram 2 shows a one-to-one mandatory connection; diagram 3 shows a one-to-many optional connection; and diagram 4 shows a one-to-many mandatory connection. The connection depicts an is-referenced-by or references relation. One end of the relation states a reference; the other end states is-referenced-by. For example, in box 2, an instance of a subclass of AbstractClassA references exactly one instance of a subclass of AbstractClassB. An R near the class indicates whether it is a referencing relationship, and the absence of the symbol means that the relationship is one of is-referenced-by. The reference relation typically translates to the ability to invoke a method.

This notation only expresses the relationship of an instance of an AbstractClassA subclass to instances of subclasses of AbstractClassB. To express the opposite relationship, a similar notation is used. For example, in Figure 2.5 each instance of a subclass of AbstractClassB may be referenced by many entities of AbstractClassA, but the instances of an AbstractClassA subclass are not referenced by any instance of a subclass of AbstractClassB.

2.3 SUBFRAMEWORK COMPOSITION

Each framework is a composition of subframeworks. When an **exit** node in one graph is connected to an **entry** node of another graph, the two graphs are said to be composed. A control flow between two subframeworks implies that there is an entity relationship between these two classes in the subframeworks and, hence, their entity relationship diagrams may also be composed. More than one class may provide such interface between subframeworks. Composed subframeworks are similar to the layers in the THE [Dyk68] operating system.

2.4 REFINEMENT OF SUBFRAMEWORKS

To support application-specific customizations, individual subframeworks are refined. The refinement process defines a set of rules for subclassing existing classes and maintaining relationships between these classes. The rules for refinement for both entity relationship diagrams and control flow graphs are as follows:

1. An abstract class may be replaced by a concrete class.
2. An abstract class may be replaced by a set of concrete classes.
3. New abstract and concrete classes may be added.
4. Relations and control flows may be added.
5. Previously defined relations or control flows may not be removed.

These rules ensure substitutability. The new entity relationship or control flow diagram may be reused wherever the old one was expected, since it obeys all the relationships and control flows of the old diagram.

2.5 CUSTOMIZING FOR PERFORMANCE

An important use of an object-oriented framework is to refine its constituent subframeworks based on performance criteria for an individual application. In this book, certain methods of certain classes are overloaded for better performance by using more suitable or specialized algorithms in a concrete subclass. In this special case the customization is an optimization for an application. A set of subframeworks may be collectively optimized for a given application. For example, experimentation shows that different message-queuing implementations are better for different applications: Certain applications perform better with circular lists, and others perform better with free lists. Both implementations are easily obtained by overloading the put and get methods of the message queue class. Similarly, depending on the number of processors available to an application, some locking algorithms are better than others. Therefore, both an optimized queuing implementation and an optimized locking algorithm may be chosen for an application.

One of the challenges of good framework design is to identify all the subframeworks and classes in these subframeworks that will be customized for per-application optimizations. This book demonstrates how this is possible for message-passing and scheduling systems.

2.6 ENHANCED PORTABILITY

The ease of portability of systems software is improved in two distinct ways using object-oriented frameworks. First, subframeworks allow the identification of a group of tightly coupled classes, one of which may be architecture dependent. This subframework is then said to be architecture dependent. On some ports this entire subframework may not be required. For example, since reliable delivery of messages is not an issue on a bus-based, shared-memory multiprocessor, the subframework that implements reliability need not be part of the framework on the shared-memory multiprocessor. Second, individual classes in an architecture-dependent subframework may be designed such that each subclass is refined to incorporate architecture-specific information. For example, a transport mechanism is needed on all architectures to move messages from one address space to another. The methods of the transport class are overloaded on a shared-memory architecture to move messages into and out of the kernel. On a distributed system, the transport mechanism performs fragmentation and reassembly of messages.

2.7 CLASSES AS INSTANCES

The motivation for representing classes as runtime instances in the operating system arises from several requirements.

- The object-oriented application interface supports the dynamic creation and removal of objects in the kernel and user space. References to the objects may be passed from object to object. Class inquiry functions allow simplified programming and monitoring.
- Instances of new subclasses of system abstract classes provide a mechanism to extend the application interface in a controlled but nontrivial manner. Classes provide query functions that return their superclass and subclasses, documenting the state and evolution of the system and providing a database of system facilities.
- Instances of a class can be listed, providing a database of system services that conform to the protocol of the class.
- The classes of objects are represented at runtime as objects. This allows runtime checking* that the protocols used in messages to objects are consistent with their definition.
- The classes of persistent objects can be recorded as such.

*C++ provides safe and efficient compile-time type checking; however, this type checking can be circumvented. One can also use runtime type checking to double-check compile-time type checking.

2.7.1 Implementation

First-class classes or class objects are implemented using a class called Class. Classes are similar to the Dossiers described in [IL90], except that Classes also support dynamic code linking. At runtime, every significant object in the operating system is associated with a specific Class. The code given in Figure 2.6 defines the interface for Class.

The `typedef` defines pointers to functions, *addressable constructors*, that initialize dynamically loaded class instances (see Section 2.9). The `Class` constructor takes a pointer to the Class's superclass, which is zero for the root of a hierarchy, and a character string name of the class. The constructor has an optional third parameter, which is a pointer to an addressable constructor. If a class does not have an addressable constructor or if its definition is deferred until runtime, then the third argument can be omitted. If an addressable constructor is supplied at runtime, a CodeLoader (see Section 2.9) may use the `setConstructor` operation to bind future invocations of the Class's `constructor` to invocations of a specific addressable constructor. The `constructor` operation provides a dynamically bound constructor that will initialize an instance of the class corresponding to the Class.

```
typedef ObjectStar (*CP)( Object * );

class Class : public Object {
                ...
public:
   Class( Class *, char * name, CP constructor = 0 );

   virtual setConstructor( CP constructor );
   virtual ObjectStar constructor( Object * );

   virtual ClassStar classOf();
   virtual int isA( Class * );

   virtual char * name();

   virtual ClassStar parent();
   virtual ClassStar child();
   virtual ClassStar sibling();

   virtual int displayMembers( OutputStream * );
   virtual int displayKindred( OutputStream * );

}
```

FIGURE 2.6 Class interface definition.

The `classOf` operation returns a pointer to the Class of which the object is an instance. The `isA` operation returns true if and only if the parameter is a superclass of the Class.

The class hierarchy is modeled as a tree of arbitrary degree, but it is implemented as a binary tree. Each Class object has a `parent` (superclass), a `child` (subclass), and a `sibling` (the next class with the same superclass). By convention, a zero indicates the parent of the root of a hierarchy, the child of a Class with no subclasses, the sibling of a Class with no superclass, or the sibling of a Class at the end of its superclass' sibling list.

Using Smalltalk terminology, an object is a *member* of the class from which it was instantiated. An object is said to be a *kind* of the class of which it is a member, and of all the class' superclasses. The `displayMembers` operation displays on the OutputStream the names of all objects that are members of this Class. The `displayKindred` operation displays on the OutputStream the names of all objects that are a kind of this Class.

2.7.2 Usage

An auxiliary program, allClasses, coordinates the definition and instantiation of Classes; it is run automatically by the make files. To simplify the allClasses program, a programming convention was adopted that requires certain lines of code to be present in both the header (".h") and source (".cc") files of a class. For example, consider the class Object. It is defined in "Object.h" and implemented in "Object.cc". The lines added to define a first-class class for Object in file "Object.h" are

```
extern ClassStar ObjectClass;

class Object ... {
            ...
public:
            ClassStar classOf();
            ...
};
```

The lines define a pointer to the Class that is assigned a value at runtime. The value is used by the `classOf` implementation shown below. The lines needed in file "Object.cc" are

```
ClassStar
Object::classOf()
{
      return( ObjectClass );
}
```

2.8 DEBUGGING FROM THE SYSTEM SHELL

It is possible to use the first-class classing mechanisms to visualize the classes and frameworks in the system.

2.8.1 Displaying the Class Hierarchy from the System Shell

Each Class is also bound to a name in the kernel's NameServer. A user of the system shell can request information about any Class's place in the hierarchy. The Class is looked up by name in the NameServer, and the requested information is displayed.

There are three commands for displaying class hierarchy information.

1. Ancestors, which recursively displays the superclasses of the given class
2. Descendants, which recursively displays the subclasses of the given class
3. Hierarchy, which recursively displays first the superclasses and then the subclasses of the given class

An example of the hierarchy command, which shows both the ancestors and descendants of class Process, is shown below.

```
Shell> hierarchy Process
Object
   Task
     Process <<<
           GangProcess
```

2.8.2 Displaying Instances of Classes from the System Shell

All instances of subclasses of class Object are inserted into a global object table when constructed and removed from the table when deleted. Classes have access to this table and can iterate through the table, searching for instances of the class that they represent.

The system shell uses the Smalltalk terminology for displaying instances of a class. There are two commands for displaying instances of classes.

1. Members, which displays all instances of the given class
2. Kindred, which displays all instances of the given class and its descendants

The following are examples of these commands.

```
Shell> members GangProcess
GangProcess[45a180]("GangProcessA")
```

```
GangProcess[466100]("GangProcessB");
2 instances.

Shell> kindred Process
Process[466000])("PagerProcess");
GangProcess[466100]("GangProcessB");
GangProcess[45a180]("GangProcessA")
3 instances.
```

2.8.3 First-Class Frameworks

Any operating system is a complex structure; it is impossible to discern the structure of most operating sytems at runtime. Although object-oriented frameworks are a convenient software design tool, thus far they have only been treated here as designs. First-class frameworks can be used to encode the design of the operating system such that the design can be inspected at runtime. First-class frameworks are representations of the object-oriented frameworks at runtime. To represent frameworks, a base class Framework was constructed. This is an abstract class. Subclasses were created for a variety of subframeworks, such as MessagePassing, Process, and FileSystem. The class hierarchy for frameworks is shown in Figure 2.7. The basic methods used on frameworks are shown in Figure 2.8. For frameworks, one would like to know the abstract classes, concrete classes (in effect at runtime), and the various entity relationships and control flow relationships between instances of the classes.

The instances of the framework class are available through the name server and the system shell. At runtime, these frameworks and framework instances may be viewed. Navigating the system thus becomes a much simpler task. The first-class representations are meant to be extensible and it is possible to refine the types of framework-specific information that are monitored by the system.

There is a shell command for each of the different methods listed in Figure 2.8 and there is a command `framework` to list all the active frameworks of a particular type. Each of the relevant types are subclasses of the abstract class Framework. In the examples shown, all instances of the message-passing framework are listed. The figure shows that there is one application-specific message-passing system present and that it supports the application named Cholesky. The third shell call

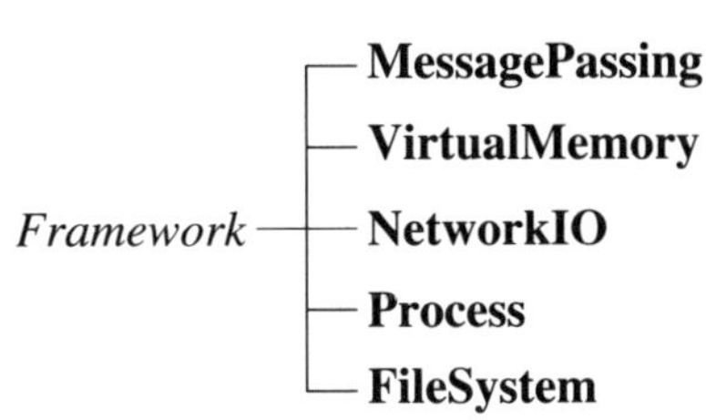

FIGURE 2.7 First-class framework class hierarchies.

```
class Framework {
public:
/*
 * List the abstract classes of this framework
 */
        void ListAbstractions()=0; // list the abstract

                                   // classes of this framework


/*
 * List the concrete classes of instance of this framework
 */

        void ListConcrete()=0;

/*
 * Show the method invocation sequence of
 * this framework.
 */
        void ShowControlFlow()=0;
/*
 * Show the entity relationship relationship between
 * the abstraction in the framework.
 */
        void ShowER();
/*
 * Show the time spent thus far in each
 * part concrete class of the framework.
 * The classes must have been instrumented.
 */
        void ShowTimings(); // performance timing breakdown

                            // Shows the amount of time

                            // spent in each class


        Framework();
        Class* classOf();
};
```

FIGURE 2.8 The interfaces of the class representing a first-class framework.

lists all of the concrete subclasses constituting the message-passing framework used by the Cholesky application.

```
Shell> frameworks MessagePassing
MessagePassing("Cholesky")
1 instance
Shell> showAbstract MessagePassing
MessagePassing("Cholesky")
   MessageContainer
   Synchronization
   Transport
   Transfer
   Reliability
Shell> showConcrete MessagePassing
   MessagePassing("Cholesky")
   MessageContainer --> NoTypeCirc
   Synchronization --> Semaphores
   Transport --> ReceivingTransport
   Transfer --> NetworkTransfer
   Reliability --> Repetitive
1 instance
```

Three other methods on frameworks exist: `showControlFlow`, `showER`, and `showTimings`. `ShowControlFlow` will display the control flow through the objects in the system (see the figures in Section 5.9.1), `showER` depicts the entity relationship between objects (see the figures in Section 5.9.4). and `showTimings` shows the time spent in the system object from the time the framework was created to the point at which the call was made.

2.9 ADDING SUBCLASSES TO A RUNNING C++ PROGRAM

An extensible application interface is provided that permits the addition of new services to the kernel without rebooting the system. Implementing an extensible kernel as a dynamic collection of objects allows a minimal kernel to be defined. New features may be added to the kernel to customize it for applications or for the target environment. Existing software in the system may invoke methods on these new services if they are subclassed from an abstract class known to the system at compile time; new software added to the system may use all methods of the new services. C++ has neither dynamic linking of code nor dynamic binding for constructors. To simplify and generalize the mechanism involved, the base classes of the system were extended to support the dynamic loading and linking of new subclasses and their methods using a scheme that has been used by several other research groups [DSS90].

To access newly loaded code from an existing, running program, the running program needs a dynamic binding mechanism that maps messages (function calls) to invocations of the new code. C++ has an ideal mechanism for performing this dynamic binding: the virtual function table, which is accessible through an object's *vtable* pointer. Once an object has been constructed, the member functions can be invoked through the object's vtable pointer. C++ constructors, however, which assign vtable pointers to objects at runtime, are statically bound and may not be called directly from an existing, running program. The problem to be solved in an implementation of dynamic, loadable C++ code is allowing existing programs to call the constructors defined in the newly loaded classes.

2.9.1 Dynamically Bound Constructors

Each class in the system is represented by a Class object, described in Section 2.7, which is accessible through NameServers. The solution to invoking traditional static C++ constructors dynamically uses a `constructor` method, which indirectly invokes the traditional static C++ constructor and is defined for Classes.

There are three interrelated constructor functions: (1) traditional C++ constructors, which have names like `Object::Object`; (2) addressable constructors, which are named `ObjectConstructor`; and (3) dynamic constructors, which are named `Class::constructor`. Traditional constructors are no longer called directly by code that is designed to take advantage of the dynamic linking facility. They are, however, still used to allocate and initialize heap storage.

An addressable constructor, which is implemented as a C++ function, is linked and loaded at the same time as the new class to which it will be bound. The linker can thus bind an invocation of the traditional constructor into the code for an addressable constructor. Unlike traditional constructors, addressable constructors return a zero in cases of failure. A failure may occur if the class of the parameter to the addressable constructor is inappropriate (because a runtime check failed).

A dynamic constructor is implemented by the `Class::constructor` function. It provides dynamic linking to the traditional static constructor function by an invocation of the addressable constructor to which the static constructor has been linked. When the code for the new class is to be loaded, a Class object is created to represent the new class. When the code is loaded, the linker installs the address of the addressable constructor in the Class object's _constructor instance variable. When the dynamic constructor of the Class object is invoked, it in turn invokes the addressable constructor stored in the _constructor instance variable. The addressable constructor then invokes the static constructor.

In detail, the following steps are performed by the dynamic constructor.

1. If the _constructor variable is zero, it creates an instance of class CodeLoader (described in the following section) and initializes it with the name of the Class.

2. Since the CodeLoader object performs all of its work when created, the dynamic constructor then deletes the CodeLoader object.
3. If the _constructor variable is still zero, then it fails by returning zero.
4. If the _constructor variable is non-zero, it calls the addressable constructor, which calls the traditional constructor. The return value of the traditional constructor is also returned by the addressable constructor, which is then returned by the dynamic constructor.

2.9.2 The CodeLoader

A subclass of the abstract class CodeLoader is defined for each type of object file format. The first such class supports the Common Object File Format (COFF) [Gir88]; thus the subclass is named COFFLoader. The CodeLoader constructor performs the following operations.

1. Open a file that contains the symbol table for the running program.
2. Look up the name of the class with the undefined constructor in a NameServer that maps class names to file names.
3. If the file name is found, open the corresponding file, which should be a relocatable, unstripped module that includes the code for the class and for closely related classes.
4. Allocate memory and read code from the file.
5. Resolve undefined symbols in the loaded code with the symbols found in the running program's symbol table.
6. Relocate symbols in the loaded code, basing them on the memory address at which the code is loaded.
7. Create Class objects for any loaded classes that do not already have them.
8. Install addresses of addressable constructors defined in the loaded code into corresponding Classes.

By making C++ classes loadable, parts of the operating system can be greatly simplified. For example, the operating system supports many types of synchronization primitives. Code for each type of primitive needs to be loaded only when a request is made to access that type of primitive. Thus, neither the kernel nor user space is penalized for the flexibility that is provided by the operating system, particularly when a large variety of synchronization primitives are available. Figure 2.9 shows some of the data structures used to support a dynamic code-loading system. All of the Classes in a running system form a single tree that corresponds to the compile-time inheritance hierarchy. Figure 2.9 shows, as an example, three of these Classes: (1) the abstract class Synchronization; (2) the concrete classes Semaphore, in which a process requesting a resource may block; and (3) TASLock, in which a process spins on a shared variable, waiting for a

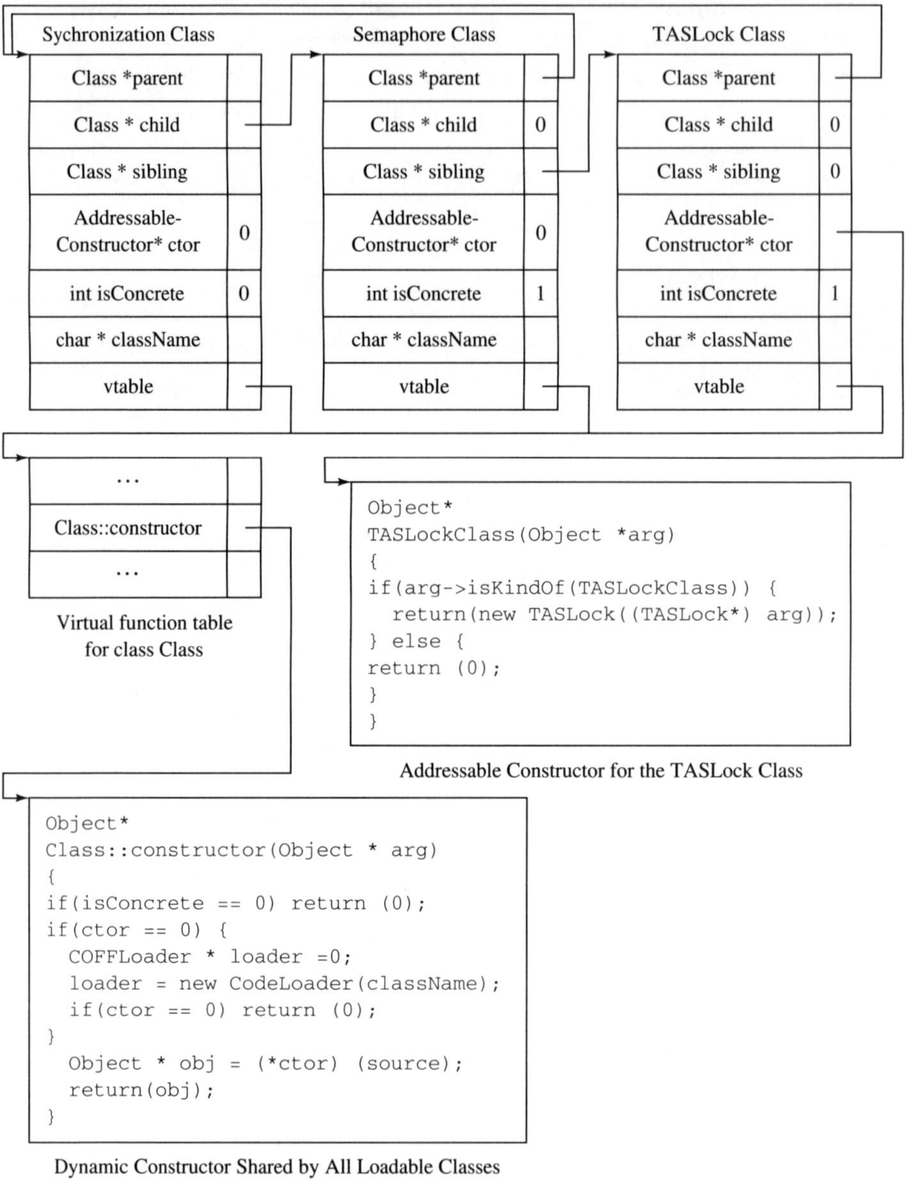

FIGURE 2.9 Dynamic code loading.

resource to become free. All three **Classes** share the same virtual function table and therefore also share the same dynamic constructor. Abstract classes do not need addressable constructors since programs do not directly create instances of abstract classes; therefore, the Synchronization class does not have one. In this example, the addressable constructor for the Semaphore class has already been loaded, and the Semaphore class contains a pointer to it. The addressable constructor for the TASLock class has not yet been loaded. If the CodeLoader successfully finds and loads the code for the TASLock class, it will update the `ctor` pointer in the TASLock class. The `constructor` method can then call the newly loaded addressable constructor, which in turn will call the traditional constructor for the TASLock class.

2.10 SUMMARY

Object-oriented frameworks are important tools for creating customized software. In particular, frameworks help in the design of portable software and allow optimizations on a per-application basis to be generated easily.

This chapter describes two new approaches to documenting the design of an object-oriented framework. These framework documentation techniques are more comprehensive than traditional techniques. In particular, the use of control flow graphs and entity relationship diagrams makes clear the relationships between system components that must be maintained when new components are added.

C++ is a popular language and it performs well. It does, however, lack certain features that are useful for large-scale systems development; namely, first-class classes and first-class frameworks. Although it is possible to put such features into a language, it is also possible to build requisite support through libraries and a methodology for using objects.

CHAPTER 3

Characterizing Parallel and Distributed Applications

This chapter presents an application taxonomy based on attributes that are concerned with the performance of customized message-passing and scheduling systems. In later chapters, these attributes guide the design of such systems. The relevance and importance of these attributes was determined by examining and executing instrumented versions of several representative parallel codes, including those for FFT [MII89], Simplex [Stu88b], Cholesky [AHP92], adaptive quadrature [And91b], Laplace [FJL$^+$88] and wave equations [FJL$^+$88], and distributed systems services such as name services and distributed schedulers. These attributes were chosen because by experimentation they were found to affect the performance of parallel and distributed applications. System optimization for parallel applications is treated differently from that of distributed applications. A major focus of the author's work, however, was to provide a uniform characterization of both types of applications. This uniform characterization is useful because it allows one to consider the customization of the operating system as being performed for the specific attributes of an application rather than for an individual application per se.

Each application has certain characterizing dynamic and static attributes. Static attributes are application programmer supplied. These attributes are the same across multiple runs of the application. Although it would be possible to provide compiler support or parser support for finding static attributes, this option is not considered in this book. The focus, rather, is on the design of the operating system once the attributes have been found. Dynamic attributes are obtained through runs of the application on an instrumented version of the operating system.

Dynamic attributes can vary from one run of the application to the next. Some of the attributes may only be used on one of the two architectures. Each attribute guides the minimization of operating system overheads.

The following are the static attributes of an application.

- `Program structure`. Programs are often written using standard structures: asynchronous, synchronous, pipeline, master-slave, or client-server. These are called *process interaction patterns* and specify the relationship between the communication and computation phases of an application. The processes in the process interaction pattern communicate by sending and receiving messages according to a *communication pattern*.
- `Invalidation`. Message data in the form of a received data segment and local data may be mapped to the same cache line. Repeated and consecutive accesses to these two structures can lead to frequent cache line invalidations. This is only important on the bus-based, shared-memory multiprocessor.
- `Types`. Many applications are written using explicit message types in their blocking receive operations. An application may require its multicast messages to be delivered in order. Application-specific types may be used to implement ordering. This is only important on distributed systems.
- `Idempotent server functions`. A server function that yields monotonically better results or the same result each time it is invoked is called an *idempotent* server function. This is only important on distributed systems.

Dynamic attributes cannot be determined by parsing the application; they vary from run to run, and depend on the input data set and user preferences. The following are the dynamic attributes of an application.

- `Message size`. The size of messages in bytes that are transferred between processes of the program. The size is generally dependent on the input data set and the number of processes into which the application is partitioned.
- `Iteration time`. The time for an iteration in an iterative application, which includes the communication overhead in the iteration. This is only important on distributed systems.
- `Concurrency`. The number of processes into which the application has been partitioned.

3.1 PROCESS INTERACTION AND COMMUNICATION PATTERNS

In this section, two of the most important static attributes of an application are discussed: (1) process interaction patterns (PIP), and (2) communication patterns (CP). PIPs describe the control structure of the application. They depict how the control flows through the application. The CPs describe the message-passing behavior between the processes that constitute the parallel application. In effect, a PIP shows when communication occurs in a program and a CP specifies the exact nature of the communication. Although there are many possible PIPs and CPs, experience has shown that it is possible to specify many applications with a small set of PIPs and CPs. Some of the optimizations described take advantage of CP knowledge to reduce sender-side buffering and to reduce the number of explicit acknowledgment messages required for the reliable delivery of messages on an unreliable network.

The processes of a parallel application generally synchronize the execution of various parts of their own computations with subcomputations of other processes. The points at which a process so synchronizes delineate the tasks of that process. The subcomputations of a process that are executed independently of other processes are the tasks executed by that process. PIPs are similar to the task graphs described by Mohan [Moh84] and the event diagrams used in ParaGraph [HE91]. PIPs show precedence relations between the tasks of an application.

In a PIP, a labeled bubble refers to a computation sequence or task in an application process, and a directed arrow represents a dependency between two tasks. Unlike the traditional task model, the model used here allows the actual points at which synchronization takes place to be called tasks as well. Therefore, there are two types of tasks in an application, as shown in Figure 3.1: work tasks (unshaded) and communication tasks (shaded). While work tasks are independent, communication tasks involve two or more processes. For example, in the synchronous PIP, there is only one communication task, even though there are several processes executing this task. The actual type of communication is specified using a CP. The following is a list of the most common PIPs found in parallel applications.

- Asynchronous, where there are no explicit dependencies between the various processes.

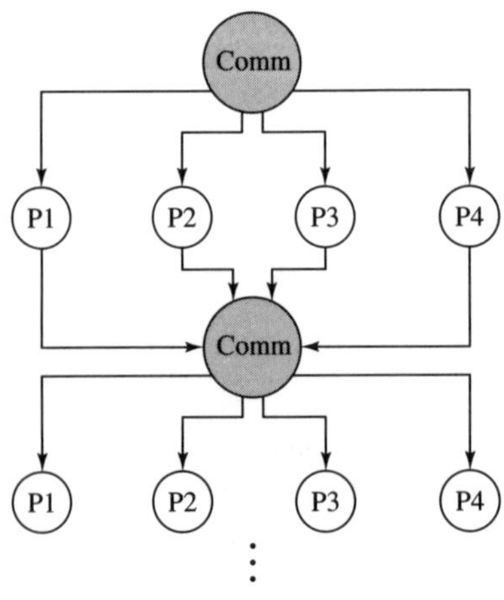

FIGURE 3.1 Process interaction pattern of a synchronous application.

- Synchronous (shown in Figure 3.1), which is often iterative with synchronization at the end of each iteration.
- Pipeline, in which data flow through the processes in a predefined order. Data enter at one end of the system and leave at the other end. Pipeline PIPs can be asynchronous or synchronous.
- Client-server, where a client process computes for a while, then communicates with one or more server processes.
- Bag-of-tasks, where one process maintains a bag of tasks and other processes query that process for tasks to work on. The bag-of-tasks PIP differs from the client-server PIP in that a client can initiate communication with more than one server, whereas in the bag-of-tasks PIP all processes communicate with only one central process.

3.1.1 Communication Patterns

Each PIP can be combined with a variety of different CPs in an application. In PIPs, the shaded bubbles refer to places where communication takes place. In a CP, a bubble refers to a process. An arrow connecting two processes refers to a message sent from one process to another. A line with arrowheads at both ends represents a message sent from both processes. The CP of an application describes the number of messages needed to implement the communication required by an application on an ideal network (one that does not lose messages and has infinite size buffers). This ideal network allows point-to-point sends between processes and supports hardware multicast. Therefore, one network message is required for a multicast, rather than $N - 1$ network messages. In a later chapter, it is shown that the number of application-level messages is not the same as the number of network messages. In this book, application-level messages are called *messages*, and messages that are actually sent on the network are called *network messages*.

The CP identifies communication locality and sender identities. Communication locality exists in an application if, when process A sends a message to process B, process B sends a message to process A sometime in the future. This information is used on unreliable networks to generate implicit acknowledgments. For example, a message-passing system may use the sending of a message from process B to process A as an implicit acknowledgment to the original communication from A to B. In most communication systems, the sender of a message is anonymous. Sender identities, however, are important for recovering from message losses on unreliable networks. CPs provide sender identity information.

The following are the basic patterns from which a complete pattern for many applications may be obtained. This list includes the most important patterns observed in a representative list of parallel applications.

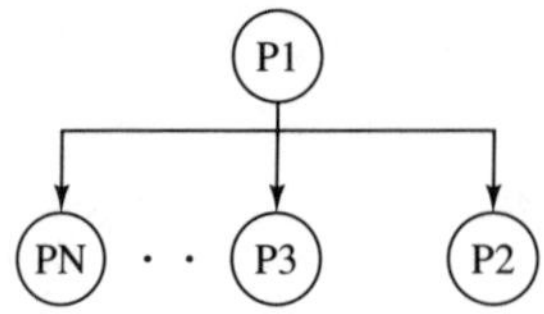

FIGURE 3.2 The multicast communication pattern.

- `Synchronous sends and receives (sendrecv)`. The sender process blocks and waits for the data buffer to which it is sending to be free, and the receiver process blocks and waits for a message to arrive.
- `Asynchronous sends (Asend)`. The sender process does not wait for the data buffer it is sending to be free. It must make separate inquiries to determine when the data buffer is free to be reused.
- `Asynchronous receives (Async)`. The receiver does not wait for a message but sets up a data buffer region, and periodically queries the system to see if the buffer has been filled with data.
- `Request-response (RR)`. A process sends a request message to another process; the first process then blocks and the second process works on the first message and sends a response. This message-passing paradigm may be used to implement a language-level remote procedure call (RPC) mechanism. Typically, the send buffer acts as the receive buffer.
- `Multicast`. A message is sent to a subset of the processes of an application.*
- `Broadcast`. A message is sent to all processes.
- `Reduction`. A process receives messages from a subset of or all the processes of an application.
- `MultiRR`. A message is sent to a group of processes and more than one reply is received. That is, a message is sent to *N* processes, and replies are sought from *M* processes, where *N* and *M* could be distinct.
- `Exchange`. Two processes exchange data simultaneously.
- `RedMulticast`. A `Reduction` followed by a `Multicast`.

As an example, the multicast CP is shown in Figure 3.2. Although it is possible to view all communications in an application as sequences of sends and receives, aggregating as many operations as possible into patterns provides a better characterization of the application for the purposes of communication optimization. An application may consist of a sequence or iteration of basic patterns. Sequences of patterns are denoted by ; and iteration by *. In later chapters, these CPs are used in the design and selection of optimized message-passing and scheduling systems. The selection procedures are described in Figures 6.10, 7.13, 7.17, and 8.9.

*This is different from hardware-supported multicast, where a subset of the hosts (machines) is addressed.

3.2 APPLICATIONS

This section characterizes several parallel applications using the attributes that have been defined. In later chapters, these attributes are used to select optimizations for the applications. Each application description consists of five parts.

1. A description of the algorithm.
2. A description of the parallel decomposition.
3. A list of the application's attributes.*
4. The minimum number of messages required to implement the communication of the parallel decomposition. This represents the messages that must be generated for a correct execution of the algorithm.
5. A list of other applications that have similar PIPs and CPs.

The applications described in this book were chosen because they are either important scientific applications or system services. Four important scientific applications are considered: (1) Simplex; (2) FFT; (3) adaptive quadrature; and (4) Cholesky. Two other scientific applications, wave and Laplace equations, are also characterized. Although implementation results are not presented on these two applications, their characterizations are performed to demonstrate the generalizability of the approach advocated in this book. Two important distributed system services are also considered: a name service, and a distributed gang scheduling facility.

3.2.1 Simplex

Mathematically, the Simplex linear optimization algorithm may be stated as follows:

Minimize $c^T x$
subject to:
$Ax = b$ where $b \geq 0$ and $x \geq 0$

c^T is an n-vector of variable coefficients that defines the objective function (the function to be minimized). The $m \times n$ linear system $Ax = b$ defines the linear constraints on the objective function x. Each of the m rows of the matrix A defines a constraint on the n variables of the objective function. The problem is to optimize the solution x.

This application was chosen because its behavior has been studied extensively on the iPSC/2 hypercube by Stunkel [Stu88b]. In the parallel version [Stu88b] of

*The use of the time-between-iterations attribute for parallel applications is discussed in Section 6.3.4.

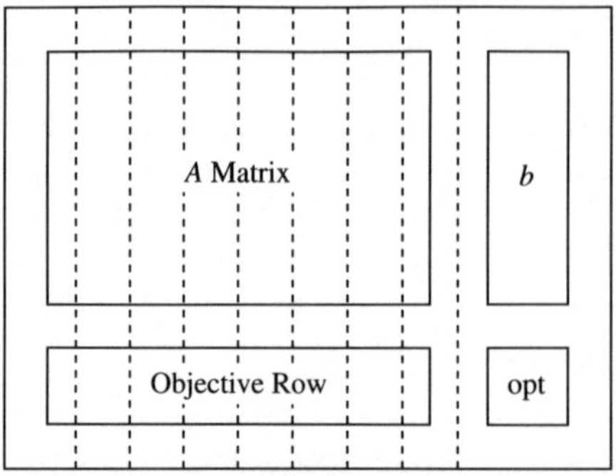

FIGURE 3.3 Simplex column data partitioning scheme.

the Simplex algorithm or application, the data of the problem may be partitioned as rows or as columns. The column partitioning strategy is shown in Figure 3.3. Each process repeatedly finds a minimum among its local data values and then participates in the identification of a global minimum, the pivot element. The process that owns this minimum value multicasts a matrix row or column, depending on the data partition chosen, to all the other processes. Thus, the pattern of interprocess communication is data dependent. Table 3.1 shows the number of messages transmitted between processes as the number of processes increases for a data set used in one of the measurements. The message sizes are input data set dependent. Table 3.2 shows a sample distribution of message sizes for a data set used in one of the measurements. The message size distribution is bimodal. Such bimodal distributions occur in many distributed systems [Che86b].

The Simplex application has the communication pattern shown in Figure 3.4. Each process finds the local minimum of the objective values for columns at each process and communicates these values to process 0, which then redistributes these values and the identity of the process that has the pivot column. This process is referred to as **piv_id**. This is a `RedMulticast` pattern.

One process owns the entire pivot column; and the identity of this process changes with each iteration of the algorithm. This process can also determine the pivot row if it has **b** (see Figure 3.3). **b** is sent to the **piv_id** by the owner of the **b** column, which is referred to as **b_node**. **piv_id** determines **piv_row** and then multicasts the entire **pivcol** and value of **piv_row**. Each process then uses

TABLE 3.1 Increasing Number of Messages as Processes Increase

Simplex Processors Versus Messages	
Processors	Messages
2	585
4	881
8	1528

TABLE 3.2 Simplex Message Size Distribution in Bytes for Two to Eight Processes for the Share2b Data Set

	Number of Process		
	2	4	8
Input Data Set Size			
16 (pivot selection)	54	74.9	80
814 (pivot and b data)	45.79	25	19
1192 (input)	0.21	0.1	0.1
Average	377.02	216.67	160.65

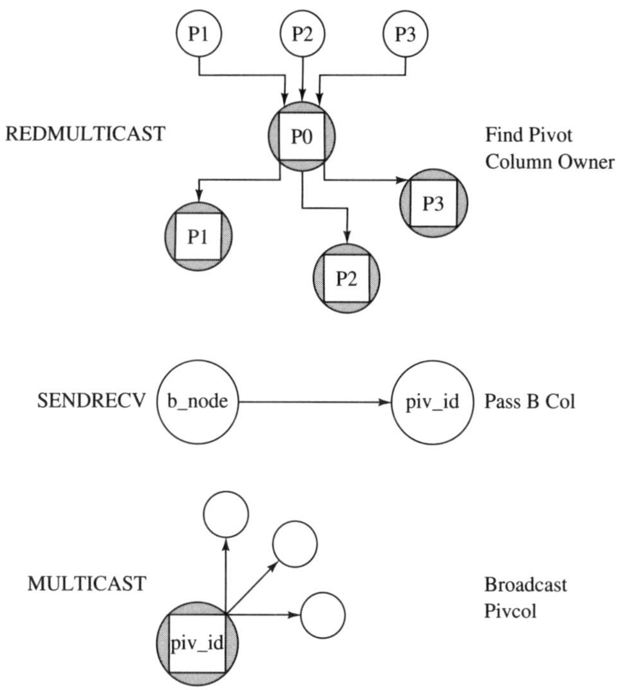

FIGURE 3.4 CP of Simplex per iteration.

piv_col to perform Gauss-Jordan elimination, exchanging the basic columns. The iteration is then complete. The CP of the entire application is a variant of the `RedMulticast` CP.

The Simplex application has a synchronous PIP. The Simplex application requires ordered and reliable multicast. The application uses message types in its blocking receives.

Minimum Number of Messages. The minimum number of messages per iteration is $N + 2$, where N is the number of processes used.

Applications with Similar PIPs and CPs. The revised Simplex application [Stu88b] has a similar PIP and CP to that of Simplex.

3.2.2 Cholesky Factorization

Cholesky factorization is an important algorithm in linear algebra. If matrix A $(M \times M)$ is symmetric positive definite, then there exists a unique lower triangular matrix G $(M \times M)$ with positive diagonal entries such that $A = GG^T$ [GL89]. This factorization is known as Cholesky factorization and G is referred to as the Cholesky triangle. Once the Cholesky factorization has been computed, it is possible to solve the triangular systems $Gy = b$ and $G^T x = y$ using $b = Gy = G(G^T)x = (GG^T)x = Ax$. Triangular systems are easier to solve than matrices with no regular structure.

There are a variety of ways to parallelize Cholesky. Two schemes for distributing the rows of the matrix are discussed: shuffle (sometimes referred to as cyclic) partitioning and block partitioning. In block partitioning, the rows are partitioned in a chunk or block. In shuffle partitioning, the rows are partitioned in a striped fashion. The Cholesky factorization of a matrix of size $M \times M$, using N processes, is considered.

In the block partitioning scheme, each process multicasts its entire set of rows to a subset of the processes before the next process in the sequence starts its communication. Each process multicasts $\frac{M}{N}$ rows of size i each, where i is the ith iteration. The number of processes receiving a multicast decreases by one after each block of *M/N* multicasts are sent [AHP92]. All $\frac{M}{N}$ rows are multicast by one process, and then the next process multicasts its set of $\frac{M}{N}$ rows. There are a total of M iterations.

In the shuffle partitioning scheme, different processes are involved in multicasting their row at each iteration. Here each process takes its turn in multicasting a row. Each multicast sends exactly i elements, where i is the iteration number. Each process multicasts a total of $\frac{M}{N}$ rows, but these are interspersed with multicasts from other processes in a regular pattern (see Figure 3.6). This pattern is referred to as `Repetitive` since the multicast pattern repeats.

In both schemes, the message size linearly increases with the number of the iteration performed. The CPs for the two partitioning schemes for Cholesky are shown in Figures 3.5 and 3.6. They both have a synchronous PIP.

Both Cholesky partitionings have a unimodal message distribution that depends on the data set size. The message size is $16 \times M$, where M is an integer value specifying the number of columns in the matrix. Only square matrices are considered in this example. The Cholesky application requires ordered and reliable delivery of its multicast messages. The application uses message types in its blocking receives.

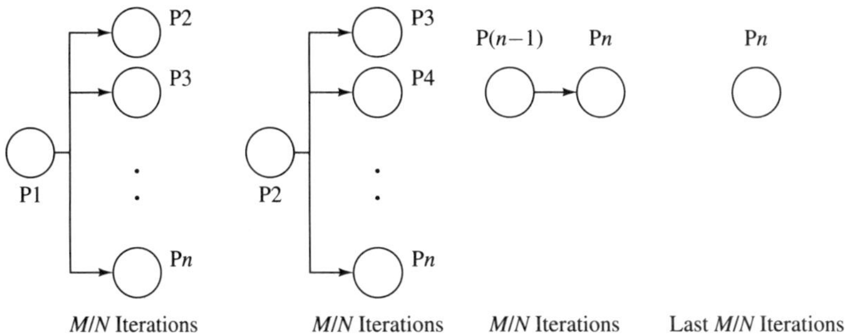

FIGURE 3.5 CP of block-partitioned Cholesky.

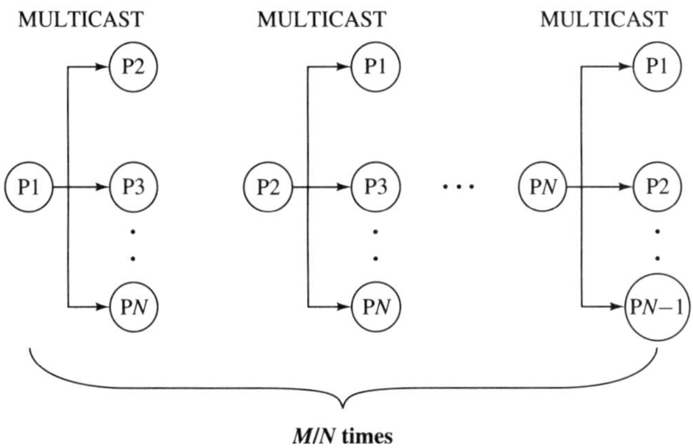

FIGURE 3.6 CP of shuffle-partitioned Cholesky.

Minimum Number of Messages. The minimum number of multicasts required is M, which is the number of columns.

Applications with Similar PIPs and CPs. The following applications have similar a PIP and CP: transitive closure of matrix, matrix multiply, and all pairs shortest path.

3.2.3 Fast Fourier Transform

The Fast Fourier Transform (FFT) [MII89] is a computational technique that is used extensively in engineering applications. In the parallel version of the FFT, the application uses N processes. For a data set of size M, the application has $\log_2(M)$ butterfly stages, $\log_2(N)$ of which are performed over the network. The $\log_2(N)$ network stages involve the transfer of $16 \times M \times \log_2(N)$ bytes of data. The FFT experiment is interesting as a scalability study: As the size M of the

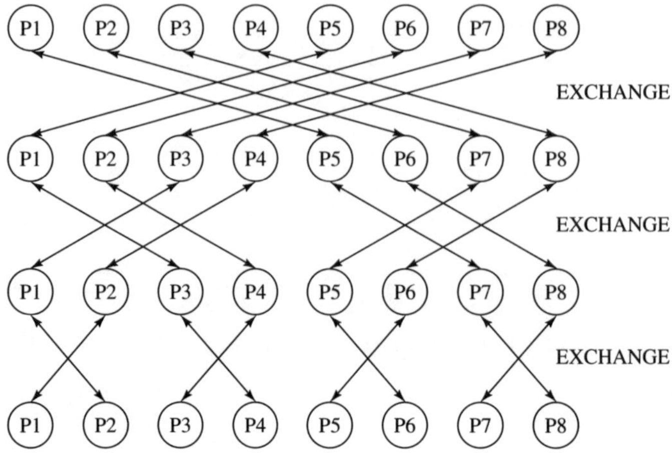

FIGURE 3.7 CP of FFT.

data increases, the message size increases linearly with M, but the computation increases as $M \log_2(M)$.

The PIP of the FFT application is synchronous. The CP for the parallel version of the FFT is shown in Figure 3.7. FFT has an `ExchangeNoLocality` pattern, which is an `Exchange` pattern without any communication locality across iterations: The pairs of processes communicating are different at each iteration.

The message size distribution for various input data set sizes and number of processes is shown in Table 3.3. On the shared-memory multiprocessor, the FFT application has the invalidation attribute, since the arrays holding the data array of two different processes may be mapped to the same cache lines.

Minimum Number of Messages. The minimum number of messages per iteration is N, since there are $N/2$ exchanges each involving two messages.

Applications with Similar PIPs and CPs. The bitonic merge, convolution, and data rearrangement algorithms [PV81] have the same PIP and CP as FFT.

TABLE 3.3 FFT Message Data Size in Bytes for Varying Numbers of Processes

	FFT Points				
Processors	128	256	512	1024	2048
2	512	1024	2048	4096	8192
4	256	512	1024	2048	4096
8	128	256	512	1024	2048

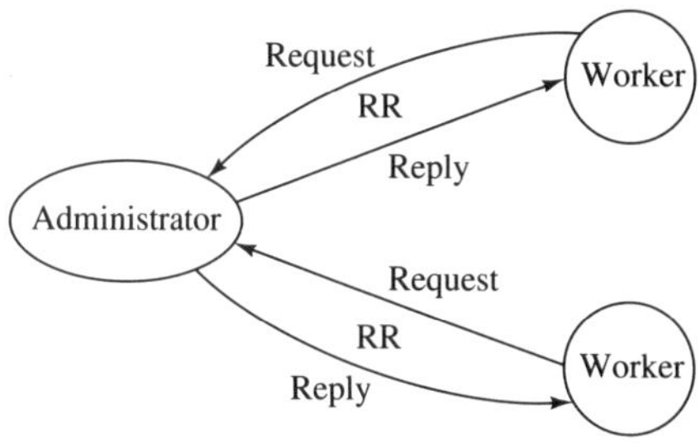

FIGURE 3.8 CP of adaptive quadrature.

3.2.4 Adaptive Quadrature

Adaptive quadrature is a technique for numerical integration. The area under the function that is to be integrated is broken into rectangles, which are used as approximations to the area under the function. The desired accuracy of the numerical integration is user specifiable.

The parallel version is structured with a central administrator process coordinating the integration. Each worker process computes a different section under the function. The worker processes either send more work back to the administrator process or send an approximation to the part of the function it was assigned to evaluate. The administrator process then decides when to terminate the application, based on the accuracy specified by the user. The application has a constant message size of 40 bytes, which is input data set-size independent. Therefore, even if the function being computed changes the message sizes do not change. The CP for the parallel version of adaptive quadrature appears in Figure 3.8. It has an RR CP and a bag-of-tasks PIP.

Minimum Number of Messages. The minimum number of messages per interaction between the administrator and a worker is two.

Applications with Similar PIPs and CPs. Branch and bound algorithms share the adaptive quadrature's PIP and CP.

3.2.5 One-Dimensional Wave Equation

The time-dependent motion of a simple vibrating string may be described by the following hyperbolic partial differential equation [FJL+88].

$$\frac{1}{c^2}\frac{\delta^2\psi}{\delta t^2} - \frac{\delta^2\psi}{\delta x^2} = 0$$

This equation is known as the *wave equation*. Figure 3.9 shows the CP for the parallel version of the one-dimensional wave equation per iteration. It has an `ExchangeWithLocality` CP, which is an `Exchange` CP with communication locality across iterations. Each process exchanges data with two neighbors at each iteration. Across each iteration these two neighbors are the same for each process. The messages are all typed and are of size *size(of)nodal element.*

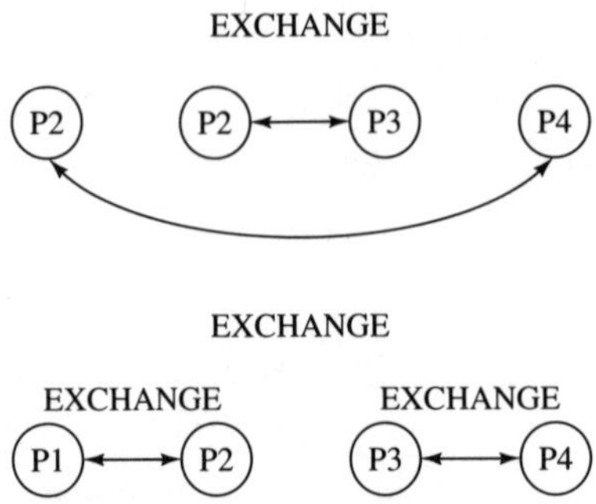

FIGURE 3.9 CP of wave equation per iteration.

Minimum Number of Messages. The minimum number of messages required per iteration is eight per process.

Other Applications with Similar PIPs and CPs. The Laplace equation solved using the method of finite differences has a similar PIP and CP.

3.2.6 The Laplace Equation Using Finite Differences

The two-dimensional Laplace equation [FJL+88] is an example of an elliptical partial differential equation. The Laplace equation may be solved by a first-order finite difference equation. The CP for a parallel version of this application is shown in Figure 3.10. It has an `ExchangeWithLocality` CP, which is an `Exchange` CP

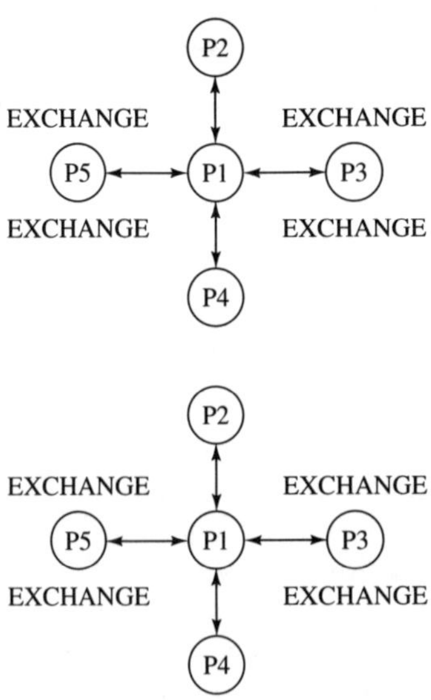

FIGURE 3.10 CP of the Laplace equation per iteration.

with communication locality across iterations. As the figure shows, there are two sets of exchanges per iteration. Each exchange has locality between each exchange and across iterations. The messages are typed, and the size of the message is *sqrt(N)*, where *N* is the number of nodal points stored on each processor.*

Minimum Number of Messages. The minimum number of messages per iteration is 16 per process.

Applications with Similar PIPs and CPs. The wave equation has a similar PIP and CP.

3.2.7 Distributed Applications

Applications written using the client-server PIP also have CPs associated with them. Two client-server applications are discussed in this book: a distributed name server and a distributed gang scheduler. Both applications have idempotent server functions. The distributed gang scheduler requires ordered and reliable multicast. The details of the algorithms and the patterns for these applications are described in Sections 7.6.1 and 7.6.2.

3.3 SUMMARY

Table 3.4 lists some of the most salient attributes of applications discussed in this chapter. Parallel and distributed applications may be characterized according to attributes that can be used to design optimized message-passing and scheduling

*Nodal point refers to domain discretization [FJL+88].

TABLE 3.4 Summary of Salient Application Attributes

Application	CP and Other Attributes
FFT	`ExchangeNoLocality*` Invalidation, Types, and Message Size = Variable
Cholesky	`Multicast*` Types, Iteration time, and Message Size = Variable
Simplex	`(RedMulticast;sendrecv;Multicast)*` Types, Iteration time, and Message Size = Small
Adaptive quadrature	`RR*`, Types and Message Size = Small
Wave	`ExchangeLocality*`, Types and Message Size = Variable
Laplace	`ExchangeLocality*`, Types and Message Size = Variable
Dist. Scheduler	`MultiRR;Multicast;Multicast` and Types, Idempotent Server functions and Message Size = Small
Name Server	`Multicast;MultiRR` and idempotent server functions and Message Size = Small

systems. All applications, except adaptive quadrature, are written with a synchronous PIP. The adaptive quadrature is written using a bag-of-tasks PIP.

Detailed implementation and performance results are discussed for the Simplex, FFT, adaptive quadrature, Cholesky, NameService, and distributed gang scheduling applications. In particular, the CP attribute allows an efficient message-passing system to be designed per application. To demonstrate the generalizability of the CP-based approach to the design of customized message-passing systems, the CP of several other applications are discussed, including those for the wave and Laplace equations.

CHAPTER 4

Optimization Selection Guidelines for Message Passing

The design of the message-passing system encapsulates basic facilities to support different message-passing primitives, such as synchronous and asynchronous message passing, multicasts, and broadcasts. The message-passing system is designed to be easily extensible to incorporate new interfaces and implementations. This chapter describes the subframeworks of the message-passing system and the classes of each subframework that facilitate easy customization. This chapter also describes how to select an optimization of the message-passing system using the application attributes discussed in Chapter 3.

One of the distinguishing features of an object-oriented design is the granularity at which customizations can be made. In server-based systems such as Mach, it is possible to easily replace an entire server with a new one. Introducing a new implementation of a Mach communication port, however, is not easy. Incrementally adding new implementations of communication ports is supported in the design presented here. Allowing fine-grained modifications to fundamental operating system primitives and implementations is an important part of application-specific customizations.

4.1 THE SUBFRAMEWORKS OF THE MESSAGE-PASSING SYSTEM

Object-oriented frameworks are used to design the message-passing system. They are chosen for three reasons.

1. Frameworks enable the design of portable software.
2. Frameworks allow a controlled environment to run experiments.
3. Frameworks enable the incremental generation of new message-passing system optimizations.

A framework consists of subframeworks [CI93a], which may be refined independently. Each subframework consists of a set of classes that are used together; each class represents a component of a subframework. Seven subframeworks exist in the message-passing system: (1) application programming interface (API); (2) naming; (3) message handling; (4) transport; (5) reliability; (6) data transfer; and (7) synchronization.

When a message is sent by an application process, it enters the message-passing system through the API subframework, passes through the various other subframeworks, and appears at the API subframework for the receiving process. The receiving process then retrieves the message from the message-passing system.

This particular decomposition of the message-passing system is chosen to facilitate easy porting of the message-passing system to various hardware architectures. It is possible to compose subframeworks for each port of the message-passing system to an architecture and thus eliminate the overhead of unnecessary subframeworks. For example, the subframeworks for the message-passing system on a distributed system and on a shared-memory multiprocessor are shown in Figures 4.1 and 4.2, respectively. The distributed system and shared-memory multiprocessor ports have differently constructed message-passing systems. The shared-memory multiprocessor port is simpler and uses only six subframeworks, whereas the distributed system port uses seven subframeworks. The distributed system port must handle reliable delivery and the fragmentation and reassembly

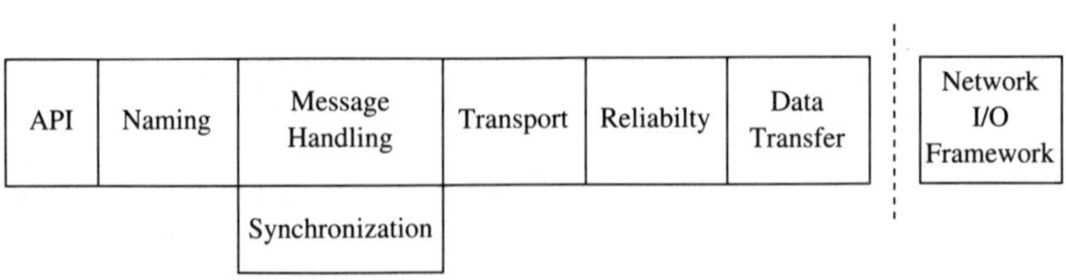

FIGURE 4.1 Subframeworks for the message-passing system on the distributed system.

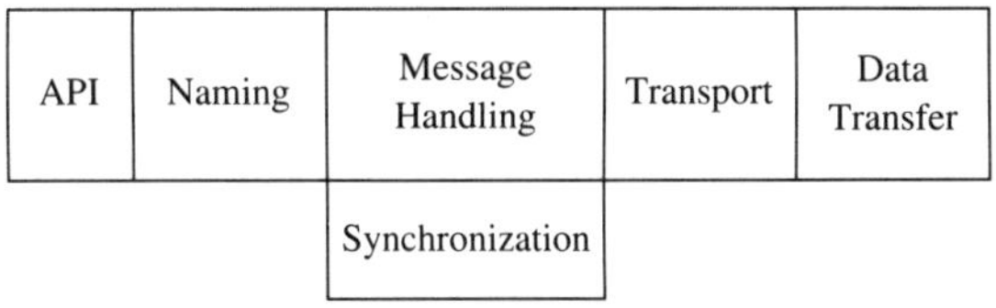

FIGURE 4.2 Subframeworks for the message-passing system on a shared-memory multiprocessor.

of messages. In addition, a network I/O framework interacts with the message-passing system framework on the distributed system to move messages to and from the network hardware.

The message-passing system supports multiple application-specific optimizations. The classes in the framework are subclassed on a per-application basis. These classes allow incremental modifications to existing designs and implementations. The classes in the subframeworks also allow controlled experimentation. Each optimization requires only a few changes to one or more classes while leaving the rest of the system intact. Experiments can measure the performance improvements resulting directly from these changes. For example, a change in the message handling subframework can be made without affecting the other subframeworks.

The message-passing system subframeworks have multiple implementations as concrete subclasses. In designing each subframework, the choice of implementation for a class is dictated by possible application attributes and how they affect performance. The subclasses were designed so that application attributes can be used to choose between them.

4.2 SELECTION GUIDE

Creating an instance of the message-passing framework that is application specific requires the selection of a set of concrete classes, instances of which at runtime form an application-specific message-passing system. This section describes how to select an optimized message-passing system for an application from an existing set of implementations (that is, concrete classes). This set of implementations is called a tool kit. Figure 4.3 illustrates the selection process, which consists of two steps, with the second step yielding an optimized message-passing system. Using the characterizing attributes (see Chapter 3) of an application, an optimized implementation of a message-passing system can be found.

Section 1.2 shows the three steps required to run an application. In this section, steps 1 and 2 are described in detail. In step 1, the characterizing attributes of an application are identified by the application programmer, and the values of the attributes for that application are recorded. For example, the FFT application has a CP attribute with a value of `ExchangeLocality*`. In step 2, a description of the message-passing system framework and the attribute value pairs are used in the

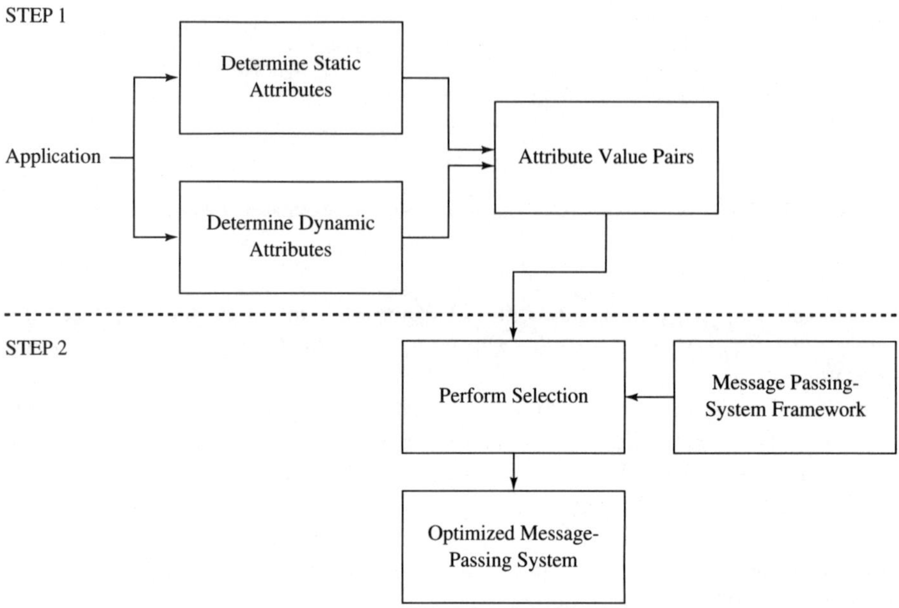

FIGURE 4.3 Selecting an optimized message-passing system for an application.

selection process. A framework consists of a set of subframeworks, each of which consists of a set of class hierarchies. Each class hierarchy is rooted in an abstract class. We refer to this as the *root abstract class*. Figure 4.4 shows a class hierarchy with three classes: A, B, and C. Abstract class A is at the root of the hierarchy, and it has concrete subclasses B and C. Distinguished classes in each hierarchy help select between implementations; they are decision points. In step 2, the application attributes and synthetic benchmarks, or analytical models that differentiate between the various implementations, are used to select an optimized message-passing system. The synthetic benchmark or analytical model would be used to select between concrete classes B and C, as is shown in Figure 4.4. For example, if B and C were to represent two separate synchronization mechanisms, and a synthetic benchmark that measured the time to acquire and release locks, the CP and other attributes would be used to select between two concrete classes. In this manner, a concrete implementation is chosen for all the root abstract classes in the message-passing framework.

It is possible for an abstract class to have other abstract classes as implementations. The selection process just determines the choice of various concrete class implementations of the root abstract classes of each implementation. The optimized message-passing system is a set of concrete classes, instances of which collectively represent an application-specific message-passing system. Once the selection is made, the names of the concrete classes are passed to the operat-

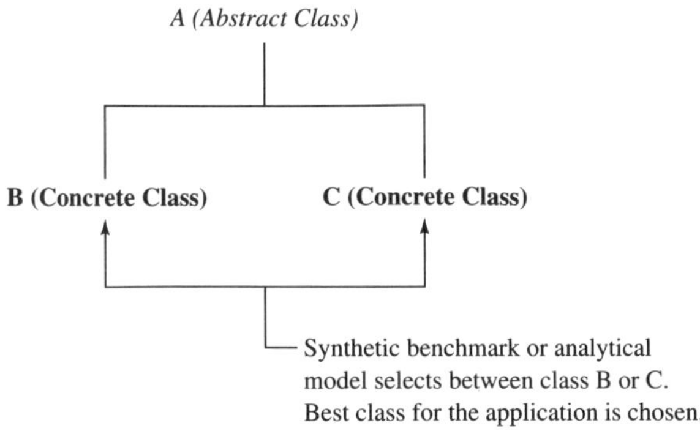

FIGURE 4.4 Selecting an implementation or concrete class.

ing system, which then loads the relevant subclasses. These classes may then be dynamically loaded using the mechanism described in Section 2.9.

To select an application-specific instance of a framework, a concrete subclass must be chosen for each root abstract class of each subframework. For example, to generate an application-specific instance of the message-passing framework on a shared-memory architecture, a concrete class of each of the abstract classes in the API, naming, message handling, synchronization, transport, reliability, and data transfer subframeworks must be chosen. The selection process assumes that each of these subframework selections can be made independently.*

The synthetic benchmark or analytical model measures a particular performance overhead of the message-passing system. For example, one synthetic benchmark measures message latency, so the implementation that reduces message latency is chosen. In another example, an analytical model evaluates the number of network messages, interrupts, and buffers required by an application running on the message-passing system. The synthetic benchmarks are carefully chosen so that they can differentiate between the various implementations, and the implementation that minimizes operating systems overheads is chosen. Chapters 6 and 8 discuss in detail the selection process for the relevant subframeworks on the distributed system and the shared-memory architecture. This semiautomatic selection procedure forms an important part of this book. Detailed selection is discussed in these later chapters because selection goes hand-in-hand with the construction of the class hierarchies. The class hierarchies are constructed to be easily selectable. Before examples are presented on how the selection works, the synthetic benchmarks and analytical models used in the selection process are described.

The use of the selection guide is now presented for the shared-memory multiprocessor and the distributed system. Although the selection procedure is

*Sometimes dependencies appear and these must be noted. Handling selection dependencies between subframeworks is addressed in a later section.

architecture independent, the actual optimizations chosen for a particular application are architecture specific.

4.2.1 Shared-Memory Selection Guide

On shared-memory multiprocessors, specialized classes are selected from five subframeworks: (1) API; (2) synchronization; (3) message handling; (4) data transfer; and (5) transport. Each subframework is optimized independently. Synthetic benchmarks are a powerful selection technique used on shared-memory multiprocessors. Although many synthetic benchmarks are possible, the five synthetic benchmarks used for customization selection on shared-memory multiprocessors are presented. Each synthetic benchmark measures the overhead of several implementations, given various application attributes. The synthetic benchmarks are constructed such that, given a set of attributes of an application, the implementation that minimizes message latency and the overhead of lock acquisition is chosen. Four of the synthetic benchmarks measure the message latency, and one benchmark measures the overhead to acquire and release locks. All synthetic benchmarks are constructed using the PIP attribute. The value of the PIP attribute is either synchronous or bag-of-tasks. The five synthetic benchmarks, along with the attributes used with them, are as follows

1. Ring. This is a basic message latency benchmark. It uses message size as a parameter.
2. Free list/circular buffer (circ/free). This benchmark measures the effect of message queue organizations on message latency for different message sizes. Free list and circular list organizations are examined. This benchmark uses message size as a parameter.
3. Multicast. This benchmark measures the message latency for sending a message to more than one process. The CP of an application is used as a parameter.
4. Invalidation. This benchmark measures the effect of cache line invalidations on message latency. It uses the invalidation and message size attributes as parameters. Although many different invalidation patterns are possible, the invalidation pattern observed in the FFT application is used as an example.
5. Acquire/release. This benchmark measures the time to acquire and release a lock and uses the concurrency attribute as a parameter.

4.2.2 Distributed System Selection Guide

On the distributed system, the reliability subframework is specialized. Analytical models are a powerful selection technique used on distributed systems to find the appropriate reliability subframework specialization for an application. On unreliable networks, error handling can be expensive and naive implementations can exact heavy penalties for communication performance. The designers of the

VMTP protocol [Che86b] and the Amoeba [KT91] multicast protocols and the results in this book concur that the following metrics characterize communication performance overheads.

- Number of network messages
- Number of interrupts
- Number of network buffers

The number of network messages refers to the number of messages generated by the implementation of the message-passing system. This number is often different from the number of application-level messages because acknowledgment messages are generated that add to the cost complexity of the protocol. The number of network messages is an important performance metric because it provides an indication of network bandwidth consumption. This metric is particularly important on low bandwidth networks such as Ethernet.

The number of interrupts generated in the system as a whole is an extremely important metric because it indicates the amount of additional processing overhead for the message-passing system. This number is the same as the number of network messages, except in cases where hardware-supported multicast is used. Then, the number of interrupts is greater than the number of network messages. Interrupts spoil locality by causing hardware cache flushes and are inherently expensive on many modern RISC architectures.

Unacknowledged messages must be buffered by a message-passing system implemented on an unreliable network, because if an error in transmission occurs, the message has to be retransmitted. The number of network buffers required is the number of messages that have to be maintained in the message-passing system until a sent message is acknowledged. Buffer management overhead is an important consideration in the implementation of ordered and reliable multicast.

4.3 EXAMPLES OF THE SELECTION PROCEDURE

The selection process is demonstrated using two examples. In the first example, an optimized message-passing system is generated for the FFT application on a shared-memory architecture, with special emphasis on selecting the synchronization mechanism. In the second example, an optimized message-passing system is generated for the Cholesky application on a distributed system, with special emphasis on selecting the reliability mechanism for the network protocol.

Figure 4.5 shows the selection procedure depicted in Figure 4.3 annotated with the relevant information pertaining to the FFT application for an input data set size of 1024. The application-specific information appears in italics outside the steps. In step 1, the attributes and their values are set by the application programmer. For step 2, a representation of the synchronization subframework is shown. It is simply the relevant class hierarchy with the abstract class *Synchronization* at its root. It has three implementations: (1) Semaphore; (2) TASLock (test-and-set locks);

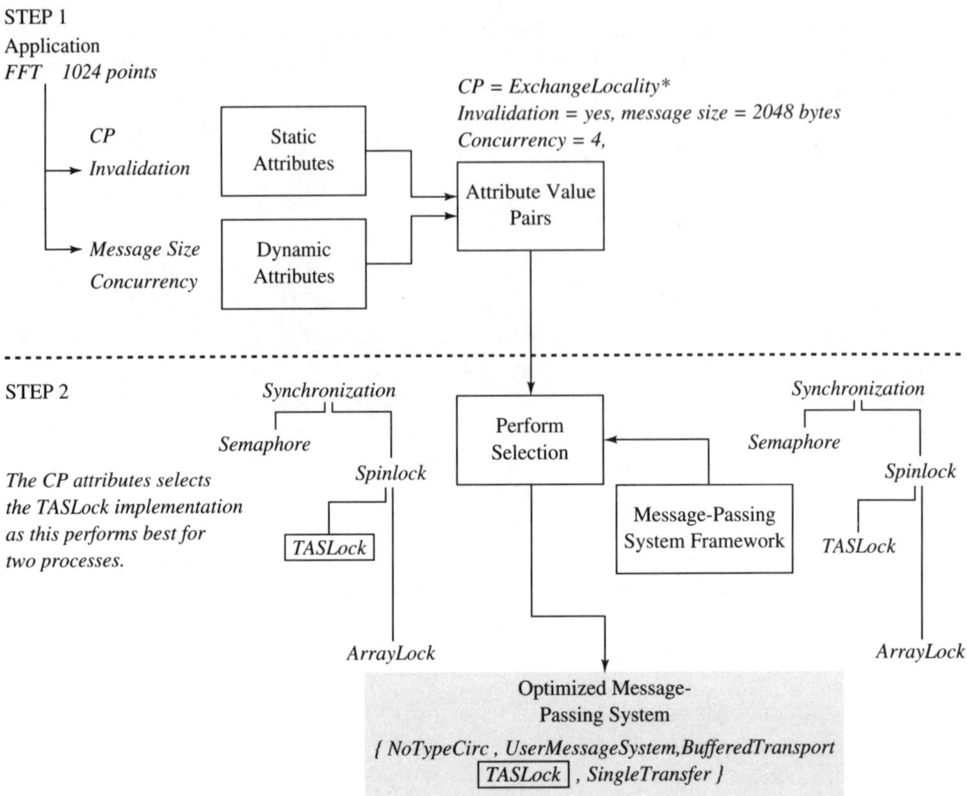

FIGURE 4.5 An illustration of how the locking subframework of an optimized message-passing system is selected for the FFT application on a shared-memory multiprocessor. The other subframeworks of the message-passing system are similarly optimized for FFT and are explained later in the book. The diagram illustrates steps 1 and 2 of the selection procedure. The selection of the TASLock for synchronization is highlighted.

and (3) Anderson's ArrayLock. In step 2, synthetic benchmarks are used to differentiate between these implementations using the CP of `ExchangeLocality*` as a parameter. The best concrete subclass is TASLock.

To find the best synchronization on a shared-memory multiprocessor, three attributes are considered: (1) PIP; (2) concurrency; and (3) CP. The selection process for synchronization is summarized in Figure 4.6. It illustrates how the three application attributes guide the selection process. The synchronization class hierarchy is shown in Figure 4.7. The selection procedure starts at the root of the class hierarchy, synchronization, and proceeds to the leaves of the hierarchy. At the root of the hierarchy, the choice is between a spinlock and a semaphore. The Ring benchmark dictates that for a synchronous or bag-of-tasks PIP, spinlocks

```
SynchronizationSelection() {
N = numProcesses;
if( PIP = synchronous or PIP = bag-of-tasks)
if((CP with more than two processes) && (N => 8)) Array Lock
        else test-and-set Lock
}
```

FIGURE 4.6 Sample selection procedure for synchronization subframework.

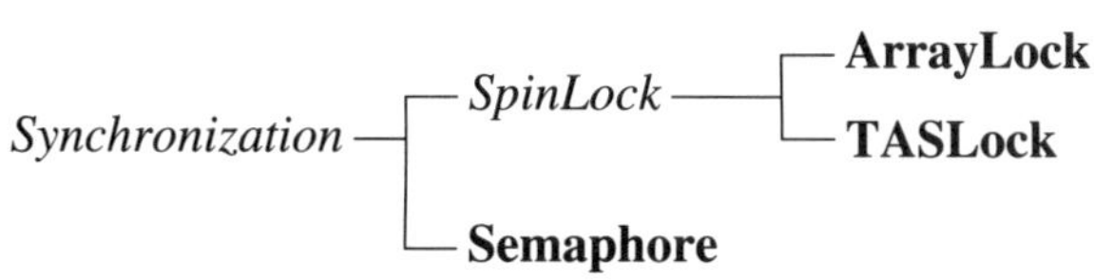

FIGURE 4.7 Synchronization class hierarchy.

are always chosen over semaphores because they always provide lower message latency. To choose the appropriate spinlock, the CP and the concurrency attributes of an application are used. If the CP can potentially involve more than two processes and the value of the concurrency attribute is greater than or equal to eight, an array lock should be chosen; otherwise a test-and-set lock should be chosen. The synthetic benchmark that selects between the array lock and spinlock is shown in Figure 4.8. It measures the time to acquire and release a lock 100,000 times. As

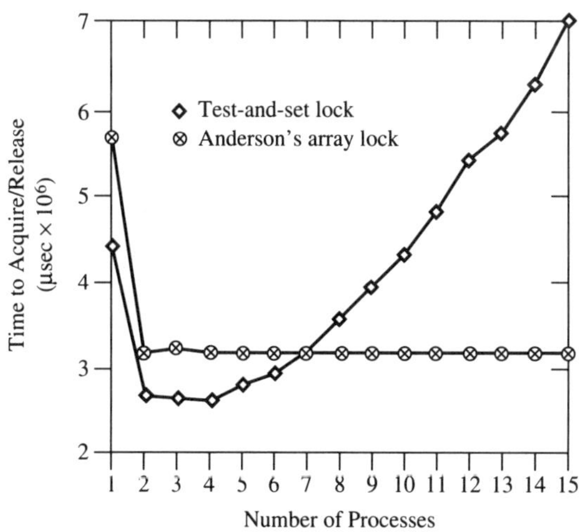

FIGURE 4.8 Time to acquire and release a lock 100,000 times.

the benchmark shows, there is a crossover point when the number of processes is seven, When the number of processes is less than or equal to seven, the test-and-set lock is preferred. When the number of processes is greater than or equal to eight, the array lock is preferred.

To select the appropriate synchronization mechanism for the FFT application on a shared-memory multiprocessor, one must know the application's attributes. It has a synchronous PIP and an `ExchangeNoLocality` CP. The synchronous PIP dictates the choice of specialization of a spinlock. Since the `ExchangeNoLocality` CP only involves pairs of processes, the test-and-set lock is chosen for the FFT application. The selection of a synchronizations mechanism is only one part of the procedure for generating the optimized message-passing system for the FFT application.

To generate an instance of the message-passing system that is tailored to the FFT application on a shared-memory architecture, optimized selections must be made in the five remaining subframeworks (API, naming, message handling, transport, and data transfer) using the attributes of the FFT application. Since the selection of the optimizations is independent, however, the attributes are used to select the appropriate concrete classes. As Figure 4.5 shows, the set of subclasses chosen for FFT are as follows: NoTypeCirc for the message-handling subframework; UserMessageSystem for the API subframework; BufferedTransport for the transport subframework; TASLock for the synchronization subframework; and SingleTransfer for the data transfer subframework. The control flow through the FFT-specific instance of the message-passing framework is shown in Figure 4.9. Note that all the abstract classes of the framework in the abstract control flow graph of Figure 5.6 (see Chapter 5) have been replaced by concrete subclasses. The method invocation sequence is an invariant of the design and has not changed in the implementation. The design of the abstract framework has been preserved in an implementation. For a complete selection of the other subframeworks for the FFT application, see Section 9.1.

The selection procedure for Cholesky is summarized in Figure 4.10, which shows how the transport subframework is specialized for the Cholesky application. Figure 4.10 depicts the application shown in Figure 4.3 with each step annotated (in italics) with application-specific information. The relevant attributes for Cholesky are CP, reliability, types, ordering, and iteration time. To find the best reliability measure on a distributed system, the CP attribute is used. The selection procedure for reliability is summarized in Figure 4.11. It illustrates how the attributes guide the selection process on a distributed system. The selection process starts at the ClientCSR decision point in the class hierarchy (shown in Figure 4.12). This class has two implementation options: CSRShuffle and Naive.

The CP application attribute is used to select a specialization of the reliability subframework. An implementation is chosen to minimize the three overheads for distributed systems: number of network messages, interrupts, and network buffers. An analytical model measures these overheads, given the different application attributes.

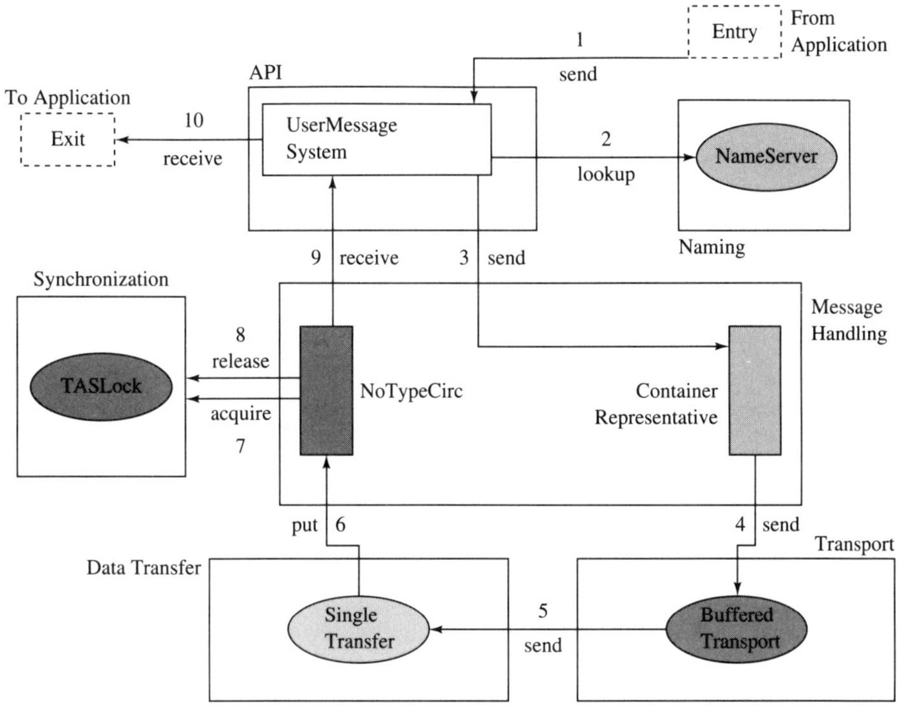

FIGURE 4.9 The control flow through an FFT-specific message-passing framework.

On unreliable networks there are a variety of ways to ensure the reliable delivery of data. Most schemes generate too many network messages for each application-level message. The goal is to aggregate the acknowledgments for application-level messages by examining the CP of an application.

For example, the Cholesky application has a `Repetitive` CP, attribute as described in Section 3.2.2. The `Repetitive` CP is shown in Figure 3.6. In the `Repetitive` CP, each process performs a multicast and then waits for all the other processes to multicast. This process then performs its next multicast. Hence, the multicast pattern repeats. Such CPs provide global knowledge about the state of the system. If the multicast pattern repeats every N iterations, this set of iterations constitutes a phase. Once a process is able to multicast again, all the activity in the previous phase is known to be complete.

Multicast communication from all other processes serves as an acknowledgment from the other processes that they have received the previous multicast communication from that process. In the optimized implementation, missing messages are retrieved by blocked receivers whose timers expire. These receivers ask the appropriate instance of the message-passing system to resend the missing multicast message. At the start of each phase, buffers kept for the previous phase may be

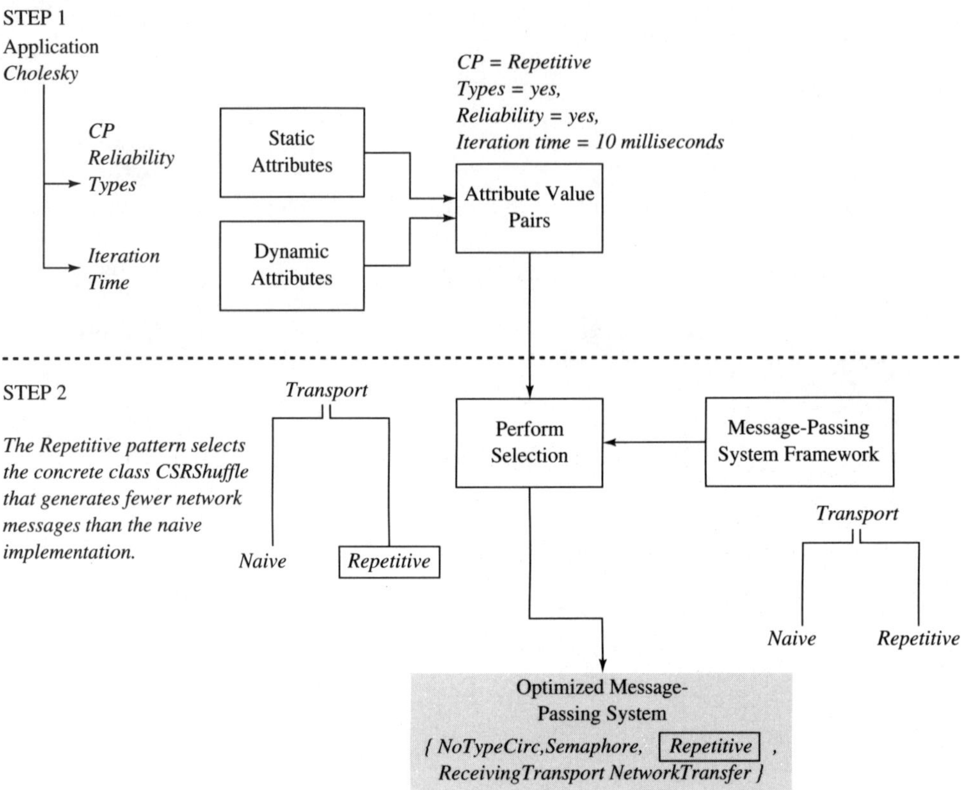

FIGURE 4.10 An illustration of how the reliability subframework of the message-passing system is optimized for the Cholesky application from start to finish. The diagram illustrates steps 1 and 2 of the selection procedure. The selection of the `Repetitive` class is highlighted

removed. A naive scheme would send point-to-point messages and acknowledge each message independently. If there are N processes in the application and one process performs the send, the optimized scheme requires N network messages*

*This assumes that hardware support for multicast exists, and requires only one network message.

```
SynchronousParallelApplicationSelection()
{
        if (CP=Repetitive)
                CSRShuffle;
        else Naive;
}
```

FIGURE 4.11 Sample selection procedure for reliability subframework.

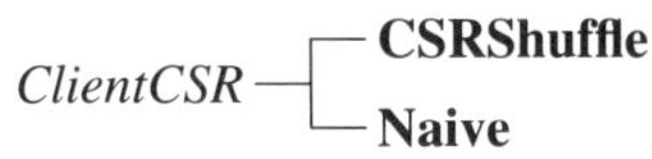

FIGURE 4.12 Reliability class hierarchy.

while the naive scheme requires $N \times 2(N - 1)$ network messages. Thus, the optimized implementation of the `Repetitive` pattern is chosen rather than the naive implementation. To generate a complete instance of the message-passing system for Cholesky on a distributed system, the six remaining subframeworks must be optimized as well. As can be seen, the same technique is used to select the other concrete subclasses to yield a concrete implementation. The remainder of the selections are shown in Figure 4.10 as KernelMessageSystem, MessageContainer, Semaphore, Repetitive, ReceivingTransport, and NetworkTransfer. The control flow through the Cholesky-specific instance of the message-passing framework is shown in Figure 4.13. Note that all the abstract classes of the framework in the abstract control flow graph of Figure 5.7 (see Chapter 5) have been replaced by concrete subclasses. The method invocation sequence is an invariant of the design and has not changed in the implementation. The design of the abstract framework has been preserved in an implementation. A more detailed account of the selection for Cholesky appears in Sections 6.3.2 and 7.2.

For each application, the attributes, synthetic benchmarks, and analytical model guide the selection of the various specializations of subframeworks. The remainder of the selection procedures for all the options in the message-passing system are discussed in detail in Chapters 6, 7, 8, and 9.

4.4 SUMMARY

In any system that provides a multitude of alternatives, there must be a mechanism for selecting among the alternatives. This chapter describes a methodology for choosing optimizations of a message-passing system. The selection process uses application attributes, synthetic benchmarks, or analytical models to select optimized message passing from a tool kit of implementations. The application attributes guide the selection of optimizations from existing implementations. There are a variety of implementations of message passing on both shared-memory multiprocessors and distributed systems. The mechanisms for adding new optimizations are presented in later chapters.

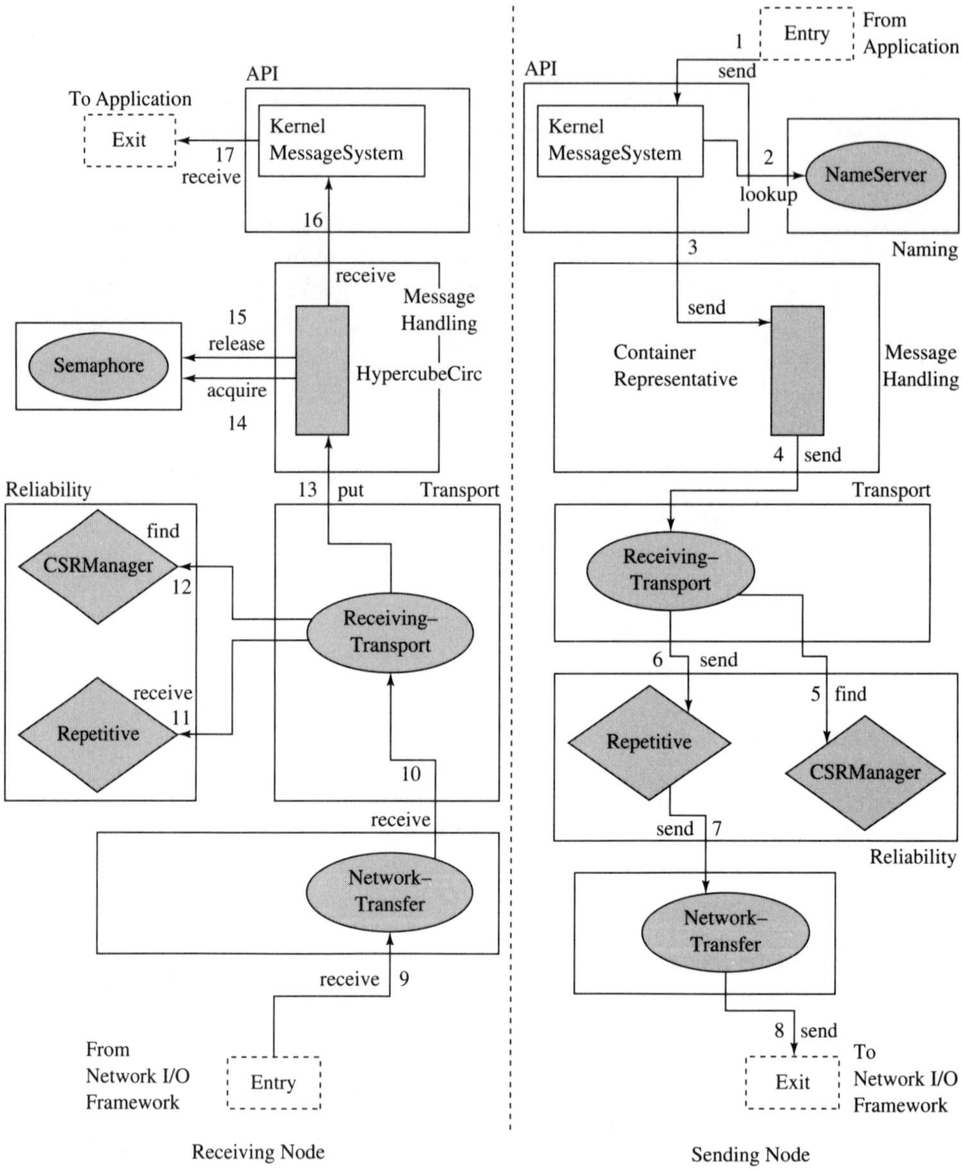

FIGURE 4.13 The control flow through a Cholesky-specific message-passing framework.

CHAPTER 5

Design of the Message-Passing System

The purpose of this chapter is to describe the overall structure of the message-passing system and introduce the major abstractions that are refined to generate the application-specific optimizations of later chapters.

The major abstract classes of each subframework are the roots of class hierarchies consisting of other abstract classes and concrete classes. There are two categories of subclasses. One category describes classes that are subclassed for functionality. The other describes those that are created solely for the purpose of application-specific performance. Descriptions of the concrete classes that are based solely on performance appear in later chapters. Those subclassed for functionality are described in this chapter. For each abstract class, the major public methods are reviewed. These methods are overloaded by subclasses for implementing application-specific customizations.

The abstractions presented in this chapter are important because they represent the granularity at which useful customizations can be made. Other decompositions of the operating system into objects are possible. The decomposition into classes and class hierarchies presented here represents one decomposition or model of the operating system in terms of objects. The decomposition reflects the use of the operating system: a decomposition that can be customized performance in parallel and distributed applications.

5.1 APPLICATION PROGRAMMING INTERFACE (API)

The API subframework has two important class hierarchies, one rooted at Message and the other rooted at MessageSystemInterface. These classes provide message-passing system primitives or interfaces that application programmers use to write message-passing programs.

The Message class is used to send and receive data. It allows an object-oriented application programming interface for message passing. A hierarchy of message types implements the most commonly encountered styles of message-passing semantics, from synchronous to asynchronous message passing. The Message class supports the `send` method for sending messages, and the `receive` method for implementing receives. The Message class has methods for managing and setting application buffers.

The MessageSystemInterface (MSI) is an adaptation layer encapsulating features specific to a particular parallel or distributed programming paradigm. Unlike the Message class, it provides a flat interface to the operating system, which allows easy porting of applications written to interfaces such as PVM, NX/2, and Mach. For example, the entire set of Intel iPSC/2 message-passing primitives [Pie86, Clo86] has been implemented [IC92a]. The kernel message system interface and user message system interface support two alternate implementations of the message-passing system, the former in the kernel and the latter in user space.

Appendix B contains examples of how programmers use these classes to write programs.

5.2 MESSAGE HANDLING

The message handling subframework has two important class hierarchies. The roots of these class hierarchies are MessageContainer and ContainerRepresentative. The MessageContainer class is a named communication entity for buffering messages. Processes communicate by sending messages to MessageContainers. The MessageContainer class has methods `receive`, `put`, and `isEmpty` to provide concurrent access to its internal message queue. The `put` method is invoked by the class Transport or by the class DataTransfer to add a message to the message queue. The `receive` method is invoked by processes to retrieve messages from the MessageContainer message queue. To receive a message, a process must create and then bind a subclass of MessageContainer with a NameServer. Processes send messages through a ContainerRepresentative obtained from a NameServer. ContainerRepresentative is a kernel-protected entity and cannot be forged by applications. The capability is accessible to all processes that are in the same address space.

MessageContainers can be customized based on the use of application-specific types, message size, and whether asynchronous receives are used. These combinations lead to the class hierarchies shown in Figure 5.1. A detailed dis-

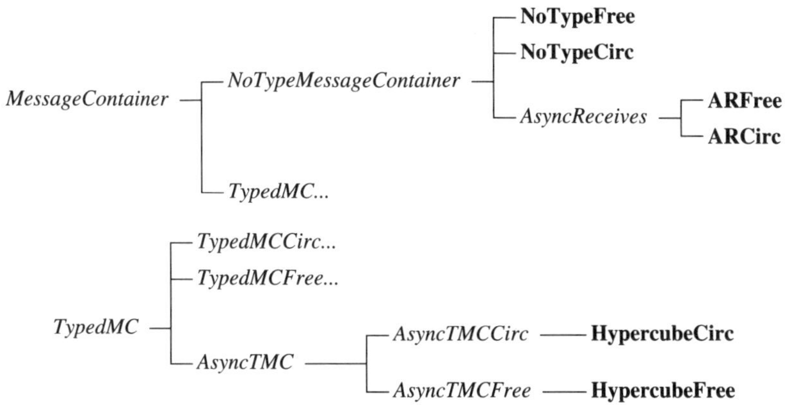

FIGURE 5.1 Message handling class hierarchies.

cussion on how to customize the MessageContainers on a bus-based, shared-memory multiprocessor appears in Section 8.4. That section describes the behavior of each of the classes shown in Figure 5.1.

The `receive`, `put`, and `isEmpty` methods are overloaded for different implementations. The `receive` and `isEmpty` methods are called by classes in the API subframework, and `put` is called by classes in the transport or data transfer subframework.

5.3 DATA TRANSFER

The data transfer subframework has one important class hierarchy rooted at the DataTransfer class. The DataTransfer class implements the buffering strategies used in sending a message. On a shared-memory multiprocessor, message sends may be double buffered, single buffered, or passed by reference. As Figure 5.2 shows, this class has two branches. The NetworkTransfer classes are used for interfacing with the network I/O framework on a distributed system. The LocalTransfer has three subclasses, each of which has different buffering strategies for multiprocessors. Section 8.1 includes a detailed discussion of the performance

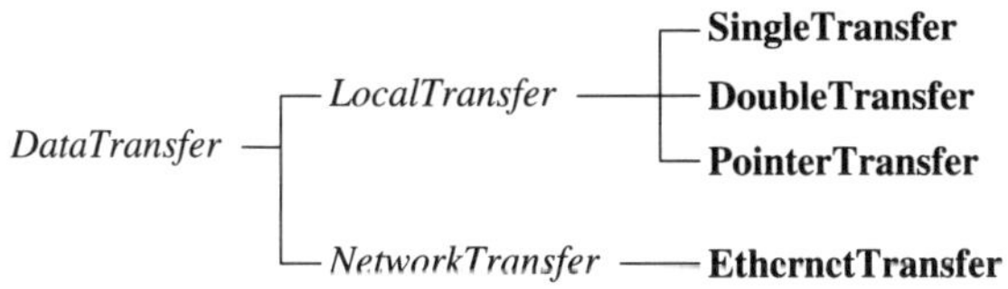

FIGURE 5.2 Data transfer class hierarchy.

characteristics of the data transfer implementation alternatives on a bus-based, shared-memory multiprocessor. The `send` and `receive` methods are overloaded for each type of data transfer. These methods may be called by classes in the reliability or transport subframeworks. On a distributed system, the `send` method is called by the reliability subframework classes and the `receive` method is called by the network I/O subframework classes.

5.4 TRANSPORT

The transport subframework has one important class hierarchy rooted at the Transport class. It has two subclasses: NetworkTransport and LocalTransport. The Transport class specifies the mechanism that is used to move a message from a sender to a receiver. Subclasses of the LocalTransport class transport a message by a separate copying process or by the process that receives the message performing the copy. The subclasses of the NetworkTransport class perform fragmentation and reassembly. The Transport class has methods `send` and `receive`. The `send` method is called by the ContainerRepresentative class, and the `receive` method is called by the DataTransfer class.

The class hierarchy for NetworkTransport and LocalTransport is shown in Figure 5.3. Table 5.1 shows the interface and code inheritance in a Transport class hierarchy. Method `dispMessage` dispatches a message to a MessageContainer; methods `fragment` and `assemble` fragment and assemble messages. Methods `send` and `receive` are used to interact with the DataTransfer class. The LocalTransport classes do not require the reconstruction of messages, fragmentation, or reassembly code. The methods defined in Table 5.1 may be refined to provide different fragmentation, reassembly, and message reconstruction algorithms. For NetworkTransport and its subclasses, it is necessary to infer message types. This is one of the primary purposes of DispatchMessage, which provides a default implementation for the `reconstruct` method, used to reconstruct the appropriate object from a network message. DispatchMessage is also responsible for putting the reconstructed message into a local MessageContainer. Further refinements implement network packet fragmentation, SendingTransport, and network packet assembly, ReceivingTransport. This abstraction allows one to adopt different network fragmentation and reassembly policies. The default policy breaks a packet into chunks equal to the network packet size, except for the last packet, which is smaller than the network packet size. These packets are then transmitted in

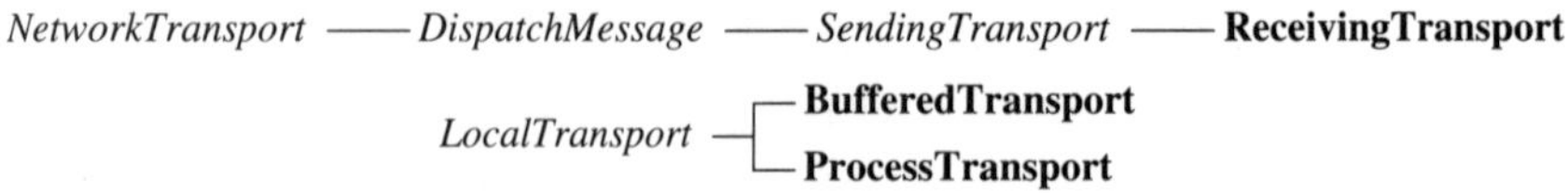

FIGURE 5.3 Transport class hierarchy.

TABLE 5.1 Interface for the Transport Class and Its Subclasses

Class::Method	dispatch-Message	reconstruct	send	fragment	receive	assemble
Transport	=0	-	=0	-	-	-
▽ NetworkTransport	=0	=0	=0	=0	=0	=0
▽ ▽ *DispatchMessage*	△	•	=0	=0	=0	=0
▽ ▽ ▽ *SendingTransport*	▽	▽	•	•	= 0	=0
▽ ▽ ▽ ▽ **Receiving-Transport**	▽	▽	▽	▽	•	•
▽ *LocalTransport*	•	-	=0	-	=0	-
▽ ▽ **BufferedTransport**	▽	-	•	-	•	-
▽ ▽ **ProcessTransport**	▽	-	•	-	•	-

order. In the Peregrine [JZ93] RPC system, large messages are fragmented into packets, and the packet that would traditionally be sent first is sent last. This, combined with some other optimizations, leads to faster RPC. The default algorithms are changed by overloading the `fragment` and `assemble` methods to implement the Peregrine system's fragmentation and reassembly policy. Thus, these methods would be overloaded to implement the Peregrine RPC optimizations.

The performance of different implementations of the LocalTransport class is examined in detail on the bus-based, shared-memory multiprocessor in Section 8.3. The `send` and `receive` methods are overloaded for the implementations.

5.5 RELIABILITY

The reliability subframework has two class hierarchies rooted at the CSR (communication state record). CSR keeps protocol connection state information and is modeled after the VMTP protocol's client state record [Che88b]. The abstract class CSR defines the interfaces for reliable delivery and error recovery semantics for the message-passing systems on unreliable networks. For example, subclasses allow messages to be sent unreliably, with at-least-once or exactly-once [Gos91] semantics. The reliability measures are implemented as a state machine. CSR provides basic methods to set (`setState`) and query (`queryState`) the current state of the state machine and provides the generic interface, `releaseBuffers`, for buffer management. The CSR class is subclassed for application-specific reliability. In Chapter 6, for example, it is customized for the Cholesky factorization application. The CSRManager class manages the allocation and deallocation of CSRs.

In Chapters 6 and 7, customizations of the CSR class and one of its subclasses, ClientCSR, are discussed for parallel applications and distributed system services. The ClientCSR class is an abstraction that can be used for both symmetric and asymmetric message-passing systems. The methods of the ClientCSR class that are overloaded by subclasses are `receive`, `send`, `awaitResponse`, `probe`, sendProbe, and releaseBuffers. The send and awaitResponse methods are invoked by the Transport class. The probe and sendProbe methods are used for error handling, and the releaseBuffers method is used for buffer management of messages that have been acknowledged. The receive method is called by the Transport class to notify the ClientCSR class of arriving messages.

A Timer class implements interval timers using hash, and hierarchical provides interval timers [VL87]. The timer has four relevant methods: (1) start, to start the timer for a specified amount of time; (2) stop, to stop the timer, (3) residual to find out the amount of time left over after a stop and before the next start; and await, which allows a process to wait for a timer to expire. The timer expires after the time specified in the call to the start expires.

5.6 SYNCHRONIZATION

The Synchronization class has two methods, acquire and release, which provide access to the shared or critical region used for implementing message passing. The performance of different implementations of synchronization on a bus-based, shared-memory multiprocessor are discussed in section 8.2. Many other subframeworks, including message handling, make use of this subframework. The acquire and release methods are overloaded to provide the necessary synchronization implementation. These methods are called by the message-handling subframework.

The class hierarchy for semaphores and locks is shown in Figure 5.4. Both blocking (Semaphore) and nonblocking synchronization primitives are supported. There are two types of spinlocks: test-and-set and Anderson's array [And91a].

5.7 NAMING

A distributed and recursive naming service was designed for processes to locate references to MessageContainers. At the top level is a NameServer, which supports the lookup and bind methods. The lookup method is used to find a reference to an object, and the bind method is used to attach a character string name to an object. Other processes can use this character string name to gain access to the object through the NameServer.

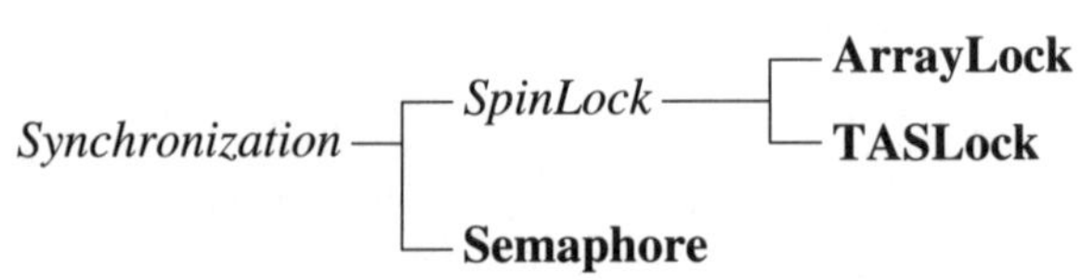

FIGURE 5.4 Synchronization class hierarchy.

Recursively, other name services, such as the distributed name service, may be obtained explicitly from the NameServer. Alternatively, given a type, the name service recursively finds the appropriate name server using the first-class class mechanism that permits the discovery of the C++ type of an object at runtime. For example, when a process invokes the `lookup` method on the NameServer and requests an object of type MessageContainer, this request will be forwarded to the DistributedNameServer. The DistributedNameServer will then return an appropriate ContainerRepresentative to the process that invoked the `lookup` method.

5.8 NETWORK I/O FRAMEWORK

The network I/O framework has three class hierarchies rooted at ProtocolDispatcher, EthernetDriver, and NetworkBuffer. One instance of the network I/O framework per machine supports multiple instances of the message-passing system framework.

The EthernetDriver class manipulates the hardware network device registers to implement different options, such as polled or interrupt-driven message passing. The appropriate subclass is hardware architecture dependent.

The ProtocolDispatcher class dispatches network messages to the appropriate message-passing system instance. This class buffers messages until a process can accompany a message through the subframeworks of a message-passing system instance. The dispatcher allows multiple application message-passing system frameworks to exist at the same time. In standard protocol terminology, this implies that multiple protocol stacks may be active at the same time.

The NetworkBuffer class interacts with the virtual memory system to manage network buffers to reduce the amount of copying for network messages. Architecture-specific optimizations are often used. NetworkBuffers are managed as part of a free list structure, NetworkBufferFreeList.

These classes provide the interface and implementations of a variety of drivers for communicating with networks (see Figure 5.5). The EthernetDriver is subclassed to work with the LANCE chip on the SPARCStation II SPARCDriver or the Encore Multimax Ethernet chip MultimaxDriver. The subclass SPARCDriver uses buffers that have been preallocated to both the direct virtual memory access (DVMA) and kernel regions. The NetworkBuffers are managed on a NetworkBufferFreelist. SPARCBuffers are a subclass that is premapped to a DVMA region as well as to other kernel regions. Thus, SPARCBuffer and SPARCDriver should be used together. Premapping the buffers substantially reduces the cost of sending and receiving messages. For example, the cost of mapping each buffer adds approximately 300 μsec to each `send` and `receive` on the SPARCStationII architecture. Table 5.2 shows the methods and the various subclasses of the device driver.

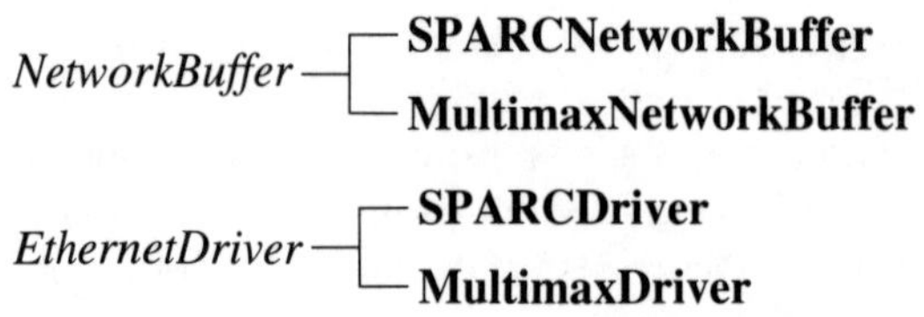

FIGURE 5.5 NetworkDriver and NetworkBuffer.

TABLE 5.2 Interface for the NetworkDriver Class and Its Subclasses

Class::Method	get/relBuffer	transmitPacket	receivePacket
EthernetDriver	=0	=0	=0
▽ **MultimaxDriver**	•	•	•
▽ **SPARCDriver**	•	•	•

Much like the mbufs used in many UNIX implementations, NetworkBuffer-FreeList is a list of network buffers that are preallocated. In addition, these buffers may be preallocated to sizes expected by applications. The message size attribute can be used to calculate the size of network buffers. The number of buffers required can also be determined from the CP in the application. Each NetworkBuffer is added to the free list once it has been used, and taken from the free list when needed. In the absence of application-specific information, the number of buffers varies based on need.

5.9 INSTANCES OF THE MESSAGE-PASSING SYSTEM FRAMEWORK

This section examines how the instances of the various classes of the message-passing system interact. Two ports of the message-passing system, one for a shared-memory multiprocessor and the other for a distributed system, are described in detail. Each port is described using entity relationship diagrams and control flow graphs. This section shows the relationships between system objects that must be maintained when application-specific customizations are made. None of the control flows or entity relationships may be removed by new subclasses. New classes, control flows, and relations may be added. The refinement techniques for exactly how these relationships should be maintained appear in Chapter 2. Deutsch [Deu89] defines similar rules for subclassing in a Smalltalk environment. He maintains that subclasses in a framework should extend and not invalidate the specification (interface protocols) of their superclasses.

An application-specific message-passing system is defined as an instance of the message-passing framework where all of the abstract classes in each subframework have been replaced by concrete classes, and application-specific attributes were used to select these concrete subclasses.

5.9.1 Control Flow through the Message-Passing System

Control flow graphs specify the control flow and method invocations that must be maintained between system objects when new optimizations are created. Control flow graphs depict an ordering on method invocations of a framework. The control flow graphs in this section attempt to capture the major control flows through the message-passing system. Although abstract classes are shown in the graph of any implementation of the message-passing system, there will be a concrete control flow representing the control flow through a series of objects that are instances of concrete classes. Figure 5.6 shows the abstract control flow graph for the message-passing system on the shared-memory multiprocessor. Rectangles are used to denote the subframeworks described in Section 4.1 and shown in Figure 4.2.

The control flow graph shows the various classes and the methods of those classes invoked for sending a message between two application processes. A message sent between two processes passes through the various classes in the framework and is processed in different ways depending on the concrete subclasses that process the message. Each subframework processes the message and then

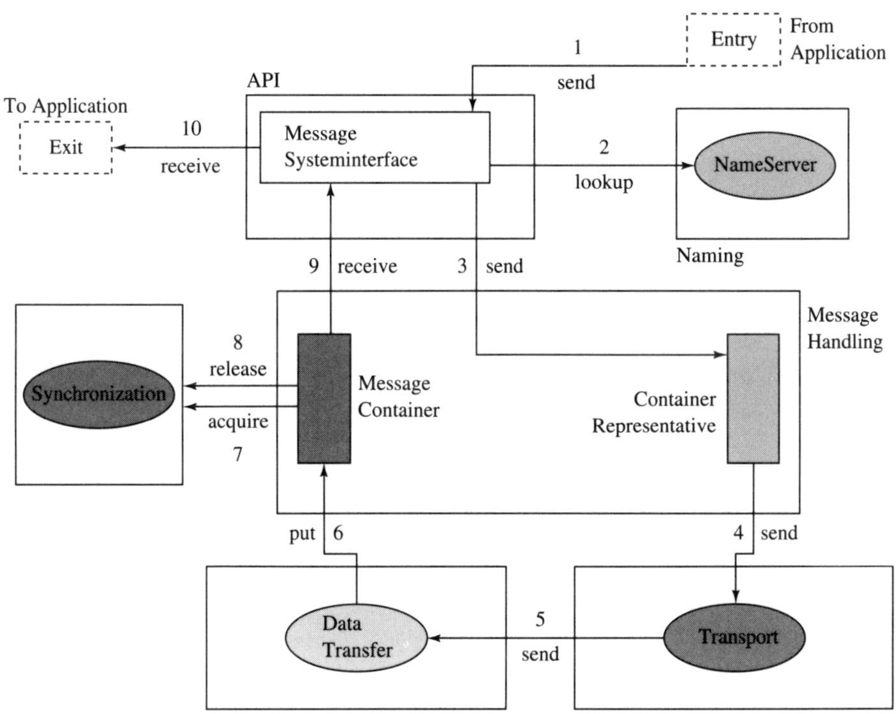

FIGURE 5.6 Abstract control flow of a message send and receive pair on the shared-memory multiprocessor.

hands it off to the next subframework for further processing. The application process invokes a `send` method on the MSI, which interacts with the NameServer to obtain a ContainerRepresentative to send the message. The `send` method is invoked on the ContainerRepresentative, which locates the appropriate Transport to send the message. The Transport will find the appropriate MessageContainer to deposit the message and will use DataTransfer for transferring the data. Another process will invoke the `receive` method on the MSI, which will locate the appropriate MessageContainer and retrieve the desired message. On the shared-memory multiprocessor, an application-specific message-passing system can replace all of the abstract classes, except the NameServer, with a specialized concrete class.*

Figure 5.7 shows the abstract control flow graph for the message-passing system on the distributed system. The arrows show the direction of the flow of control as a message is sent by a process on the node labeled "sending node" and received by a process on the node labeled "receiving node." The arrows are labeled with the names of the methods invoked. The initial and final flow of control sequences is similar to the shared-memory version. In the distributed system, however, the reliability subframework introduces more classes to implement reliable delivery of messages on a unreliable network, and a network I/O framework moves messages to and from the Ethernet.

An important aspect of the reliability framework is how the different state machines that are subclasses of CSR are located and garbage collected. An instance of the CSRManager class keeps a list of all instances of concrete subclasses of CSR per application. CSRManager uses a timer-based mechanism to garbage collect CSRs. In addition, there are timers associated with CSRs on which processes may wait for events to occur, such as the arrival of a message.

The Transport then invokes the `send` method on the appropriate instance of the CSR class. The message then passes through the DataTransfer to the network I/O framework. There is one instance of the network I/O framework per node. Network messages are dispatched to the appropriate application-specific message-passing framework instances.

The control flow graph of the network I/O framework is shown in Figure 5.8. Method `transmitPacket` is used to send a network packet to the physical network, and `receivePacket` is called at interrupt level when a packet is received from the network interface chip. EthernetDriver network buffers are managed by the `getBuffer` and `relBuffer` methods. These methods interact with the NetworkBufferFreeList to get buffers. The figure also indicates how the ProtocolDispatcher can dispatch packets to different instances of the message-passing system framework on the same machine. Each instance of the message-passing system framework has a unique identifier that is used by the ProtocolDispatcher for dispatching each packet. There is only one instance of the ProtocolDispatcher, NetworkBufferFreeList, and EthernetDriver per machine.

*Although it is possible to customize the NameServer, this is not discussed in this book.

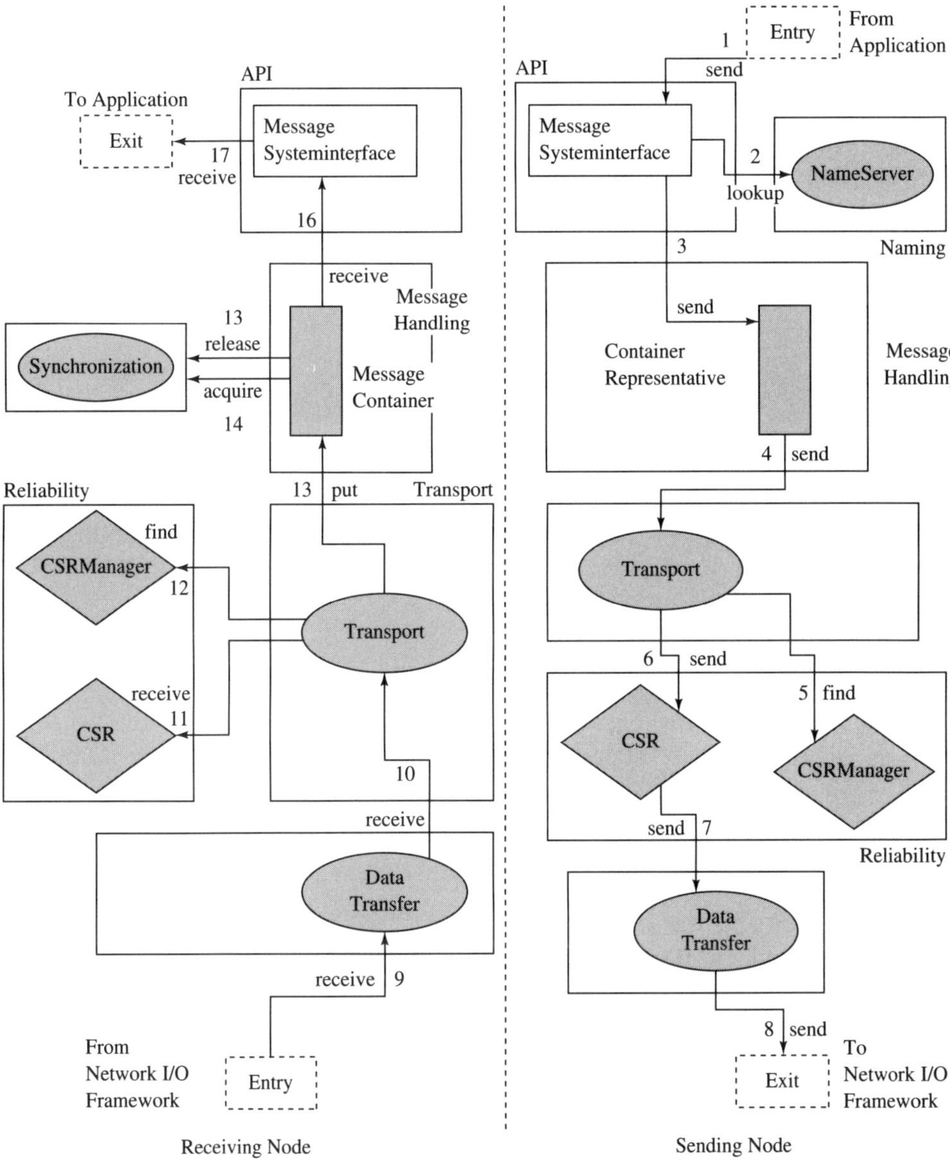

FIGURE 5.7 Abstract control flow of a message send and receive pair on the distributed system.

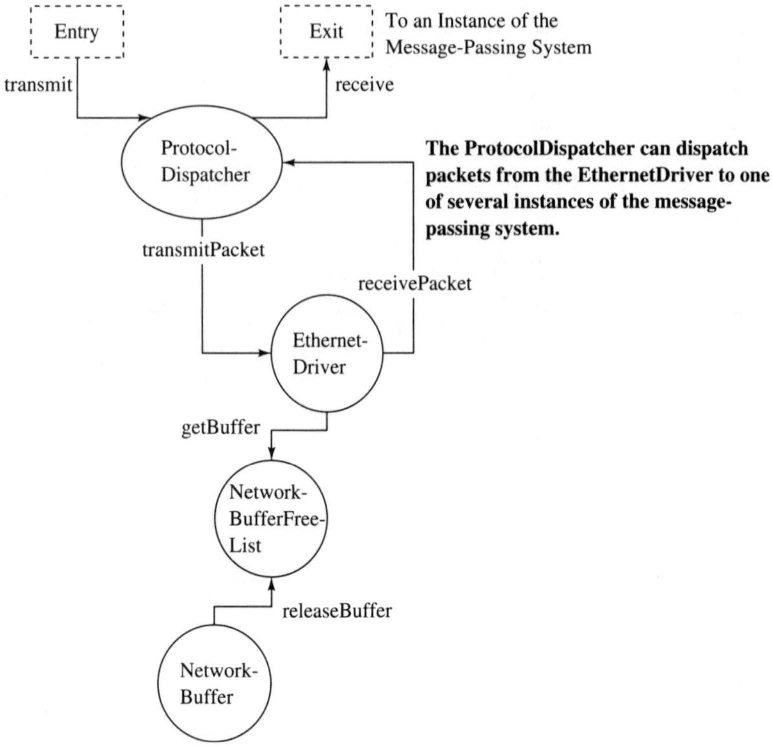

FIGURE 5.8 Network I/O framework.

The ProtocolDispatcher uses method `transmit` to transmit network messages, and selects an appropriate instance of a message-passing framework to dispatch an arriving network message by invoking the `receive` of an appropriate DataTransfer class. In this software architecture, each instance of a framework provides a set of processes to move messages through it.

5.9.2 Process Model

One of the key factors influencing the implementation performance of a communication protocol is the process model. For example, in Dykstra's original model [Dyk68], a process was associated with each layer, leading to a context switch each time two layers passed information. Thus, interlayer communication was slow. The *x*-kernel adopted a process per-message model, where a process shepherds a message to and from the network interface and incurs no context switches in the absence of contention.

Although processes are also discussed in Section 10.2, they are discussed here to demonstrate how messages flow through the communication subsystem. When an application process sends a message, that process shepherds the message from user space into kernel space through the objects into the network interface. In the absence of contention, no context switches occur. When a packet is received, a receiver process is typically waiting for the message, and this process will shepherd the message to the application. However, individual packets are put into the ProtocolDispatcher by an interrupt process. Application processes blocked in `receive` then move the messages up the protocol stack. In the absence of contention, there is one trap into the kernel and an additional context switch due to the interrupt process. As far as protection boundaries are concerned, the network I/O framework must be in the kernel, but the message-passing framework can be in user space. Thus, the application-specific message-passing protocols run in at the user level.*

On a shared-memory multiprocessor there are two context switches, one into the kernel for a `send` and one out of the kernel for a `receive`. In both cases the application processes trap into the kernel run on a kernel stack and perform the necessary operations inside the kernel. There is a version of the message-passing system that runs all the message-passing code at user level on the shared-memory architecture. In this case, no kernel trap overheads are encountered for sending or receiving a message.

5.9.3 Virtual Memory Support

There are no explicit copies of data between the various classes as messages are sent between processes; only pointers to objects are passed around. Data are only copied when a protection boundary is crossed. When a message is sent, there is a copy from the user address space into the kernel address space, and when a message arrives there is a copy from the kernel to the user address space. More sophisticated memory mapping techniques are clearly possible but not implemented (for example, it is possible to change the protection on pages instead of performing copies).

5.9.4 Entity Relationship Model

The entity relationship (ER) diagrams of this section describe the relationships between system objects that must be maintained when new optimizations are introduced in the system. One instance of a *uses* relation can translate to a method invocation of an instance of a particular class at runtime.

Figure 5.9 shows the abstract ER diagram for the message-passing system on a shared-memory multiprocessor. An important relationship exists between the MessageContainers and ContainerRepresentatives. There are multiple ContainerRepresentatives per MessageContainer and exactly one MessageContainer for each ContainerRepresentative. The diagram shows that there is exactly one instance of the Transport and one instance of the DataTransfer mechanism per application. The transport subframework only supports local communication on the shared-memory multiprocessor.

*In the current implementation, the trap actually occurs in the message system interface class.

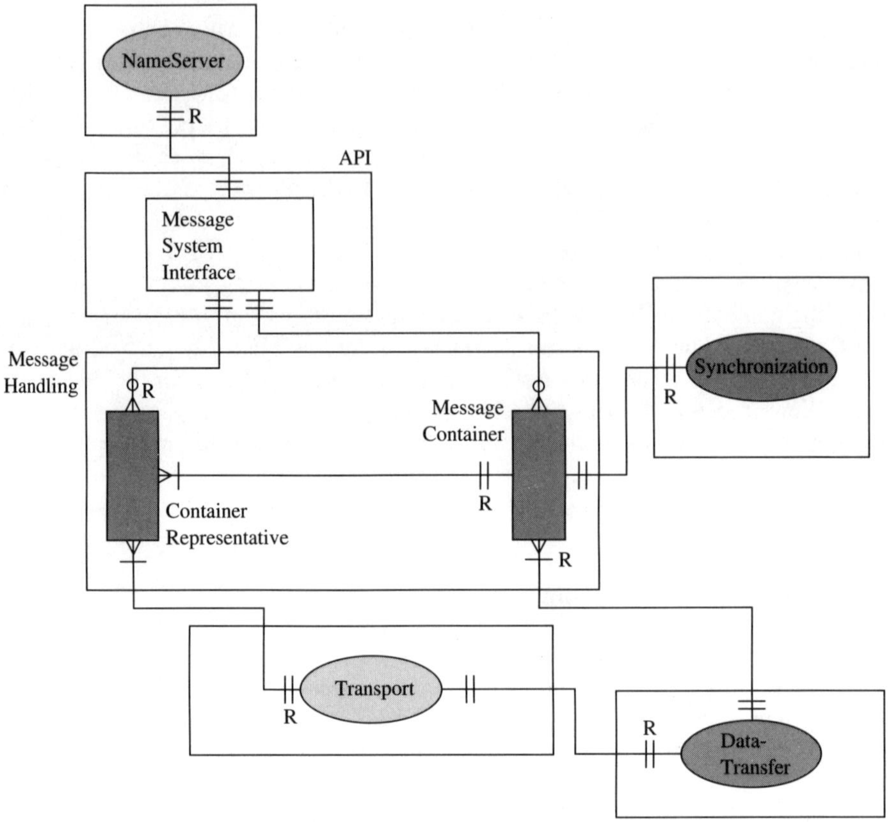

FIGURE 5.9 Abstract ER diagram for shared-memory multiprocessor.

Figure 5.10 shows the abstract ER diagram for the message-passing system on a distributed system. The relationship between ContainerRepresentatives and MessageContainers is the same on the distributed system as on the shared-memory multiprocessor. The diagram shows that the CSRManager manages multiple CSRs. Each state record, however, is only associated with one CSRManager. There are two instances of the Transport, one for local and the other for remote communication; and one DataTransfer mechanism is in effect at any one time per application.

5.10 SUMMARY

This chapter describes the major abstractions of the design of the message-passing system, detailing where fine-grained, application-specific customizations are possible. This information is important for programmers extending the set of optimiza-

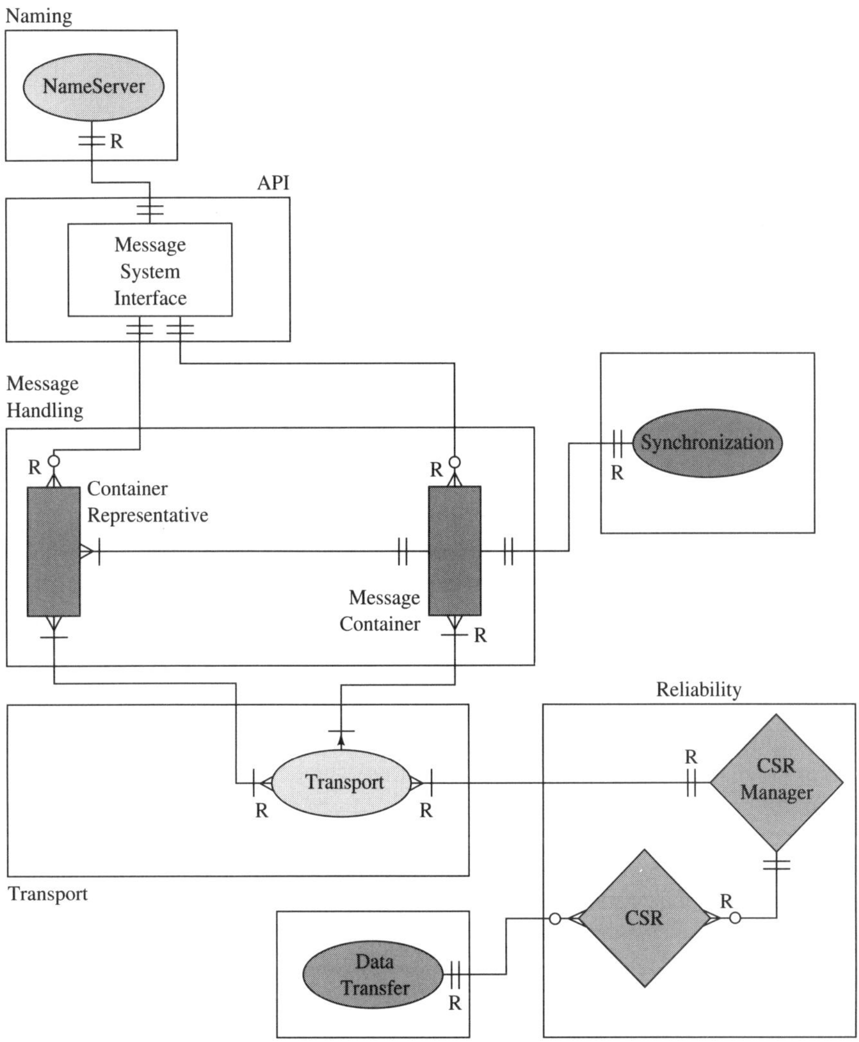

FIGURE 5.10 Abstract ER diagram for distributed system.

tions. In order to better explain how to customize the message-passing system, entity relationship diagrams and control flow graphs are used.

This chapter also describes how the message-passing system is decomposed into subframeworks that allow easy porting to new architectures. Two ports are described, one to a bus-based, shared-memory multiprocessor and the other to a distributed system.

CHAPTER 6

Customized Message Passing on a Distributed System

This chapter describes application-specific customizations of the message-passing system for distributed systems consisting of unreliable networks. Message-passing systems for distributed systems, such as PVM and Amoeba, often generate too many network messages for each application-level message. These additional messages are generated as part of the reliability measures for recovering from message loss, but they degrade performance. They are not always necessary, and it is possible to reduce the number of network messages using application-specific information.

This chapter addresses three issues. First, it describes how application attributes guide the selection of appropriate message-passing system optimizations. Second, the message-passing systems for four sample communication patterns are discussed. Third, a detailed description is provided on how to easily generate new application-specific optimizations to the object-oriented message-passing system framework.

6.1 DESIGNING AN OPTIMIZED MESSAGE-PASSING SYSTEM

Most of the overhead and extra network messages sent between computers in a distributed system consist of reliability provisions in the network protocols that are required to overcome unreliable network hardware. In this section, the cost of reliability is examined and techniques for minimizing this cost are described. In these discussions, message loss and corruption are treated as errors. Any reliability measure must handle errors; error handling comprises three parts.

1. Error detection. Detecting that an error has occurred.
2. Damage confinement. Restricting the damage due to the error.
3. Error recovery. Resending the lost or damaged message.

The terms used in this section are similar to those used by Anderson et al. [AL81] except that fault treatment is not discussed.

Cost Models. A cost model is proposed that sums the overhead contributions of each CP in an application. The objective is to minimize the cost.

$$\min \sum_i Cost(CP_i) \tag{6.1}$$

CP_i is the overhead performing the ith CP in the application. Following is an examination of the contribution of each of the four overhead metrics to the cost function for a particular CP. The contribution from the number of network messages for a CP, assuming that the probability of two or more errors is negligible, is

$$Cost(CP) = p * (S + R) + (1 - p) * [(1 + F) + S + R] \tag{6.2}$$

where the probability of network message loss is $(1 - p)$. The number of messages required by the CP on an idealized reliable network is S,* and a further R messages implement error detection and reliability provisions. Acknowledgment messages are included as part of R. Since the network is mostly reliable, the cost of recovery† after an error is detected is $(1 + F)$. F consists of probe messages, and 1 represents the retransmission of the original message.

Although systems such as PVM assume that messages are frequently lost ($p \approx 0$), in practice on many networks messages are rarely lost ($p \approx 1$). Assuming that $p = 1$ and S is a constant, the objective is to minimize R. The overhead for interrupts is similar. The overhead for buffers measures the number of buffers per node required to implement the CP. In the optimal case, this is one, and in the worst case this is S, the number of messages sent. Generally, time-outs used for timers are set to a value that is independent of application computation. Techniques for setting application-specific time-out values are explored.

The overheads are not independent. There is a tradeoff between minimizing the number of buffers and reducing the number of acknowledgment messages. The number of buffers can be minimized by acknowledging each message. Alternatively, by increasing the number of buffers, the number of acknowledgments can

*Note that some systems may choose not to use hardware-supported multicast, and, hence, this number varies between implementations.

†Assuming one message gets lost.

be reduced—for example, by aggregating acknowledgments between two communicating nodes. First the number of messages is minimized, and then ways to reduce the number of buffers are sought. In practice, this technique optimizes both the number of messages and the number of buffers, with a few exceptions. In these exceptional cases, acknowledgment messages can be added to reduce the number of sender-side buffers. The use of the five attributes is now explained.

6.2 THE USE OF ATTRIBUTES IN OPTIMIZATION

This section describes a methodology for reducing the number of network messages, interrupts generated, and buffers required for implementing the message-passing system using application attributes. The following five application attributes are used to design efficient message-passing systems.

1. Communication pattern (CP)
2. Type of message
3. Idempotent server functions
4. Message size
5. Time between iterations

Communication Pattern. The CP identifies communication locality and sender identities. Communication locality occurs when a process receives a message generated as a consequence of an earlier message that it sent. In most communication systems, the sender of a message is anonymous. Sender identities, however, are important for recovering from message losses on unreliable networks.

As an example, the use of the CP attribute to reduce the number of acknowledgment messages is demonstrated. The technique involves examining the CP of an application to determine how to aggregate the acknowledgments for messages sent. Communication locality allows acknowledgments to be implicitly piggybacked CPs on application-level messages that are part of the natural communication of the application. The remaining unacknowledged application-level messages require explicit acknowledgment.

The following example illustrates this technique using a simple CP. Process **A** sends a message to process **B**, which then sends a message to process **A**. The message from **B** to **A** allows an implicit acknowledgment of the communication from **A** to **B**. If either the message from **A** to **B** or from **B** to **A** is lost, then the message-passing system must provide error recovery in the form of retrieving the lost message. Error detection is achieved using a timer, which, when it expires, initiates error recovery. If the message-passing system supporting process **A** times out, it will resend the original message. If this pattern repeats in a loop, then the optimizations used by the message-passing system supporting process **A** may be used by the message-passing system supporting process **B**. Applying the cost model in a globally optimized message-passing system, $S = 2$ and $R = 0$.

Alternatively, a naive implementation of this CP on an unreliable network could generate an acknowledgment for each message sent. Applying the cost model to the naive implementation gives $S = 2$ and $R = 2$. The implicit acknowledgments also allow the release of the message buffers held by the message-passing system. This technique can be used on more complex CPs of the four applications.

Type. Type may be used to implement efficient error detection. The receipt of a message of the wrong type signifies that an earlier message is missing and will trigger the search for a missing message. This optimization is used for all four applications.

Idempotent Server Functions. Servers that call idempotent functions can reduce receiver-side buffering. For example, request-response protocols can be implemented as either at-least-once or exactly-once semantics [BN84]. At-least-once semantics require no receiver-side buffers to be kept. This optimization is used in the protocol of the distributed scheduler.

Message Size. For large messages, a blast protocol [Che86b] is used, which generates a single acknowledgment (implicit or explicit) for a group of network packets representing one message. Missing messages are selectively retransmitted. Results of this technique are presented for the FFT application.

Iteration Time. Most communication systems do not support application-specific time-outs. They typically provide default values of a few seconds. Application-specific values may be shorter. The following technique is used to calculate time-out values for parallel iterative applications. The maximum time to compute an iteration T_{max_iter} is found for the one node case for a particular data set. The maximum possible communication time $T_{max\_comm\_iter}$ is factored in to obtain $T_{max} = T_{max\_iter} + T_{max\_comm\_iter}$. It is assumed $T_{max\_iter} > T_{max\_comm\_iter}$ and thus, $T_{max} = 2T_{max\_iter}$. When a parallel version of the application runs on the same data set, the system keeps track of the time spent in the current iteration, $T_{timeSoFar}$. The time-out values are set to $T_{time-out} = T_{max} - T_{timeSoFar}$. This technique works well when all the processes of the applications are gang scheduled (see Chapter 10), since other system effects are minimized. Using this technique, T_{max} is 88 ms for Cholesky and 200 ms for Simplex for the data set sizes presented in this book.

6.3 SAMPLE USE OF APPLICATION ATTRIBUTES IN OPTIMIZATION

In this section, some of the application attributes described in Section 3.2 are used to illustrate how to generate optimized message-passing systems. Much of the discussion centers around the CP attribute, though other attributes are considered as necessary. The CPs discussed include `RedMulticast`, `ExchangeNoLocality`, `ExchangeWithLocality`, and `Repetitive`. There are N processes in the group communication algorithm descriptions.

The analytical cost models allow the message-passing overheads of PVM and Amoeba to be compared with those of the optimized message-passing system. PVM was chosen because it is a popular message-passing library used on networks of workstations. Amoeba was chosen because it has an efficient implementation of ordered and reliable multicast.

For each send, PVM generates two network messages: one application data message and one acknowledgment. In PVM, multicasts are point-to-point, and each point-to-point, message requires an acknowledgment. Thus, PVM multicasts are synchronous. The Amoeba multicast protocol as described in [KT91, KTHB89] is used in the comparisons. The Amoeba multicast protocol is also described in Chapter 11. For point-to-point sends, Amoeba uses the Flip protocol [KRST93], which generates three network messages for each point-to-point send. On the SPARCStationII* each send and each receive generates an interrupt.

The next few sections describe the minimization of the three cost functions (Equation 6.1) for sample CPs of applications. These sections also demonstrate the inefficiency of systems such as PVM. In particular, for Equation 6.1 the cost of implementing each CP when no errors occur (that is, when $p = 1$) is considered. The implementation of error detection is briefly considered. The different systems are evaluated on their error-handling abilities in a later section.

6.3.1 Reduction Followed by Multicast

Reduction is a simple collective communication pattern. The `Reduction` CP is shown in Figure 6.1. To execute the CP for `Reduction`, PVM requires $4(N-1)$ interrupts and $2(N-1)$ network messages, and the Amoeba system requires $6(N-1)$ interrupts and $3(N-1)$ messages. Since there are no application-specific attributes to exploit, a customized message-passing system performs like PVM rather than Amoeba. All systems employ point-to-point communication. Error recovery in point-to-point communication is initiated by timers. When a timer expires, the original application message is resent.

In some applications, a multicast follows the `Reduction` CP, as shown in Figure 6.2. For this CP, PVM generates $8(N-1)$ interrupts and $4(N-1)$ network messages. Amoeba generates $6(N-1) + N + 2$ interrupts, and $4(N-1) + 2$

*Details of the experimental platforms can be found in Appendix A.

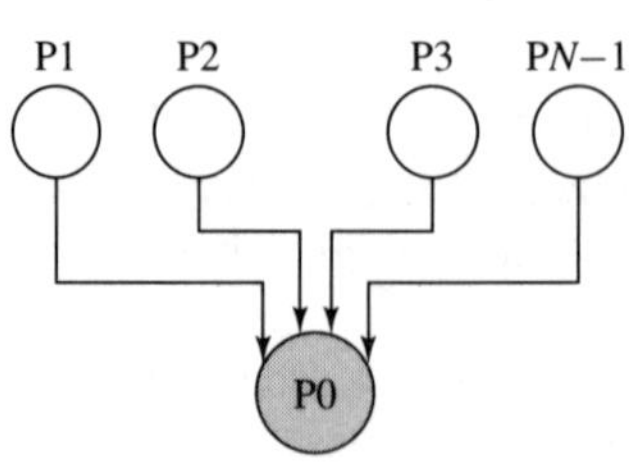

FIGURE 6.1 CP for `Reduction`.

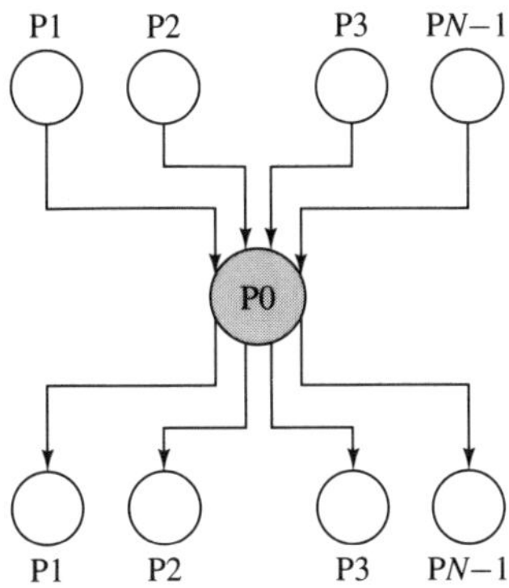

FIGURE 6.2 CP for `Reduction` followed by a multicast.

network messages. Customized message passing can use the multicast as an acknowledgment to the original message send. The customized message-passing system generates N network messages and $3(N-1)$ interrupts. Clearly, the customized message-passing system performs better than either Amoeba or PVM. The primary reason is that acknowledgments are piggybacked on normal future communication that is not taken into consideration in PVM or Amoeba. To guarantee reliable delivery, a timer is set to wait for the multicast. If the multicast is not received within a certain time-out period, error recovery procedures are initiated.

Many parallel applications are iterative. In these applications, the CP repeats across loops. In such cases, a buffer allocation problem arises. In systems such as Amoeba, if the multicaster is the same in each iteration, then the multicast message buffers stored in the sequencer become large. The number of message buffers required at the sequencer depend on the number of iterations executed. PVM only requires one buffer at a time, but this effectively synchronizes the multicast operation. PVM's approach to implementing reliable multicast results in a situation in which the multicast is point-to-point with acknowledgments for individual messages. In the customized message-passing system, the `Reduction` acts as a point of synchronization. The completion of a `Reduction` implies that all communication from the previous iteration is complete, and the multicast buffer from the previous iteration may be released. Note that in all systems the `Reduction` CP communication buffers are released at each iteration and do not pose a buffering problem.

In an application there may be more communications that follow the `RedMulticast` pattern, as shown in Figure 6.3. In that figure, process 2 performs a multicast after the `RedMulticast`. In this case PVM generates an additional $2(N-1)$ messages and $4(N-1)$ interrupts, and Amoeba generates an additional two messages and $N+2$ interrupts. The customized message-passing system, however, generates one additional message and N interrupts. To detect lost messages, the customized message-passing system uses timers at each of the receiving instances. Simple error recovery is possible because the name of the sender of the

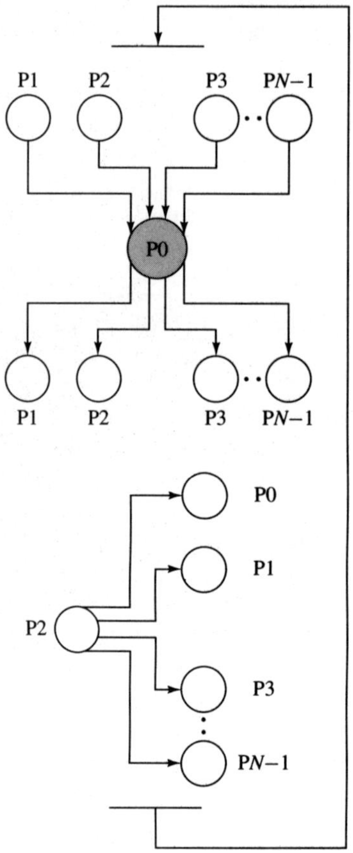

FIGURE 6.3 CP for `Reduction` followed by multicast and an additional multicast.

multicast message is provided as part of the CP, and a request can be made of the sending process to resend the lost message. Since the CP repeats, buffer allocation is restricted to two message buffers at any time in the customized message-passing system (one on the machine holding process 0, and the other on the machine holding process 2). In the Amoeba sequencer, buffers may again become large.

There is still a chance that in a particular iteration the two multicasts may be received out of order by a process. Application types are used to distinguish these messages. An event-based error recovery mechanism is then used to retrieve the missing messages.

This example illustrates how optimizations are incrementally made as the communication pattern becomes more complex in the customized message-passing system. For the customized implementations of the `RedMulticast` CP and its variant (which occurs in the Simplex application), the number of network messages is the same as the number of application-level messages.

6.3.2 Repetitive Multicasts

In some applications, multicasts from the same process may repeat. For example, a group of processes may take turns multicasting. In such a CP, each process performs a multicast and then waits for all other processes to multicast. This process then performs its next multicast. Hence, the multicast pattern repeats. This pattern is referred to as `Repetitive` (see Figure 3.6). Such CPs provide global knowledge about the state of the system. If the multicast pattern repeats every N iterations, this set of iterations constitutes a phase. Once a process is able to multicast again, all the activity in the previous phase is known to be complete. To implement this communication pattern, PVM requires $N \times 2(N-1)$ network messages and Amoeba requires $N \times 2$ network messages. The customized message-passing system requires N network messages. In the customized message-passing system, missing messages are retrieved by blocked receivers whose timers have expired. These receivers ask the appropriate instance of the message-passing system to resend the missing multicast message. The repeat pattern also uses event-based error detection. If a message of the wrong type is found by the message-passing systems, it can retrieve the missing messages.

Multicast communication from all other processes serves as acknowledgment that they have received the previous multicast communication from that process. At the start of each phase, therefore, buffers kept for the previous phase may be removed. In Amoeba the number of buffers required is N per phase, and for PVM it is one. The customized message-passing system requires one buffer per phase per node. The number of interrupts generated is $N \times N$ for the customized message-passing system, $N \times (N+2)$ for Amoeba, and $N \times 4 \times (N-1)$ for PVM. In the customized message-passing system, the number of network messages generated is the same as the number of application-level messages. The `Repetitive` pattern occurs in the Cholesky factorization application.

6.3.3 Exchange

In this section, the various implementation issues for the `Exchange` CP are described. `Exchange` is a common CP in parallel iterative applications and has two variants. In both variants, `Exchange` repeats within a loop. In the first variant, the communicating process pairs are the same at every iteration. This is an example of communication locality. This CP is referred to as `ExchangeWithLocality` and its CP is shown in Figure 6.4. If locality exists (for example, the CP of the wave equation consists of `ExchangeWithLocality`), the communication is similar to an inverse request-response CP. Thus, a successful `receive` in one iteration indicates that the `send` from the previous iteration succeeded. The number of outstanding messages oscillates between one and two. But there is an upper limit of two on the number of messages that need to be buffered by any one message-passing system instance. If a network message is lost, the message-passing system instance that is blocking on the relevant `receive` times out and resends the lost

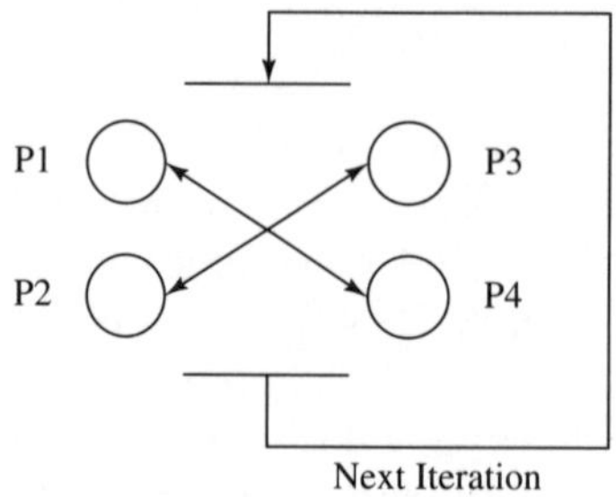

FIGURE 6.4 Exchange CP when locality exists between loop iterations.

message of the previous iteration. This scheme generates two network messages and four interrupts per exchange. PVM generates four network messages and eight interrupts, and Amoeba generates six network messages and 12 interrupts.

If there is no communication locality, the pattern is called an `ExchangeNoLocality`. In this case, explicit acknowledgments are needed. Since the identities of the processes involved in the exchange communication are known in advance, however, it is possible to force one process to perform a send and the other to receive first and then send. The first instance then generates an acknowledgment. An alternative implementation would allow both processes to send at the same time and then would generate separate acknowledgments for each application-level message. The first option is chosen, since it generates fewer acknowledgments.

Figure 6.5 shows the optimization in which only one acknowledgment is generated, rather than the two that would be generated by a naive implementation. A naive implementation would use two separate request-responses. The exchange CP with no locality appears in the FFT application (see Figure 3.7). Note also that message-passing systems supporting processes P1 and P2 have timers associated with them that are used for error detection. This scheme generates three network messages and six interrupts per exchange. Per exchange, PVM generates four network messages and eight interrupts, and Amoeba generates six network messages and 12 interrupts.

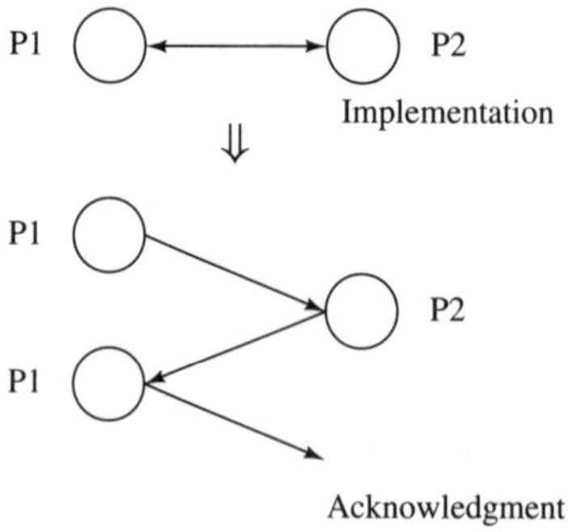

FIGURE 6.5 Exchange CP with no locality between loop iterations.

The analysis shows that the performance of the PVM and Amoeba systems does not change for the two communication patterns but the customized message-passing systems adapt to take advantage of the communication pattern.

6.3.4 Error Recovery

This section investigates what happens when a message is lost in several CPs, including `RedMulticast`, `Repetitive`, `ExchangeWithLocality`, and `ExchangeNoLocality`. $(1 + F)$, the overhead associated with a single message loss on an unreliable network, is investigated. The buffering analysis is not relevant since buffers simply support error recovery. F is the overhead associated with additional probe messages, and 1 represents the retransmission of the original data. Table 6.1 lists the number of additional network messages generated for a lost message, and Table 6.2 shows the number of additional interrupts generated for a lost message. Error recovery for multicasts in all systems involves point-to-point communication only. A multicast is never redone, since the assumption is that only very few (typically one) of the message-passing system instances do not receive the multicast message.

When a message is lost or corrupted, the customized message-passing systems generate one or two additional messages as part of their error recovery mechanism. One additional message is generated in cases where a process sends a message and then immediately waits for a reply. This type of error recovery is implemented by the message-passing systems for the `RedMulticast`, `ExchangeWithLocality`, and `ExchangeNoLocality` CPs. For all other cases, two additional messages are generated. In this second situation, a probe message is first generated by the message-passing system instance that times out, and the lost message is resent by

TABLE 6.1 Additional Network Messages Due to a Lost Message

Communication pattern	PVM	Amoeba	Customized
`RedMulticast`	1	1	1
`Repetitive`	1	2	2
`ExchangeNoLocality`	1	1	1
`ExchangeWithLocality`	1	1	1
`RedMulticast; Multicast`	1	1 or 2	1 or 2

TABLE 6.2 Additional Interrupts Due to a Lost Message

Communication pattern	PVM	Amoeba	Customized
`RedMulticast`	2	2	2
`Repetitive`	2	4	4
`ExchangeNoLocality`	2	2	2
`ExchangeWithLocality`	2	2	2
`RedMulticast; Multicast`	2	2 or 4	2 or 4

TABLE 6.3 Network Messages Generated by Various Systems

Attributes	PVM	Amoeba	Optimized
`RedMulticast`	$8(N-1)$	$4(N-1)+2$	N
`Repetitive` and Types	$2(N)(N-1)$	$2(N)$	N
`ExchangeNoLocality` and Types (per exchange)	4	6	3
`ExchangeWithLocality` and Types (per exchange)	4	6	2

TABLE 6.4 Interrupts Generated by Various Systems

Attributes	PVM	Amoeba	Optimized
`RedMulticast`	$8(N-1)$	$6(N-1)+N+2$	$3(N-1)+N$
`Repetitive` and Types	$4(N)(N-1)$	$(N)(N+2)$	$N(N)$
Exch and Types (per exchange)	8	12	6
`ExchangeLocality` and Types (per exchange)	8	12	4

TABLE 6.5 Buffers Required by Various Systems

Attributes	PVM	Amoeba	Optimized
`RedMulticast`	1	Unknown	1
`Repetitive` and Types	1	N	1 per phase per node

the message-passing system instance supporting the original sending process. In PVM, one additional message is always generated when a message is dropped. In the Amoeba multicast protocol, receiver timeouts generate a probe message and the original message is then resent. Therefore, two additional messages are generated. For point-to-point communication in the Amoeba system, one additional message is generated.

Tables 6.3, 6.4, and 6.5 summarize the number of network messages, interrupts, and buffers for the set of attributes discussed in Sections 6.3.1, 6.3.2, and 6.3.3, then compare them with implementations on Amoeba and PVM for the four sets of attributes described previously. The column labeled "Optimized" refers to the implementations that take advantage of application attributes in the message-passing implementation.

6.4 DISTRIBUTED SYSTEMS SELECTION

The generic methodology for transforming a set of application attributes to an implementation is used to build a tool kit of optimized message-passing systems that minimize the three performance metrics discussed previously. Each class in the tool kit has an annotation that describes the attributes relevant to it. A selection procedure is a procedure that selects between the various implementations using the attributes. Thus, given a new application and its attributes, there are two rules for finding an implementation of an optimized message-passing system for it.

6.4.1 Ease of Customizing the Message-Passing Framework: Rule 1

This section describes how the message-passing system framework described in Chapter 5 can be customized (rule 3 of 6.4) to incorporate new message-passing systems. This section demonstrates the ease with which new application-specific optimizations are created using the message-passing system framework. There are two classes of interest: CSR, and its subclass ClientCSR. ClientCSR is used for application-specific message passing for parallel and distributed applications on distributed systems. The CSR is subclassed for other distributed applications, such as distributed systems services, addressed in Section 7.4.

The abstract ClientCSR class provides the interface and reusable code for the new custom message-passing systems. The salient methods of the class are shown in Figure 6.6. There are three types of methods. First, there are methods that are used for the regular processing of messages: `receive`, `send`, and `awaitResponse`. These methods maintain the normal state machine for communication in the absence of message loss, and subclasses overload these methods to provide the relevant state machine transitions for a new CP. The `send` method saves the message for retransmission and notes that a message has been sent. The method `awaitResponse` is used for waiting for application messages. The `receive` method is called when a message arrives. All three methods are invoked by the Transport class.

Second, there are error-handling methods (`sendProbe` and `probe`) that are invoked when messages are lost or corrupted. These methods are called by either the `send` or `awaitResponse` methods when errors are detected using timers or an event-based mechanism. For error recovery, messages are resent or probe messages are sent that request corrective action. For example, the Exch class resends the original message and the Repetitive class generates probe messages. Further details about error recovery are given in Section 6.3.4. The `probe` method is called to handle probes, and the `sendProbe` method either sends a probe or resends a lost message, depending on the protocol. Subclasses overload these methods to implement the necessary error recovery steps.

Third, buffer allocation is handled by method `releaseBuffers`. It is called by one of three regular communication processing methods; `send`, `awaitResponse`, or `receive`. When a new subclass is added, each of these methods is overloaded and a few new methods may be created to provide the necessary functionality for further application-specific message passing. There is

```
class ClientCSR {
public:

/*
 * regular processing
 */
        virtual void awaitResponse();
        virtual void send(Message*);
        virtual Message* receive();
/*
 * handle errors
 */
        virtual void sendProbe();
        virtual void probe();
/*
 * Handle buffer allocation
 */
        virtual void releaseBuffers();

};
```

FIGURE 6.6 The methods of the ClientCSR class.

a set of state management methods that are inherited without any modifications but are not shown for purposes of clarity. These are inherited directly from the abstract class CSR, which is the superclass of ClientCSR.

The concrete subclass CSRShuffle of the abstract class ClientCSR is shown in Figure 6.7. This class implements the specialized message-passing system for the `Repetitive` CP described in Section 6.3.2. The six methods of the ClientCSR class are overloaded and some additional methods are defined to handle application-specific actions. These additional methods are `receiverTimeout`, `askForMissingRows`, `outOfOrder`, and `deliverInOrder`. The CSRShuffle implements both timer-based and event-based error detection. When a timer expires on a blocking `awaitResponse`, the `receiverTimeout` method is invoked. This method then invokes the `askForMissingRows` method to locate the missing row or rows and then invokes the `deliverInOrder` method to deliver the messages to the appropriate MessageContainer. If an out-of-order message is received, the method `outOfOrder` is invoked and the method `askForMissingRows` is used to locate missing rows. Finally, the messages are delivered in order to the appropriate MessageContainer using the `deliverInOrder` method. The method `mappingOfRow` is used to determine which process is needed to probe for missing messages. The `releaseBuffers` method is invoked just before the `send` method is invoked to release the multicast messages that were stored for retransmission purposes.

```
class CSRShuffle : public ClientCSR {
public:
/*
 * overload
 */

        virtual Message *receive();
        virtual void send(Message *);
        virtual void awaitResponse();

        virtual void sendProbe();
        virtual void probe();

        virtual void releaseBuffers();

/*
 * Application-specific methods
 */
        virtual void receiverTimeout();
        virtual void askForMissingRows();
        virtual void deliverInOrder();
        virtual int outOfOrder();
/*
 * This is the function f, such that pid = f(row)
 */
        int mappingOfRow();
}
```

FIGURE 6.7 The methods of the CSRShuffle class.

The ease of extension is supported explicitly by two features. In examining Figure 5.7, it can be seen that all the other classes of the framework are used without change. The CSRShuffle class fits in with the framework and preserves the control flow and entity relationships defined in Figures 5.7 and 5.10. CSRShuffle inherits these constraints from the ClientCSR class. The CSRShuffle class can be used without any further changes for both the Cholesky factorization and Matrix Multiply applications. Other applications with different data decomposition functions can use this class just by overloading the `mappingOfRow` method. This last example demonstrates the power of incremental modification of the message-passing system.

As another example, consider the implementation of the `ExchangeNoLocality` CP. The methodology requires creating a new subclass of the ClientCSR class called Exch. The methods of the Exch class are shown in Figure 6.8. Six of

```
class Exch : public ClientCSR {
public:
/*
 * overload
 */
        virtual void awaitResponse();
        virtual void send(Message*);
        virtual Message* receive();

        virtual void sendProbe();
        virtual void probe();

        virtual void releaseBuffers();
/*
 * Application-specific methods
 */
        virtual void sendLastAck();
        virtual void gotLastAck();


};
```

FIGURE 6.8 The methods of the Exch class.

the methods of ClientCSR are overloaded, as is done for CSRShuffle and two new methods, `sendLastAck` and `gotLastAck`, have been added to accommodate the additional acknowledgment that is generated because there is insufficient locality of communication. Once again, the Exch class interacts with the rest of the message-passing system according to control flow and entity relations defined in Figures 5.7 and 5.10. The implementation for `ExchangeWithLocality` is similarly constructed. The FFT application can use the Exch class without any changes. The class RedMulti implements generic `RedMulticast`, and subclasses are used to implement the optimized message-passing system for the Simplex application. The class hierarchy for these optimizations is shown in Figure 6.9. The implementations are annotated with attributes. The attributes and framework classes are inputs to a selection procedure. The pseudocode for the selection procedure and the attributes used to select between the classes are shown in Figure 6.10.

6.4.2 Direct Selection: Rule 2

If the application attributes match the annotations of a particular class, choose that class. Figure 6.10 is an example of such a selection procedure. More on this topic appears in later chapters.

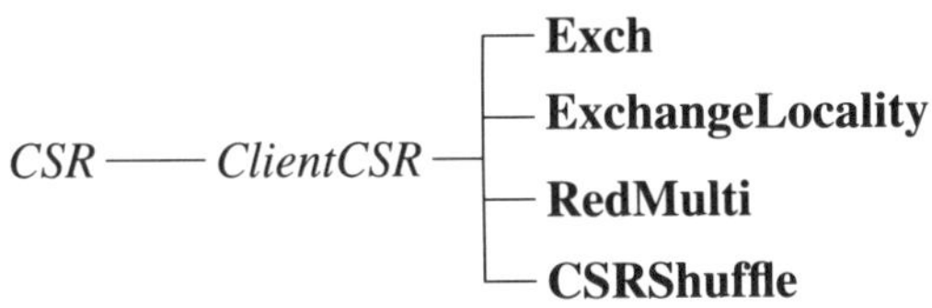

FIGURE 6.9 Distributed system optimizations.

```
/*
 * This procedure shows how to
 * use CPs to select optimizations.
 * All the choices assume the reliability attribute.
 */

SynchronousParallelApplicationSelection() {
        if(CP==ExchangeWithLocality)
                ExchangeLocality;
        else if (CP==ExchangeNoLocality)
                Exch;
        else if (CP==Repetitive and Types)
                CSRShuffle;
        else if (CP==RedMulticast)
                RedMulti;
        /*
         * Subclass one of the above classes or CSR

         * for the new message passing system.
         * Best when sufficient locality
         * of communication is present.
         */
        else if (best optimization required)
                        subclassExistingClass();
        /*
         * Compose existing implementations.
         * Optimized but better may be possible
         * by direct subclassing.
         */
        else SequentiallyCombineExistingClasses();
}
```

FIGURE 6.10 Synchronous application selections on distributed systems.

6.4.3 Composing Implementations: Rule 3

If the application attributes under consideration are a combination of existing attribute implementations, a combination of existing classes can be used by composition. Each class is used sequentially, one after the other; however, it may not generate the minimal number of network messages. The resulting implementation is optimized, but it may not be the best solution because it may be possible to use the combined attributes together to obtain a better implementation. In this case, the cost optimization function becomes

$$\sum_i \min \; Cost(CP_i) \tag{6.3}$$

This equation states that the optimized cost of an application's communication is the sum of all individual patterns, each of which has been separately optimized. This formula assumes that each pattern implementation has error-handling mechanisms independent of other pattern implementations. That is, each pattern implementation is responsible for its own error recovery mechanism, which is independent of the communication and error recovery mechanism of the other pattern implementations. Campbell et al. [CR86] advocate similar techniques in which recovery operations provided by a fault-tolerant system should be implemented within atomic actions.

> *If successful, any fault tolerance measures employed within an atomic action are invisible to the rest of the system. This provides a framework for encapsulating such measures into modular components.*

Atomic actions provide damage confinement [AL81], which supports the modularity argument of [CR86]. Systems such as PVM use explicit acknowledgments to provide damage confinement and detection. The global optimization techniques described in Section 6.2 show how damage confinement and detection can be part of the natural communication of the application. Each class is created to manage its own error recovery procedure independent of other classes. Thus, a class encapsulates the largest possible atomic action whose errors can be confined and optimized. Each class, therefore, performs damage confinement by making sure it can recover from the loss of any of its messages.

Each of the subclasses of the ClientCSR class were constructed to have independent error handling. It is possible to compose sequentially any of the classes to construct an optimized message-passing system for an application. For example, if an application had a `RedMulticast` CP followed by an `ExchangeWithLocality`, then the classes RedMulti and ExchangeLocality could be used sequentially for the message-passing system of the application. In this example, the minimum number of messages is generated, since each constituent CP implementation generates the minimum number of messages. On the other hand, if the CP in an application were to have a `RedMulticast` and then an `ExchangeNoLocality`, then the minimum number of messages would not necessarily be generated if the classes RedMulti and Exch were used one after the other in loop. In this case, it is possible to use the `RedMulticast` CP to eliminate explicit acknowledgments. An optimization subclassing RedMulti to incorporate the communication pattern in the `ExchangeNoLocality` would yield a better implementation. The user of the tool kit has the option to choose one implementation or the other. In either case, the system performs better than PVM or Amoeba.

6.5 SUMMARY

This chapter describes a methodology for constructing and selecting optimized message-passing systems on distributed systems. It discusses how to use a tool kit of optimizations. Classes from the tool kit may be used as is, classes may be composed, or classes may be subclassed to generate new implementations. Composition is particularly useful since it allows a variety of optimizations to be created from existing implementations. As the tool kit matures, a point will be reached when it is rich enough that optimizations for most applications can be generated through direct use or composition rather than through subclassing.

CHAPTER 7

Distributed System: Application Results

In this chapter, message-passing systems are designed for three sample parallel applications, Simplex, Cholesky, and FFT, and several systems services. All of the parallel applications have a synchronous PIP. The error-handling overheads for these parallel protocols are described in Section 6.3.4 and are not discussed here. This chapter presents comparisons between applications running on the optimized message passing system and those running on PVM, as well as analytical comparisons with PVM and Amoeba. The results reported are for runs of the applications when no messages are lost. In the following sections, each application has an instance of an application-specific message-passing system running on each node of the network. The applications of the customized message-passing system were run using the distributed gang scheduler described in Chapter 10.

7.1 CUSTOMIZED MESSAGE-PASSING SYSTEM FOR SIMPLEX

The CP of the Simplex application is shown in Figure 7.1. Tables 7.1, 7.2, and 7.3 show the number of resources used and messages that are generated for PVM, Amoeba, and the customized message-passing system, respectively. The CP is analyzed by breaking it into four phases. These phases are identified in Figure 7.1. The PVM and Amoeba systems generate messages additively, giving rise to the

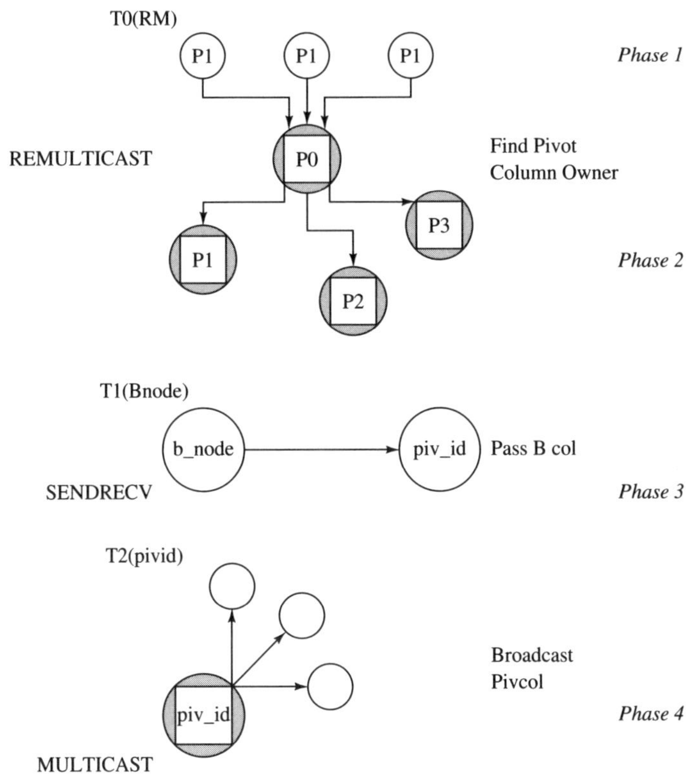

FIGURE 7.1 CP of Simplex with timer locations.

TABLE 7.1 PVM Communication Overheads

Phase	Network Messages	Interrupts	Multicast Send Buffers
Phase 1	$2(N-1)$	$4(N-1)$	—
Phase 2	$2(N-1)$	$4(N-1)$	1
Phase 3	2	4	—
Phase 4	$2(N-1)$	$4(N-1)$	1
Total	$6N-4$	$12N-8$	1

TABLE 7.2 Amoeba Communication Overheads

Phase	Network Messages	Interrupts	Multicast Send Buffers
Phase 1	$3(N-1)$	$6(N-1)$	—
Phase 2	2	$3+N-1$	Unknown
Phase 3	3	6	—
Phase 4	2	$3+(N-1)$	Unknown
Total	$3N+4$	$8N+4$	Unknown

TABLE 7.3 Customized Message-Passing System Communication Overheads

Phase	Network Messages	Interrupts	Multicast Send Buffers
Phase 1	$N-1$	$2(N-1)$	—
Phase 2	1	N	1
Phase 3	1	2	—
Phase 4	1	N	1
Total	$N+2$	$4N$	2 (max)

numbers in the tables. The buffers in the sequencer of the Amoeba protocol are unknown, because for certain input data set sizes no multicast messages are generated by some of the processes. Thus, acknowledgments cannot be piggybacked on regular communication, and as a result, the message buffers in the sequencer become full. In this case, probe messages are generated by message-passing system instances that are supporting a process blocked on a receive operation. This lets the sequencer know which messages have been received by these non-multicasting processes. For example, if process 0 is the pivot holder (**pivid**) for all iterations, then all other message-passing system instances time out constantly throughout the application's run, and the sequencer may potentially run out of buffer space and may have to invoke special protocols to free message buffers. The number of network messages generated by the customized message-passing system is the same as the number of application-level messages specified by the parallel data partitioning.

As discussed in Section 3.2, the Simplex application has a `RedMulticast` pattern. After the `RedMulticast`, each message-passing system instance can release all the buffers stored for the previous iteration once it receives the multicast message. In addition, the multicaster is free to release all buffers from the previous iteration as soon as it completes the reduction.

The two other CP implementations following the `RedMulticast` release their message buffers when the reduction is complete, since the completion of a reduction signals the end of the previous iteration. Each message-passing system instance supporting the sender for the reduction performs a send operation and then waits for a reply from the message-passing system instance supporting process 0. Each sender has a timer set to the value T0(RM). The message is sent again until a reply is received.

The message-passing system instance supporting the **Bnode** row sender then performs a send and waits for the message-passing system instance supporting the process labeled **pivid** to reply. The instance supporting process **Bnode** has a timer set to T1(Bnode). If this timer expires, the instance resends the original message until a message is returned. Finally, the instance supporting **pivid** multicasts the pivrow number and pivot column. As the sender of pivcol/pivrow, the message-passing system instance supporting **pivid** "knows" all instances have received its multicast when it receives the multicast (of the `RedMulticast` CP) in the next iteration. Each instance supporting a process that is blocked and waiting for a multicast has a timer set to the value T2(pivid). If this timer expires, the appropriate message-passing system instance requests the pivot column from the pivot column holder. The exact location of the three timers for the message-passing system instances is shown in Figure 7.1. The two multicasts generated per iteration are typed; therefore, these message types must be used to differentiate between the two multicasts in case multicasts are received out of order by a message-passing system instance.

Customized Message-Passing System Implementation. A careful analysis of the CP of each process shows that there are three different traces. These traces are shown in Figure 7.2. For each trace a state machine is implemented as a subclass of RedMulti. All the processes are potential pivot column owners, and, thus, all message-passing system instances must share the code to handle the pivot multicast and error recovery for that multicast. Pivot column management is implemented in class SimpCSR, which implements the data dependent behavior and recovery for the message-passing system. SimpCSR inherits from RedMulti the code to handle the reliable implementation of the `RedMulticast` pattern. The SimpCSR augments the behavior of that message-passing system to handle the reliable delivery of the pivot column. Three additional classes implement the differences between the three types of processes: (1) PZero, the state machine for the message-passing system supporting process 0; (2) Bnode, the state machine for the message-passing system instance supporting process bnode; and (3) All,

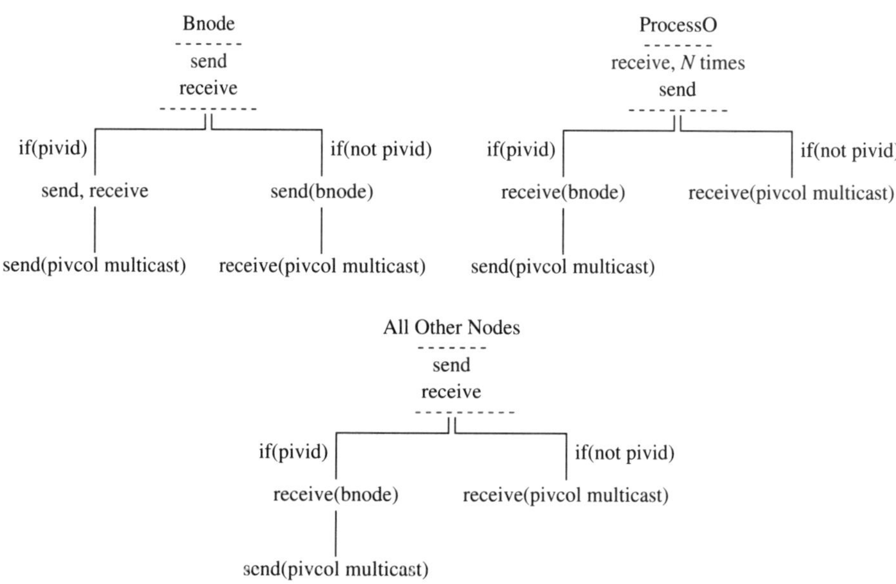

FIGURE 7.2 Per-process communication patterns.

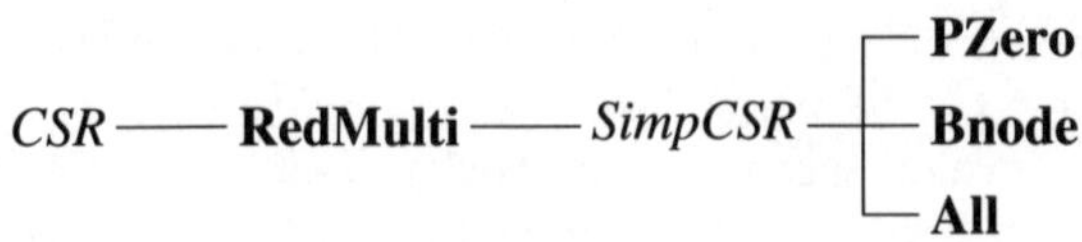

FIGURE 7.3 Classes to implement protocol for Simplex application.

the state machine for all other message-passing system instances. This description shows how it is possible to enhance the basic RedMulti class to generate variants. The classes are shown in Figure 7.3.

Performance. Figure 7.4 shows the speedup for the Simplex algorithm. The customized message-passing system performs better, particularly as the number of nodes is increased. The percentage of improvement is shown in Table 7.4. The greater the number of nodes, the better the customized message-passing system performs. In particular, with eight nodes the customized message-passing system performs 21 percent faster than PVM. Comparing Tables 7.1 and 7.3, it can be seen that approximately six times fewer messages and three times fewer interrupts are generated by the customized message-passing system. The customized message-passing system has increased speed and has the same buffering requirements. Most of the speed increase is a result of the decrease in the number of messages and interrupts. As the number of nodes is increased, this difference becomes more noticeable. These results were obtained from runs with no network message loss. A test compared computation times, and they were found to be the same on

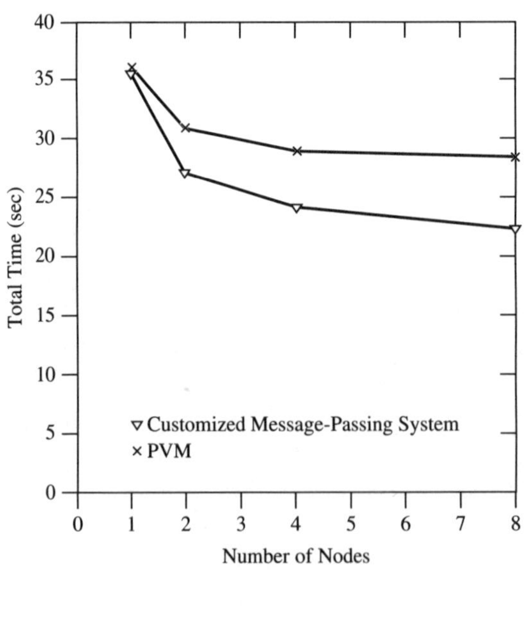

FIGURE 7.4 Speedup of Simplex.

TABLE 7.4 Benefits of Customized Message-Passing System for Simplex

Number of Nodes	2	4	8
Percentage Improvement for Simplex	10	14	21

both systems. The difference in performance is therefore due solely to the CP optimizations.

Alternate Data Partitionings: Row Partitioning. Other data partitionings are possible for the Simplex algorithm. For example, the data may be partitioned as rows instead of as columns. In both partitioning schemes, however, a global minimum is computed that requires the `RedMulticast` pattern. In the row partitioning scheme, one additional global minimization is required to find the pivot column. Thus, two `RedMulticast` patterns are computed, one after the other, with some minor computation in between. Implementing the message-passing systems for these CPs requires subclassing the SimpCSR class.

7.2 CUSTOMIZED MESSAGE-PASSING SYSTEM FOR CHOLESKY

The CP for the Cholesky shuffle partitioning scheme is shown in Figure 3.6. Table 7.5 shows the performance of the communication for Cholesky on the three communication systems; this follows directly from the analysis in Section 6.3.2. Clearly, the customized message-passing system performs the best. The customized message-passing system generates the same number of network messages as application-level messages. This is possible because there is sufficient locality inherent in the CP of the program.

In the Cholesky application, each message is tagged with the row number. Each process blocked on a `receive` knows which row it is going to receive next and from which message-passing system instance that row will come. In addition, there exists a function *f*, such that *pid* = *f*(*row*). This implies that any message-passing system instance can find the location of the owner of any row of the matrix.

In the shuffle partitioning scheme, multicast send buffers need only be kept by each message-passing system instance until it sends the next row. When the

TABLE 7.5 System Overheads for Shuffle Partitioned Cholesky

System	Network Messages	Interrupts	Multicast Send Bufs
PVM	$2(N^2 - N)$	$4N^2 - 4N$	1
Amoeba	$2N$	$N^2 + 2N$	N per round
Customized	N	N^2	1 per node per round

message-passing system instance sends the next row, it knows that all other processes have received its previous multicast. Each message-passing system instance supporting a multicast receiver has a timer set to the value TO(R). Each instance must keep at most one buffer of the multicast from the previous phase to satisfy these timeout requests. Each instance may release its buffer before it initiates a send of the next row. If a message-passing system instance times out while supporting a blocking receive, it searches for the row it is missing. If it receives a message out of order, it also searches for missing messages (that is, previous rows) and buffers all the messages that have been received out of order.

Customized Message-Passing System Implementation. Since the pattern is `Repetitive`, according to the selection guide in Section 6.6, the CSRShuffle should be used as part of the message-passing system. Although the class CSR-Shuffle is used without change, a different view of the implementation of that class is presented to further illustrate how the class implements the `Repetitive` CP. The state machine of the customized message-passing system implementing the `Repetitive` CP is shown in Figure 7.5. N processes are used to solve the problem. The state at which each message-passing system instance starts is shown in the figure. Each application process computes, performs a `receive` operation, and eventually performs a multicast send and executes $N-1$ receives before the next send.

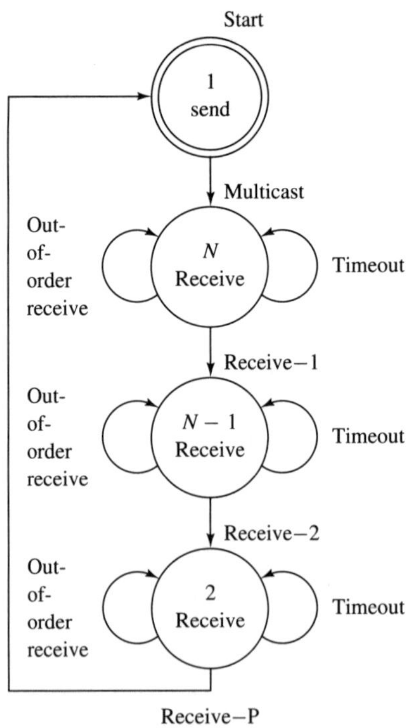

FIGURE 7.5 State diagram for the customized message-passing system for Cholesky.

Each process executes the same state machine as implemented by CSRShuffle. The sender state is maintained by methods `send` and `releaseBuffers`. The method `send` sends the buffer and retains a copy to handle probes for it. The method `releaseBuffers` releases buffers when the next send operation is invoked from the same process.

The receiver state machine is implemented by the methods `awaitResponse`, `OutofOrder`, `deliverInOrder`, and `mappingOfRow`. The method `awaitResponse` is called to block on an application receive call, `receiverTimeout` is invoked when a timer expires on an `awaitResponse`; and the method `mappingofRow` is the data-partitioning function of the Cholesky application that provides the owner of a missing row when given the row number as input. The method `awaitResponse` performs a point-to-point send to request a lost multicast row. Since there could be up to $N-2$ out-of-order messages, there needs to be $N-2$ receive buffers.

Performance. Figure 7.6 shows the performance of the customized message-passing system compared with that PVM. The benefits of using a customized message-passing system are summarized in Table 7.6 which shows the

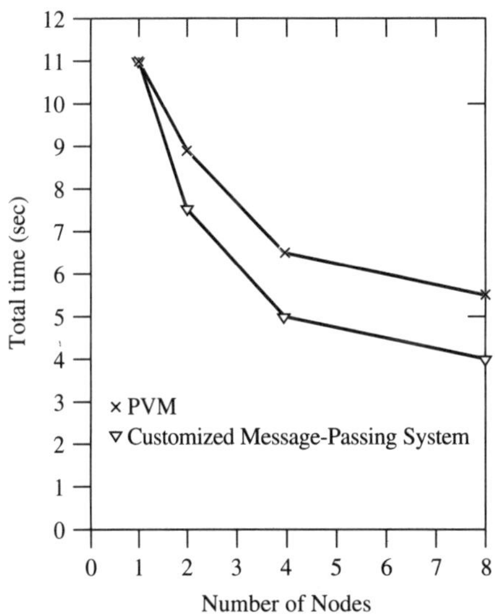

FIGURE 7.6 Speedup of the Cholesky application: Input data set size of 1024.

TABLE 7.6 Benefits of Customized Message-Passing System for Cholesky

Number of Nodes	2	4	8
Percentage Improvement for Cholesky	15.7	22.4	27

percentage improvements of the customized message-passing system over PVM as the number of nodes is increased. As with the Simplex, the performance differences are more marked as the number of nodes is increased. At eight nodes, the customized message-passing system is 27 percent faster than PVM. The improvement in the speedup of the Cholesky application is better than in the Simplex because the number of network messages is dramatically reduced from $O(N^2)$ on PVM to $O(N)$ for the customized message-passing systems, and there was a substantial reduction in the number of interrupts. The results are from runs of the application when no application-level messages were lost. The customized message-passing systems were also able to keep the number of buffers the same as in PVM while making the multicast asynchronous. A test compared computation times, and they were found to be the same on both systems. The difference is therefore due solely to the CP optimizations.

7.3 CUSTOMIZED MESSAGE-PASSING SYSTEM FOR FFT

The CP for FFT is shown in Figure 3.7. It has an `ExchangeNoLocality` CP, as discussed in Section 6.3.3. Table 7.7 shows the number of messages per iteration generated for FFT in the various systems. The numbers are for each iteration and are derived directly from Section 6.3.3. Amoeba generates the greatest number of messages, followed by PVM. The customized message-passing system generates the fewest messages and interrupts. Since the FFT application does not have multicast as part of its CP, there are no multicast send buffering requirements.

Customized Message-Passing System Implementation. Since the CP matches exactly the `ExchangeNoLocality` CP, the **Exch** class implementation is used without any changes. The number of network messages is greater than the number of application-level messages since this CP has insufficient locality of communication.

Performance. Figures 7.7 and 7.8 compare the performance of PVM with the customized message-passing system on a two-node and four-node configuration. In both cases, the customized message-passing system performs better than PVM for all data set sizes on two- and four-node configurations. The larger the data set size, the better the message-passing system performs. This is due in part to the blast protocol used in the customized system.

TABLE 7.7 System Overheads for FFT

System	Network Messages	Interrupts
PVM	$4\ (N/2)$	$8\ (N/2)$
Amoeba	$6\ (N/2)$	$12(N/2)$
Customized	$3(N/2)$	$6\ (N/2)$

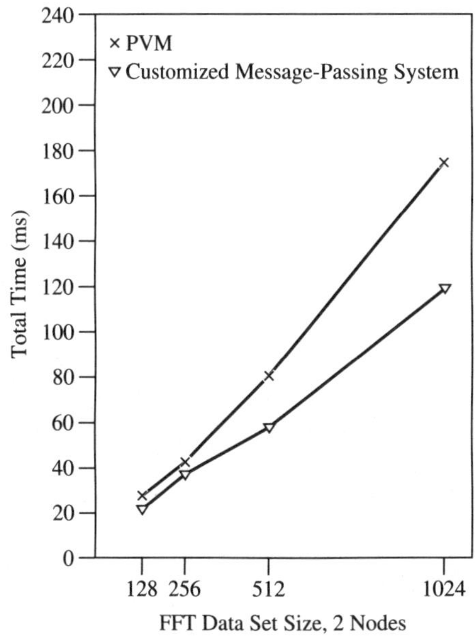

FIGURE 7.7 Execution times for FFT with two nodes with varying data set sizes.

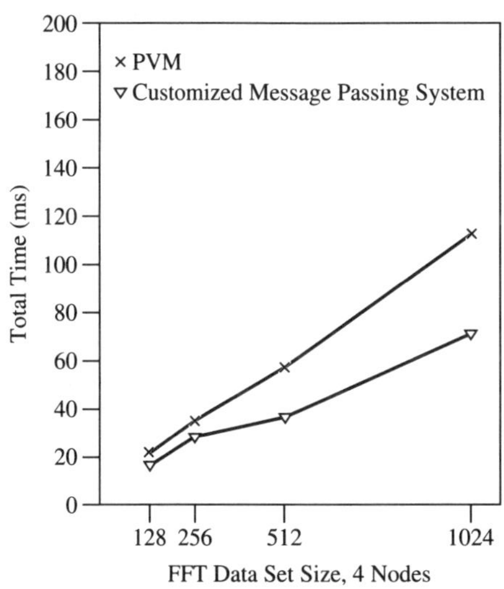

FIGURE 7.8 Execution times for FFT with four nodes with varying data set sizes.

The speedup of the FFT application is shown in Figure 7.9, which clearly shows that the customized implementation performs better than PVM regardless of the number of nodes used. Table 7.8 shows the benefits of the customized message-passing system as compared to PVM. The improvements are fairly constant for FFT as the number of nodes is increased. The dramatic increase in speedup observed for the other applications is not evident here since FFT does

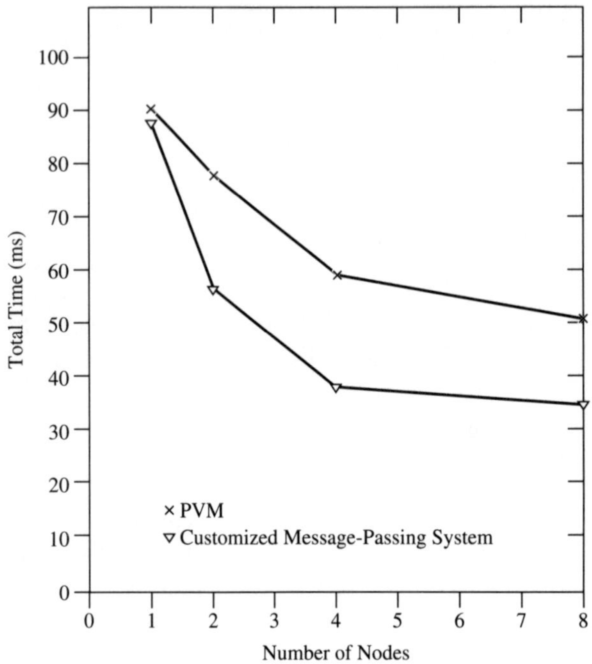

FIGURE 7.9 FFT speedup for data set size of 512.

TABLE 7.8 Benefits of Customized Message-Passing System for FFT

Number of Nodes	2	4	8
Percentage Improvement for FFT	28	22	29

not use multicast. For the eight-node case, the FFT application is 29 percent faster than PVM. A test comparing computation times found they were the same on both systems. The difference is therefore due solely to the CP optimizations.

7.4 CUSTOMIZED MESSAGE PASSING FOR SYSTEM SERVICES

In the following sections, the message-passing systems for client-server programs are described. Like synchronous parallel applications, certain patterns exist in system services. These sections demonstrate the ease with which an existing message-passing system, the V operating system primitives, may be incorporated into an object-oriented framework. The V primitives were prototyped because they provide high-performance request-response (RR) performance, and their implementation using the VMTP protocol is a special case of the techniques discussed in Section 6.2. A new set of tool kit options is described; these options are generated using the methodology presented in Section 6.1. They are used to generate optimized message-passing systems for two distributed systems services. The services discussed are a name service and a distributed gang scheduling facility.

7.5 CUSTOMIZED MESSAGE PASSING FOR REQUEST-RESPONSE CP

The RR CP is a common pattern of communication in distributed systems such as V [Che88a]. In this section, the various options and customizations for the client-server PIP are discussed. In the client-server PIP, several client processes may communicate with several server processes. The communication is asymmetric and is usually RR.

The basic message-passing system is based on the VMTP protocol of the V system. It is a considerably simplified version of the protocol and does not support forwarding and streaming. One important feature of VMTP and timer-based protocols is that they avoid the setup and teardown costs per connection that are associated with connection-oriented protocols such as TCP. VMTP is an implicit, or lightweight-connection-based, protocol, whereas TCP is an explicit, or handshake-based, protocol. Timer-based protocols require one basic guarantee: that the maximum network message lifetime can be bounded. To implement an RR protocol PVM uses four messages and Amoeba uses three. The VMTP protocol generates two messages.

The RR CP has two possible implementations: at-least-once (ALO) and exactly once (EO). EO requires the recipient to get the message exactly once; ALO means the recipient may get the message more than once. The ALO implementation requires the server function to be idempotent (see Chapter 3). Unlike parallel applications that require each application-level message to be delivered once, the ALO implementation for client-server programs allows an application-level message to be lost and regenerated by the application. In this sense, the ALO option does not require the strict, reliable delivery of every message.

The class hierarchies for the RR CP are shown in Figure 7.10. The intermediate classes ClientCSR and RemoteCSR facilitate the construction of different

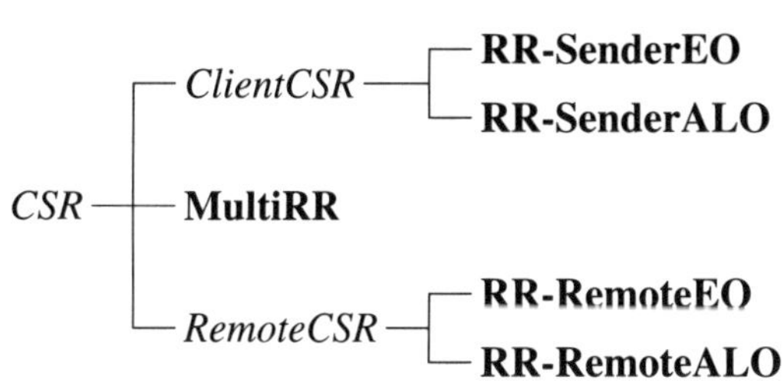

FIGURE 7.10 Reliability class hierarchies.

implementations of the RR CPs. The **ClientCSR** class and how it is to be subclassed are described in Section 6.4. The **RemoteCSR** class is introduced to keep a history of the communication on the remote machine. The implementations of the RR protocol are asymmetric and communication is driven by the client side. The **ClientCSR** and **RemoteCSR** classes have matching concrete subclasses that must be used together to obtain the different implementations. When client-server programs use an optimized message-passing system, the client side message-passing system will use subclasses of **ClientCSR** and the server side message-passing system will use subclasses of **RemoteCSR**. Therefore, to construct a complete message-passing system for a client and a server, two classes are chosen, one for the client and one for the server. The interface protocols for the client-server message-passing systems implementing EO and ALO reliability semantics are shown in Tables 7.9 and 7.10. The tables show the important methods of the classes. Probe management is considerably simpler in the classes implementing ALO semantics. The `recvRequest` and `requestDone` methods control the start and finish of a request from a client.

RR-SenderALO is used with **RR-RemoteALO** for ALO semantics and **RR-SenderEO** is used with **RR-RemoteEO** for EO semantics. The state diagram implemented by the **RR-SenderEO** class is shown in Figure 7.11, and that implemented by the **RR-RemoteEO** class is shown in Figure 7.12.

The primary difference between ALO and EO is that the **RR-RemoteALO** class does not handle probes for responses, since the response is never saved and, thus, the `handleResponseProbe` method is missing. The `handleResponseProbe` method is defined and implemented by **RR-RemoteEO**. All subclasses of **RemoteCSR** must determine when to call the method `releaseBuffers` to free message buffers and manage additional state information concerning responses to client requests. The `sendProbe` method of **RR-SenderALO** resends the entire message rather than a probe message.

TABLE 7.9 Interface for Client State Machines

Class::Method	send	receive	awaitResponse	releaseBuffers	sendProbe	probe
ClientCSR	=0	•	•	•	•	•
▽ **RR-SenderEO**	△	△	•	•	•	•
▽ **RR-SenderALO**	•	△	△	•	•	•

TABLE 7.10 Interface for Remote Client State Machines

Class::Method	recvRequest	handleResponseProbe	requestDone	releaseBuffers
RemoteCSR	=0	-	=0	•
▽ **RR-RemoteEO**	•	•	•	▽
▽ **RR-RemoteALO**	•	-	•	▽

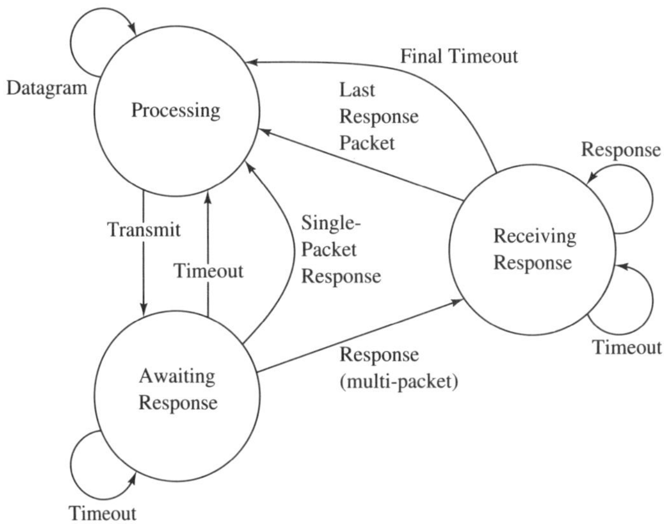

FIGURE 7.11 Exactly-once client state transitions—RR-SenderEO.

For group communication in the client-server PIP, a variety of options are possible. One common group CP is `MultiRR`, in which a client communicates with a number of servers. Two implementations of `MultiRR` exist, depending on whether the server is idempotent. The MultiRR class provides reliable group RR, in which one sender may wait for 1 to N replies before returning. It is used with the RR-RemoteEO class when the server is not idempotent and with the RR-RemoteALO class when the server is idempotent.

7.5.1 Selecting the Appropriate Request-Response Implementation

ALO semantics reduces the buffering requirements for the operating system; it is used by applications where the server function is idempotent. Examples include time servers, real-time sensing (for example, sensing the temperature of a device), and weather monitoring. Idempotent applications have a choice between EO and ALO. The choice involves a tradeoff between space and time considerations. This choice may be made by the system service designer. For example, a reasonable choice might be to use EO for small messages and ALO for large messages. The selection procedure for the various `RR` CP implementations is summarized in Figure 7.13.

Request-Response Performance. This section discusses the performance of the RR protocol. It also discusses the overhead of the software structure of the message-passing system using object-oriented frameworks. The results are for the pair of classes RR-SenderEO and RR-RemoteEO. The server function used in

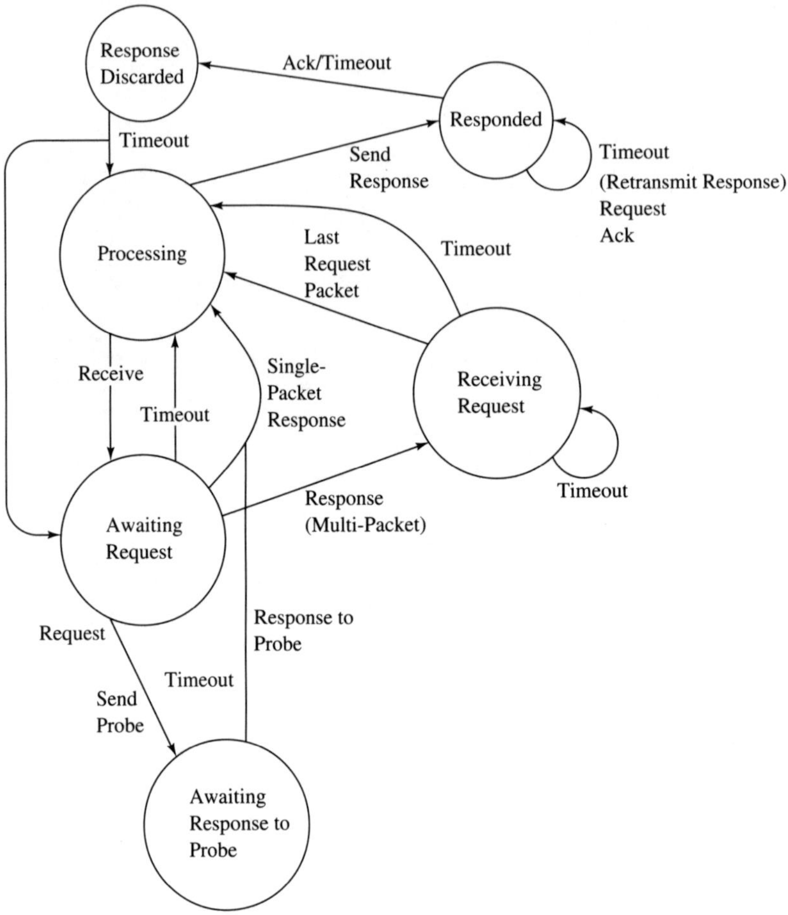

FIGURE 7.12 Exactly-once remote client state transitions—RR-RemoteEO.

this experiment is the null function; it does nothing. Figure 7.14 shows the message latency for the EO instance of the message-passing system and an equivalent PVM implementation.

The distributed system implementation is smooth until the message size requires the system to fragment the messages for transmission over the Ethernet. The distributed system port fragments messages over 1400 bytes. For large messages, the implementation uses a simple blast protocol. For very large messages, latency is dominated by data copy, fragmentation, and Ethernet transmission overheads.

Table 7.11 shows the breakdown of the various parts of the RR message-passing system for a null user message. The row labeled "Endpoint Lookup" refers to binding to the appropriate MessageContainer. This value is high because of

```
/*
 * On distributed systems
 * for applications with a client-server
 * PIP the CP as well as whether or not
 * the server has idempotent functions
 * is used for selection.
 * The following psuedo-code shows how to
 * select the various classes from the toolkit of
 * options.
 */

ClientServerSelections() {
        if(CP==RR) {
                if(idempotent server) {
                        if( space limited )
                                RRSenderALO with RR-RemoteALO
                        if( fast response important)
                                RRSenderEO with RR-RemoteEO
                }else RRSenderEO with RR-RemoteEO
        } else if(CP==MultiRR) {
                if(idempotent servers) {
                        if( space limited )
                                MultiRR with RR-RemoteALO
                        if( fast response important)
                                MultiRR with RR-RemoteEO
                } else MultiRR with RR-RemoteEO
        }
}
```

FIGURE 7.13 Client-server selections.

the recursive name service. Several levels of lookup are performed before the appropriate ContainerRepresentative for theMessageContainer is found.

The object-oriented framework structure is supported by the use of the C++ virtual function call mechanism [Str91]. The overhead of the C++ virtual function call mechanism is only 2 percent.* The number of virtual function calls made in a round trip is shown in parentheses. The number increases with the complexity of the underlying message-passing system. The low overhead of the virtual functions suggests that object-oriented frameworks are an efficient technique for structuring message-passing software. The message-passing system on the distributed system includes the overheads of fragmentation, reassembly, data copying, and context

*All of the virtual functions are not shown in Figure 5.7.

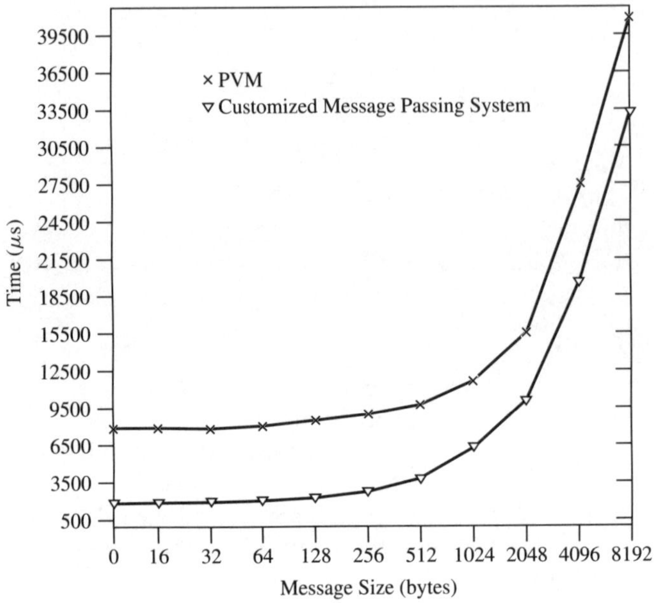

FIGURE 7.14 Request-response protocol performance.

TABLE 7.11 Request-Response Protocol Overheads in μs

Number	Activity	μsec	%
4	Proxy Calls	61	14
4	Endpoint Lookup	23	5
	Virtual Functions	2 (×28)	2
4	Network Interrupt Handler	103	23
2	Network Transmission	48	5
	Protocol Processing	910	51
	Total	1800	100

switches between operating system and application. A context switch takes 150 μs on the distributed system.

The message-passing implemented by PVM on UNIX has very large latencies. This is primarily due to the inefficient protocol that generates too many messages and network interrupts. In an effort to be general, the implementation also uses xdr [Inc90] on each communication even when messages are being exchanged between machines of the same architecture. When sufficient information is available about the nature of the application and the environment in which it is running, the additional messages and interrupts can be eliminated. PVM clearly suffers from being overly general; as a result, the customized protocol performs much better than PVM.

7.6 CP OF SPECIFIC SYSTEM SERVICES

In the following sections, the CPs of two system services, a name service and a scheduling service, are discussed. These system services use a composition of the CP implementations described in Section 7.5. The following applications have client-server PIPs.

7.6.1 Distributed Name Service

This section describes the message-passing system that is used in the distributed name service. When a process invokes the `bind` method on a NameServer, with a MessageContainer as an argument, this binding is multicast without explicit acknowledgment to the other NameServers on the network. When a process on another machine performs a `lookup` on a NameServer searching for this MessageContainer, the remote reference to the MessageContainer may already be in the local NameServer. If it is not in the local NameServer, the local name server will use a `MultiRR` CP to search for the missing object reference on behalf of the requesting process.

The NameServer protocol is idempotent and, therefore, the RR-ReceiverALO class is used for remote history maintenance and MultiRR for the local history. The NameServer database acts as a repository of the names, and the message-passing system explicitly asks the NameServer for the data if they are not found.

If Amoeba were to implement this CP, it would employ the Amoeba reliable multicast protocol, which would incur two messages. PVM uses $3 \times (N - 1)$ messages. The customized message-passing system uses one message in the best case and three messages in the worst case.

7.6.2 Distributed Scheduling

The distributed scheduling system uses an algorithm with a CP that differs from that of the NameServer. The CP for one instance of the scheduling system is shown in Figure 7.15. The attributes of this application are ordered and reliable multicasts, application types, and idempotent server functions. There are three multicasts one after the other. The first CP must be a `MultiRR` since resource information must be collected from the various message-passing system instances on the network. The resource allocation mechanism is an idempotent service and, hence, the matching class for the MultiRR class is RR-ReceiverALO. The collecting message-passing system then determines the subset of machines to use for running the parallel application's processes as a gang. This subset membership information is sent to the original group.

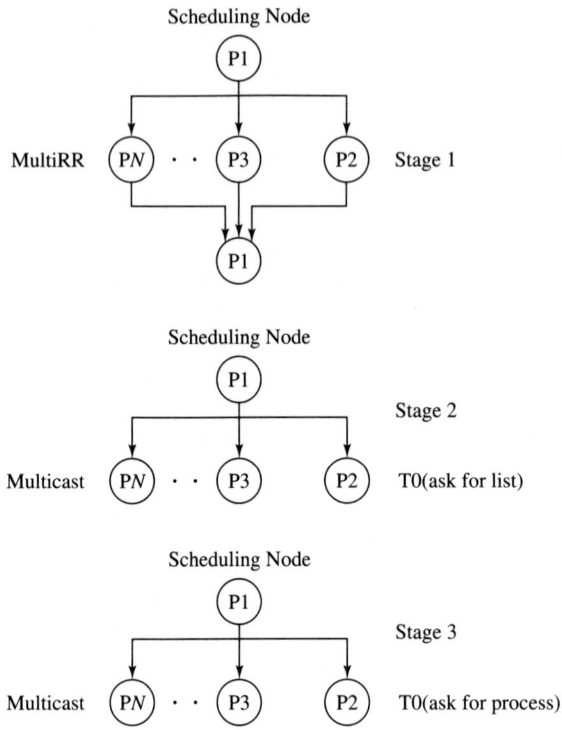

FIGURE 7.15 CP for gang scheduling.

Each of the message-passing system instances that replied in the first round sets a timer and waits to see if it was selected. If a message-passing system instance does not receive the next expected message within a few milliseconds, then it times out and requests the list of selected members from the collecting message-passing system (labeled "scheduling node" in Figure 7.15). Only those message-passing system instances that have been selected continue to listen for multicasts.

The third and final multicast from the scheduling node is a multicast of the process itself or a request to load the process from the local disk. Each receiving instance of the message-passing system will set a timer and wait for the gang process or the request to launch the gang process to arrive. If any of the timers expire, a probe packet is sent to the collecting message-passing system to ask it to resend the process or request. When the application finishes running, it exits and all state associated with the gang is removed.

The primary advantage of this scheme is that the second and third multicasts do not require explicit acknowledgments and each waiting message-passing system instance knows exactly which message-passing system instance to ask for a lost message. The last two multicast messages are differentiated by application-specific types. Ordering is not relevant across multicast groups, however, since multicast groups cannot overlap. Each replying message-passing system instance will be part of only one group and will reply only to the first request and deny further requests. If several gangs are being scheduled simultaneously, deadlock is possible. To prevent deadlock, each gang request will time out if it waits too long for a `MultiRR` request to be completed. It can retry a fixed number of times before giving up altogether. The gang must free the processes it has temporarily allocated using another `MultiRR`.

The PVM or Amoeba systems are unable to exploit this CP inherent in the gang scheduling algorithm. A comparison of overheads is shown in Table 7.12. It is extremely difficult to implement `MultiRR` on top of Amoeba, although it is quite simple in the customized system. Amoeba does perform very well for the other two multicasts, as the fast Amoeba multicast protocol can then be used.

The total time to execute this CP on the customized message-passing system and on PVM is given in Figure 7.16. The customized message-passing system shows dramatic improvements over PVM. This analysis ignores the costs of transporting data segments of a process, evaluating only the cost of the coordination.

TABLE 7.12 Performance of the Scheduler on Different Systems

System	Network Messages	Interrupts	Multicast Send Bufs
PVM	$8N - 8$	$16N - 16$	1
Amoeba	$3(N - 1) + 4$	$6(N - 1) + N + 2$	3
Customized	$N + 2$	$N + 2(N - 1)$	2

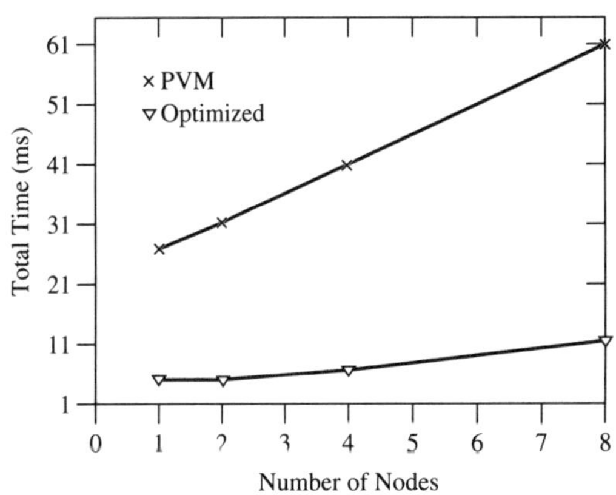

FIGURE 7.16 Distributed gang scheduling performance in ms.

7.6.3 Error Handling

For the `MultiRR` CP, if a message is lost, it is resent and the replies are collected again. Since group membership information is not known, all the results are regenerated. This situation is extremely rare, since in most cases there are more than enough machines to satisfy the query. For the other multicasts, two additional messages are generated; a probe from the receiver and the actual message from a sender. When a message is lost in transit, PVM generates one additional message; Amoeba generates two messages for a lost multicast message and one additional message for a lost point-to-point message.

7.7 SUMMARY

This chapter discusses performance results for both parallel and distributed applications on a distributed system.

Parallel Application Performance Summary. Customized message-passing systems substantially improve the performance of parallel applications. The applications also scale better using the customized message-passing systems than the general-purpose systems. The analytical models show that when communication locality is present the number of messages generated is exactly that required by the parallel decomposition of the application. For example, the customized message-passing systems for Simplex and Cholesky generate the minimum number of messages. The customized message-passing systems improve substantially on generic methods for implementing ordered and reliable multicast. The results given show that systems such as PVM generate too many network packets to implement multicast, particularly when a large number of processes are used to solve the application. Therefore, applications running on PVM do not speed up as well as on an optimized message-passing system. The experimental results show that for the eight-node case, Simplex ran 21 percent faster, Cholesky ran 27 percent faster, and FFT ran up to 29 percent faster on a customized message-passing system than on PVM.

The individual optimizations presented in this chapter are global optimizations across all communications of each application. These optimizations generate the best possible optimizations for the applications considered.

It is important to note that the optimizations used for the three applications are substantially different. Each optimization is application specific. Each of the three optimizations only works with the application for which it was designed. It is not possible to use the Exch for the Simplex application, as it does not handle multicasts at all. Similarly, it would not be possible to use CSRShuffle for the FFT application, as it does not understand error handling for the `ExchangeNoLocality` CP. Even though Cholesky and Simplex have multicasts, the message-passing implementations for the two applications are different because the error recovery mechanisms are different; the resultant state transitions for error recovery are very different. For example, CSRShuffle uses explicit communication locality to reduce the number of buffers it has outstanding, whereas the customized message-passing system for the Simplex application uses implicit information for buffer reduction. The message-passing system performs runtime checks to determine whether an application is using the correct protocol. A wrong method invocation signals a runtime error.

System Service Performance Summary. CPs exist in system services as they do in parallel applications and can be optimized. This chapter describes implementations of various RR CPs, and their basic performance is investigated. The chapter shows how easy it is to create a variety of message-passing systems for the client-server PIP. In the RR CP the customized message-passing system outperforms PVM for large and small messages. For large messages, the blast protocol helps the performance of the customized protocol.

This chapter also discusses how optimized message-passing systems can be implemented for CPs in systems services, such as a name server and a distributed scheduler. A summary of the selection procedure is shown in Figure 7.17. In this procedure the ; operator is used to describe sequential composition and * is used to denote repetition. In these examples the compositional approach to optimization selection is used. The analytical results show that the customized message-passing systems are better than both Amoeba and PVM. Practical implementations perform better than PVM on UNIX. For the eight-node case, the customized message-passing system implementation is about five-and-a-half times faster than PVM.

```
/*
 * This procedure shows the selection process
 * using communication patterns in
 * client/server PIPs.
 * These patterns occur in system services.
 */

SystemPatternSelection() {

        if(CP==MultiRR)
                MultiRR;
/*
 * This pattern occurs in the distributed
 * scheduler
 */
        else if(CP==MultiRR;(Multicast)* and Types)
                ((MultiRR and RRReceiverALO);(Multicast)*)
/*
 * The following pattern
 * occurs in the distributed NameServer
 */
        else if(CP==Multicast;MultiRR)
                (MultiRR and RRReceiverALO)

        else if(best optimization required)
                subclassExistingClass()
        else SequentiallyCombineExistingClasses()
}
```

FIGURE 7.17 Distributed system service selections.

CHAPTER 8

Customized Message Passing on a Shared-Memory Multiprocessor

Although the common mode of programming shared-memory multiprocessors is through shared variables, for reasons of portability it is convenient to have a message-passing interface for these architectures. There are a variety of ways to implement message-passing on shared-memory multiprocessors, with differing performance characteristics. Just as it is possible to improve the performance of message-passing systems on distributed systems based on application attributes, it is also possible to improve message-passing system implementations on shared-memory multiprocessors.

This chapter describes how to design and select an optimized message-passing system on a shared-memory multiprocessor using application attributes. Although the notion of a customized message-passing system is used, the optimizations presented in this chapter are fundamentally different from those presented for distributed systems. In particular, the bus in a shared-memory multiprocessor is a reliable delivery mechanism for data, so no software provisions are needed to guarantee reliable delivery. Instead, the optimizations concern overheads associated with the application's interactions with the memory architecture of the machine.

Many application attributes used to select optimizations are different from those used in distributed systems. On the shared-memory multiprocessor, attributes such as message size and data access patterns are used in addition to CPs. In this part of the book, subframeworks that are not specialized on a distributed

TABLE 8.1 Parameters Measured in Ring Synthetic Benchmark

Experiment	API (Location)	Transport	Synchronization	DataTransfer
1 ◇	Kernel	Buffered	Spinlock	Single copy
2 ▽	Kernel	Buffered	Spinlock	Pointer
3 ⊗	Kernel	Process	Semaphore	Double copy
4 ×	Kernel	Buffered	Semaphore	Double copy
5 ⊕	User level	Buffered	Spinlock	Single copy
12 ○	Kernel	Buffered	Spinlock	Double copy

system are specialized, illustrating again the extensible nature of the message-passing system. Customizations are presented for five of the subframeworks of the message-passing system that were shown in Figure 4.2. All are customized except the naming subframework. For each subframework the methods overloaded for a particular optimization are listed.

The basic overheads minimized in this chapter are message latency and the time to acquire and release a lock. Four benchmarks are presented that measure message latency for different application attributes and one benchmark measures the time to acquire and release a lock.

Ring is a basic message latency benchmark. It is used throughout this chapter for selecting among various implementations. The ring benchmark measurements allow comparison of the performance benefits of each of the design alternatives introduced in Chapter 5. Table 8.1 is a list of the different implementations of the message-passing system. The ring synthetic benchmark consists of six experiments. Each experiment measures the performance of the ring synthetic benchmark when using a message system constructed with the components specified in Table 8.1.* As shown in Table 8.1, the ring synthetic benchmark consists of six experiments. These experiments are used as part of the selection procedure on a shared-memory multiprocessor. Message sizes greater than the cache line size (16 bytes) are of primary concern to this work. Figure 8.1 shows the performance of each experiment in μs per round-trip for different message sizes, and the performance of each system is discussed in the subsequent sections.

8.1 DATA TRANSFER SELECTIONS

The selection of the best data transfer scheme involves the use of three synthetic benchmarks, invalidation, multicast, and ring, and two application attributes, invalidation and multicast, to choose an optimized message-passing system. The customized implementations are compared with the NX/2 implementations on the iPSC/2 because similar effects of the data transfer mechanism are observed.

*Each round-trip experiment was conducted in a loop of 10,000 iterations. In addition, the tests were individually run 20 times. The numbers reported are the averages of the test runs. The numbers do not vary by more than 4.25 percent from run to run.

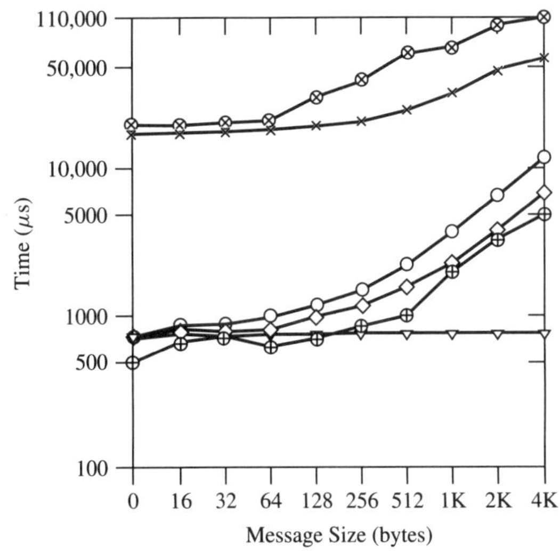

FIGURE 8.1 Round-trip message times on the shared-memory multiprocessor.

The interface for data transfer for the shared-memory multiprocessor is provided by the LocalTransfer class. Three subclasses of LocalTransfer implement three copy semantics, as defined here, by overloading the `send` and `receive` methods.

- **Double copy** (represented by Experiment 6 in Table 8.1). The message is copied into a kernel buffer by the sender process and copied out into a user buffer by the receiver process. This implementation allows hypercube programs to be ported without change to the shared-memory multiprocessor. It makes no use of shared memory between users. This is implemented by class DoubleTransfer.
- **Single copy** (represented by Experiment 1 in Table 8.1). The message is copied once into a buffer of the receiver process by the sender process. This is also known as restricted message-passing [TA91]. Buffers are located in shared memory accessible to both the sender and receiver processes. This is implemented by class SingleTransfer.
- **Pointer** (represented by Experiment 2 in Table 8.1). A message pointer is sent from the sender process to the receiver process. The pointer points to a buffer that is in a shared memory region accessible to both processes. This is implemented by class PointerTransfer.

Any transfer of data from one process to another involving a copy depends on the rate that data can be moved from one buffer to another. A minimalist copy program for the Encore Multimax consists of a loop that repeatedly reads and writes four bytes of data into memory. The Encore Multimax executes approximately two million instructions per second so that a copy could not transfer more than four bytes per μs. The maximum data rate can be decreased by indexing, by loop instructions, and by memory contention since the Encore Multimax is a multiprocessor. The measured rate for copying data between buffers on an Encore Multimax is approximately two bytes per μs. Thus, a processor performing a copy will use only a fraction of the bandwidth of the Encore Multimax backplane (8 bytes per 80 ns). The copy data rate has a major impact on the performance of the single- and double-copy message system implementations.

Results. Figure 8.1 shows the message latency between the three message transfer mechanisms. In the pointer implementation (Experiment 2), message latency remains constant as the message size increases. Both the single-copy and double-copy implementations suffer copy overhead and have similar performance behavior. As would be expected, a single copy implementation is faster than a double copy. For a 2048 byte message size, the difference between the single copy and double copy is 2690 μs. The 2048 μs can be accounted for by the extra copying of 4096 bytes of data.

Analysis. The operations involved in sending and receiving a message for single and double copy transfers are shown in Figure 8.2. In the scheme labeled `single copy`, a process receives a message by copying it from the sender's buffer into its local buffer, shown as the arc labeled (1).* When a write memory operation occurs, it writes the data to the cache (2). The cache is write-through and the message data are written out to the buffer concurrently with further processor operations (3).† The receiving process sends the message back. This requires the new receiving process to read the data (after a write-through has occurred) into its buffer (4). In one complete cycle of the message, the message data are written from cache to memory and read from memory to cache a total of four times.

To simplify comparison of the two machines, the round-trip of a message is represented as a string of operations on the underlying hardware. The notations R_m^i and W_m^i represent a read from and a write to the memory of processor i, respectively, in a multiprocessor system. For distributed-memory multiprocessor traces, the subscript designates independent memories. For shared-memory multiprocessor traces, the subscript refers to the same memory.

R_c^i and W_c^i represent a read from and a write to the cache of processor i, respectively. The symbol [] is used to indicate when the receiver process becomes a sender process. The message benchmark program corresponds to the following string of operations performed on each datum in the message for the single-copy message system.

$$R_m^2, R_c^1, W_c^1, W_m^1[\,]R_m^1, R_c^2, W_c^2, W_m^2$$

Because the buffers in user memory do not change, the write-through does not have to first read the data in the buffer. There are $2 \times \mathit{write} + 2 \times \mathit{read}$ operations in this trace.

*A read from the cache puts eight bytes from memory into the cache line.

†A write to the cache stores four bytes back into memory in the write-through.

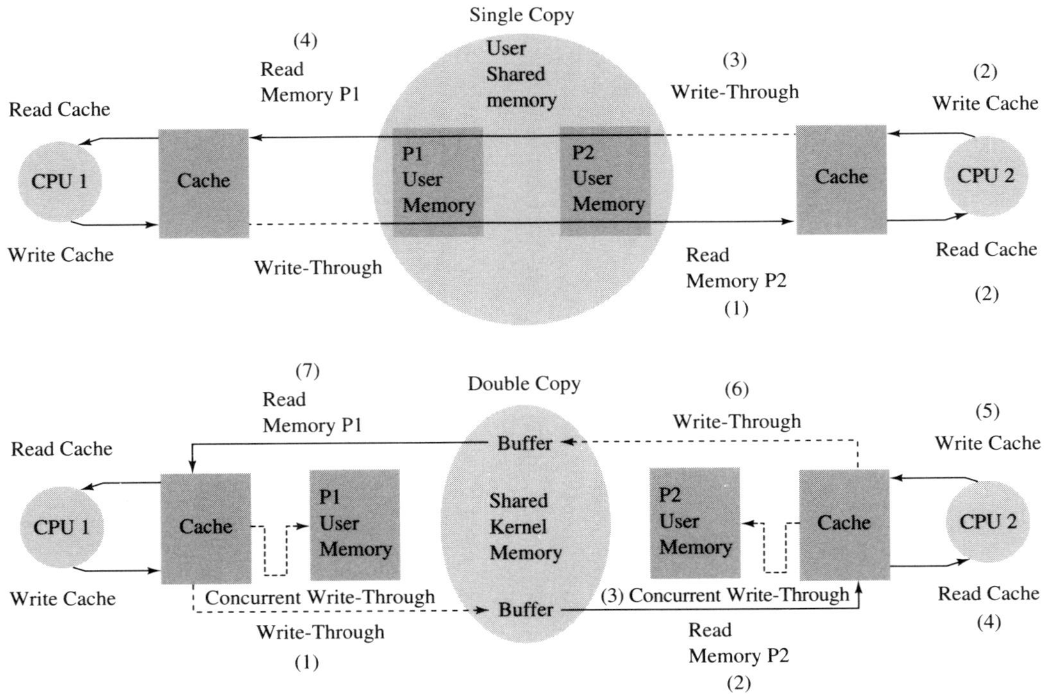

FIGURE 8.2 Cache behavior for single- and double-copy implementations.

In the scheme labeled `double copy`, a process sends a message by copying it into a kernel buffer, shown as the arc labeled (1). The process receiving the message reads it from this kernel buffer (after write-through has occurred) and writes it to a local buffer in user memory (2 and 3). This process then reads the local buffer again (4) and writes it to a kernel buffer (5 and 6) to send the message back to the original process. The original process then reads the kernel buffer and writes it to its local buffer (7). Unless the message data are very large, receiving a message primes the cache with the message data. Thus, copying the message data into the kernel buffer does not require reading the data from memory. The write-through to local memory during receipt of a message can occur concurrently (3).

R_m^K and W_m^K represent a read from and a write to a kernel buffer. Parentheses are used to delimit concurrent write-throughs. The message benchmark program corresponds to the following string of operations performed on each datum in the message for the double-copy message system.

$$R_c^2, W_c^2, W_m^K, R_m^K, R_c^1, W_c^1, (W_m^1)[]R_c^1, W_c^1, W_m^K, R_m^K, R_c^2, W_c^2, (W_m^2)$$

There are $2 \times read_{cache} + 2 \times write + 2 \times read + 2 \times write_{through}$ operations in the string, indicating that the double copy is slower by two cache read and two concurrent write-through operations. The concurrent write-throughs are somewhat faster than a write to memory. Figure 8.1 shows that the difference between the single copy and the double copy is more than the time to copy the message data twice. The remainder of the difference includes overhead from cache invalidation and interference between instruction retrieves and data retrieves in the cache.

Analysis of NX/2 Message Latency in the Control Experiment. Despite the Intel iPSC/2 processor being twice as fast as the Encore Multimax processor, Figure 8.3 shows that the message latency of Experiment 6 is similar to that of NX/2 for small message sizes. At message sizes larger than 512 bytes, the double copy message-passing system performs poorly. For example, a 4096 byte message has a round-trip message time of 4360 μs on the NX/2. A similar message, using Experiment 6, has a round-trip time of 12,171 μs. As the message size increases to more than 512 bytes, the time to execute copy instructions dominates the cost of interprocess communication. The pointer message system of Experiment 1 outperforms the NX/2 message-passing system for all message sizes. The round-trip time for Experiment 1 is a constant 770 μs.

A message is sent between two iPSC/2 nodes by transferring the message data from the memory of one node to the memory of another using the hardware message-passing support. There is a fixed communication overhead for realigning the message data, generating a header, and processing the special protocol for large messages. The message data are not accessed by a processor and are never copied into a cache. The symbol <> groups iPSC/2 actions that may be overlapped concurrently on the sender and receiver processors. The string of operations can

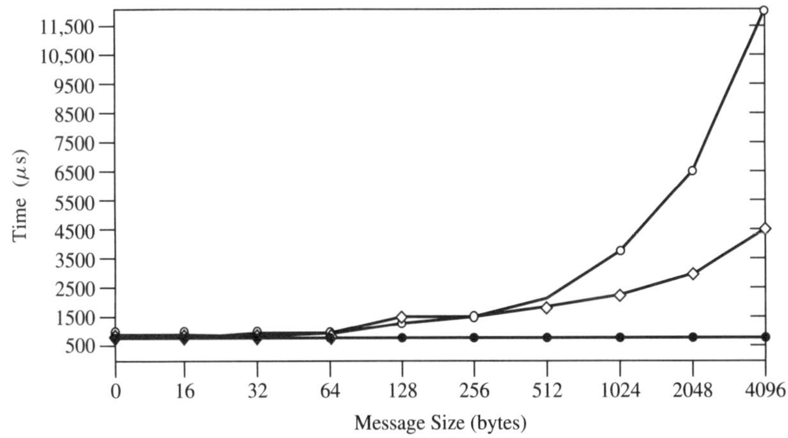

FIGURE 8.3 Variation of round-trip message times with message size

be described as

$$< R_m^2, W_m^1 > [] < R_m^1, W_m^2 >$$

The string has $2 \times read/write_{overlapped}$ operations. For large message sizes, this data transfer overlap will make the NX/2 perform better than the double copy message-passing system (Experiment 6).

8.1.1 Read and Write Access to Message Data

Actual applications rarely receive a message without accessing its contents. Experiments 1, 2, and 6 were modified to access the message data. In the read variation of the experiments, the message contents are read before being resent, forcing data into the cache.

In the write variation, the message contents are changed before being resent. Figure 8.4 shows the round-trip times measured by the benchmark for Experiments 1, 2, and 6 with no access, read access, and write access to the message data. Figure 8.5 shows the results measured for the NX/2 with no access, read access, and write access.

Results. Figure 8.4 shows that accessing the data on the Encore Multimax degrades the performance of all the experimental implementations. In particular, the pointer implementation (Experiment 2) no longer has a constant overhead if the contents of the message are accessed. Figure 8.5 shows that the results for the NX/2 are similar. In general, read access performs better than write access.

Analysis. The difference between no access, read access, and write access experiments can be attributed to the overhead of reading or writing a buffer. For 4096 bytes, a read takes 632 μs, a write takes 1190 μs, and a copy involving both a read and a write takes 1761 μs on the Encore Multimax.

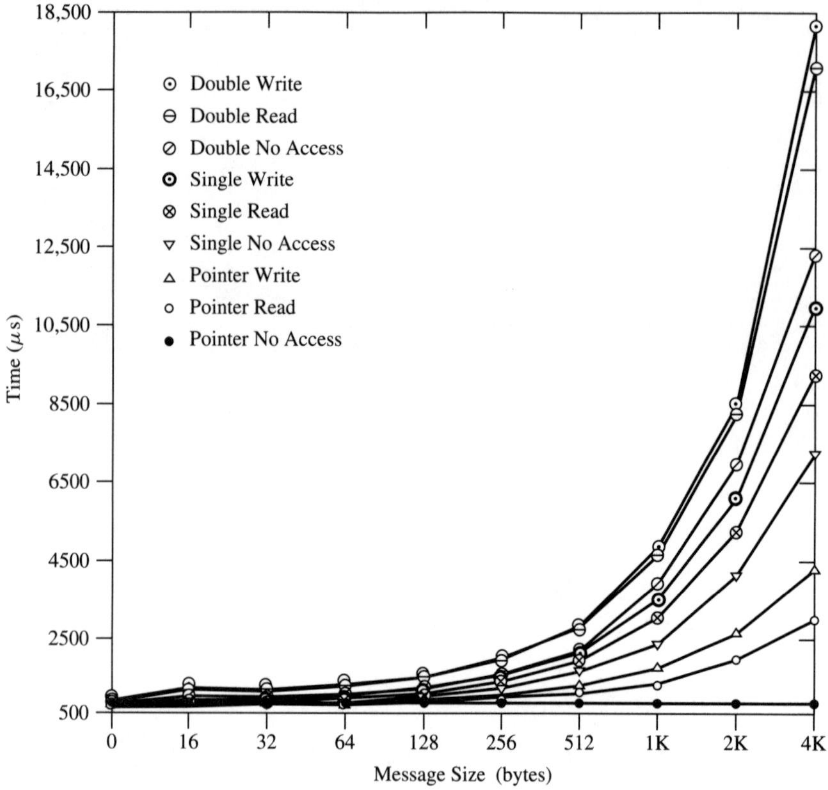

FIGURE 8.4 Message passing latency for various implementations.

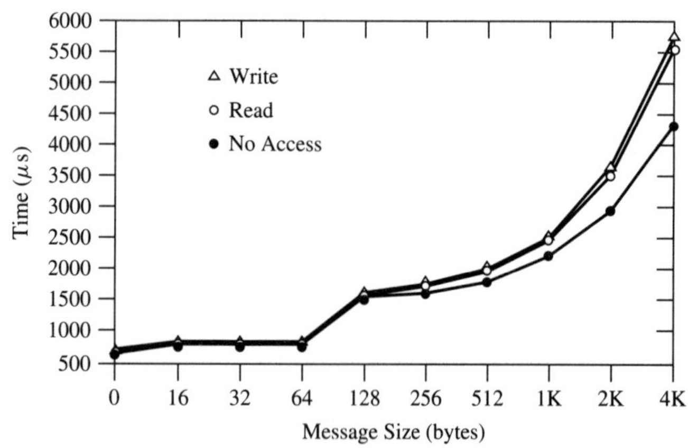

FIGURE 8.5 NX/2 message latencies with various types of data accesses.

Adding the measured overhead of read or write access to the measured round-trip time for a message with no access does not quite account for the round-trip times of messages with read or write access. For example, in the pointer experiment, the message latency for read access to a message of 4096 bytes is 2884 μs. No access message latency for the same size message is 770 μs. Reading 8192 bytes of data (round trip) takes 1264 μs. Thus, the measurements account for only 2034 μs of the 2883 μs latency. The timings for the single-copy (Experiment 1) and double-copy (Experiment 6) message system are similar to the pointer version. The remainder of the difference includes overhead from cache invalidation and interference between the instruction and data retrieves in the cache.

Analysis of NX/2 Message Latency with Read and Write Access. Figure 8.5 shows how the NX/2 message latencies change when the data in the message are referenced or written. The behavior is remarkably similar to the Multimax experiments. The pointer message system implementation on the Encore Multimax, however, is still faster than the NX/2 message-passing system for the ring benchmark.

The results show that the access time has a significant impact on latency. For example, a 4096 byte message has a round-trip message time of 5700 μs for read access and 5870 μs for write access on the NX/2. The round-trip message latency for a 4K message with no access is 4360 μs, as shown in Figure 8.5. The time to read 4K data twice is 1300 μs, and the time to write 4K data twice is 1480 μs. The results show that the additional message latency of NX/2 is caused by reading or writing the message.

To transfer the data, the system must perform interprocess communication. To access the data, the CPU must read the data into its cache. The following string of references results from this model.

$$< R_m^2, W_m^1 >, R_m^1, R_c^1[] < R_m^1, W_m^2 >, R_m^2, R_c^2$$

There are, therefore, $2 \times read/write_{overlapped} + 2 \times read$ operations. Similarly, a write access leads to $2 \times read/write_{overlapped} + 2 \times write$ operations.

The worst performance occurs on the NX/2 with write access when a message is sent but the receiver is not ready to receive the message, and the message is stored within the kernel of the receiver. Superscript ik refers to a message stored in the kernel network buffers of processor i. The string of actual memory operations is

$$< R_m^2, W_m^{1k} >, R_m^{1k}, R_c^1, W_c^1, (W_m^1)[] < R_m^1, W_m^{2k} >, R_m^{2k}, R_c^2, W_c^2, (W_m^2)$$

The string has $2 \times read/write_{overlapped} + 2 \times read + 2 \times write_{through}$ operations. To confirm the iPSC/2 worse-case behavior, a program was written that forces kernel message buffering on the receiver. When kernel buffering occurs, a 4K message takes 6920 μs, which is 1050 μs (18 percent) more than the 5870 μs observed for the normal write access case. Most of the difference is caused by copying the kernel buffer.

The double-copy message system on the Encore Multimax has a similar trace to the NX/2, except that it has two cache reads and two writes instead of the overlapped read and write operations. The double-copy write access round-trip time is 17,872 μs. Adding the time for write access to the double copy, however, no access round-trip time gives a total of 13,720 μs. The remainder of the difference includes overhead from cache invalidation, and data and instruction retrieve interference in the cache. The NX/2 message-passing system is faster than that of double copy for large messages because of the longer time to write to memory on the Encore Multimax and the concurrency of the sender and receiver processes with the DMA transfer mechanism on the iPSC/2.

8.1.2 Data Transfer and Multicast

Just as multiple implementations of multicast exist in distributed systems, alternatives for multicast exist on a bus-based, shared-memory multiprocessor. The multicast benchmark was constructed to determine which of the three data transfer mechanisms was the best for implementing multicast. The multicast benchmark shows that, for the eight-processor case, the double-copy version is roughly 7 percent faster than the single-copy scheme for message sizes less than 2K.

Figure 8.2 depicts how data copying occurs in the single- and double-copy implementations and helps explain why the double copy is faster than the single copy. In the single-copy version, all processes receiving the message make a copy of that message concurrently. This results in read-memory access contention, as all processes access the memory module containing the original message at approximately the same time. The double-copy scheme is more efficient because the sender process copies the multicast message data from its hardware cache into the kernel buffers destined for other processes. These processes copy the data from their individual kernel buffers and avoid memory-bank contention. For the eight-processor case, the read contention was significant, leading to a 7 percent degradation in the performance of multicasting. In iterative programs this behavior will manifest itself at each iteration, leading to significant performance gains for the double-copy version of the system. The pointer version is also slow for similar reasons. The processes make local copies, resulting in a situation similar to the single-copy approach.

8.1.3 Data Transfer and Invalidation Patterns

The invalidation synthetic benchmark shown in Figure 8.6 illustrates the subtle hidden cost of implementing message passing using the pointer transfer scheme.* When an invalidation pattern is present in an application, the single copy is best since the cost of the pointer version is dominated by cache invalidation costs. A

*The invalidation benchmark actually measures the overhead of the FFT invalidation pattern on eight processors.

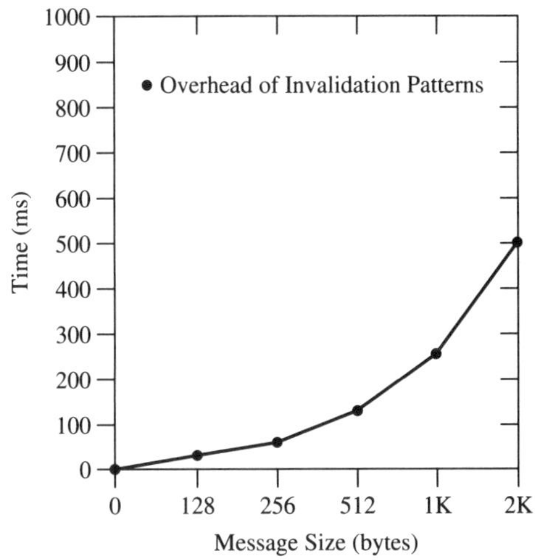

FIGURE 8.6 Effect of invalidation on the round-trip times on the Encore Multimax.

simple invalidation pattern is described; in this pattern, x and y are mapped to the same cache line.

```
read x
read y
read x (forced read into cache)
read y (forced read into cache)
```

In the pattern, there are two forced reads into the cache. This added cost is not present if x and y map into different cache lines. If this pattern repeats in a loop, the overhead due to cache invalidation is significant.

The invalidation pattern observed in the FFT application is now presented. It serves as the invalidation benchmark. In the following discussion, y and x are two arrays; x_j and x_i fit in the same cache line; y_i and x_i get mapped into the same cache line; and $i = j + 1$.

```
read y_j --> read
read y_i --> in cache
read x_j --> read x_j (and x_i)
read x_i --> in cache
read x_j --> in cache
write y_j --> read (not in cache)
read x_i -->  read (not in cache)
write y_i --> read y_i (not in cache)
write x_j --> read x_j (not in cache)
write x_i --> in cache
```

The Encore Multimax has a 64K direct mapped cache that is write through with write allocate. In the previous sequence, all entries marked as `not in cache` show additional memory reads that must occur due to the invalidation pattern that is present in the application. If this pattern repeats in a long loop, as it does in the FFT, comprehensive cache line invalidation results. A simple copy of arrays to two different locations would obviate this problem for future computations.

There is an additional problem with multiple processes. All reads from the different processors will access the same memory bank simultaneously. This will lead to further delays in accessing memory. These two factors explain the overhead due to this invalidation pattern. The dramatic impact of this pattern is shown in Figure 8.6.

8.1.4 Summary of Data Transfer Selections

In previous sections, it was shown that pointer copying is the best transfer mechanism to choose in the absence of multicast and invalidation patterns. When an invalidation pattern is present in the application, the single-copy version of the transfer semantics is best. In this case, the difference between single copy and double copy is the added data copy overhead. If multicast is present, then the double-copy version is best.

8.2 SYNCHRONIZATION SELECTION

There are a variety of implementations for synchronization. In this section, the use of the ring and acquire/release synthetic benchmarks, and the PIP and concurrency attributes to make an implementation selection is discussed. In particular, the customized system supports both semaphores (implemented by class Semaphore) that block and spinlocks that busy-wait. A simple interface of `acquire` and `release` is defined at the top of the hierarchy for the abstract Synchronization class. Concrete subclasses of Synchronization overload the methods `acquire` and `release` to implement different locking algorithms.

The synchronization experiment compares spinlocks, in particular TASLocks, which are test-and-set locks (Experiment 6), against Semaphores (Experiment 4) while keeping other message system parameters the same, as shown in Table 8.1.

Results. Figure 8.1 shows that the change from spinlocks to semaphores increases the message-passing latency by a factor of 27 for a null message and a factor of 10 for a 4K message.

Analysis. A process performing an `acquire` operation on a semaphore may block. When a `release` operation occurs, the first blocked process may run on any processor. A process context switch results in the invalidation of the translation lookaside buffer, page tables, and the data cache. A rescheduled process may have to refill the cache with appropriate data. Mogul [MB91] has shown in simulation studies that context switches have a significant effect on data caches. On the other hand, processes synchronized using busy-waiting are gang scheduled. This means that they are simultaneously started and are uninterruptable. A process releases the processor on which it is running when it has been completed.

The context switch time [RMC90] is 412 μs for application processes that perform floating point operations. Experiment 6, the spinlock implementation of the message system, indicates that a small message takes about 800 μs for a round-trip. Using a semaphore implementation; a round-trip causes two context switches. Therefore, spinning is chosen over blocking when message latency is the measure of interest, as is confirmed by the Experiment 4 measurement, shown in Figure 8.1. For large messages, Experiment 6 has a round-trip time that is far in excess of 824 μs. Most of the overhead is in copying the message data. In Experiment 4, a process will block, waiting for this copying to be completed. As can be seen from the results in Figure 8.1, for this unusual case the performance of the semaphore implementation does not improve dramatically as the waiting times increase. The processors executing the ring benchmark processes cannot perform any additional application computation while the processes of the benchmark wait for a message. This is a counterexample to the studies of Ousterhout [Ous82], which conclude that, in general, spinning should not be chosen over blocking when the waiting time is more than two context switch times.

8.2.1 Spinlock Selection

For parallel applications with a synchronous or bag-of-tasks PIP a subclass of spinlocks is used. A detailed description of each lock described in this section can be found in [MCS91].

TASLocks use a word as the state for the test-and-set instruction; the ArrayLock implements Anderson's array-based queuing lock [And90] and thus requires an array of words as state. The synthetic spinlock benchmark is shown in Figure 8.7. The figure shows the time to perform 100,000 acquire and release operations. When more than one processor is available, some concurrency is introduced: While one processor is executing the critical section, another processor can execute the acquire and release code. This concurrency is observable for both locks. As the number of processors is increased: the concurrency is overshadowed by the contention for the shared variable in the implementation of TASLock. The ArrayLock avoids this contention problem altogether by having each processor spin on a different memory location. Therefore, ArrayLock scales very well.

8.2.2 Synchronization Selection Summary

For applications with synchronous or bag-of-tasks PIPs, a subclass of spinlocks is always chosen, since semaphores do not perform well. Appropriate spinlock selection depends on the number of processes* involved in a particular act of

*The number of processes is equal to the number of processors for the acquire/release synthetic benchmark.

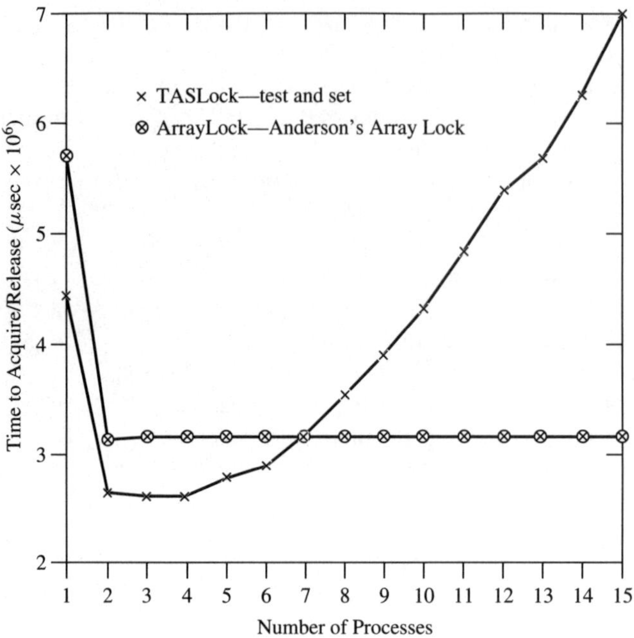

FIGURE 8.7 Time to acquire and release a lock 100,000 times.

synchronization. If the number of processes is less than or equal to seven, the TASLock is used. If the number of processes is greater than or equal to eight, the ArrayLock is used. For point-to-point communication, the TASLock is best. For multicast communication, lock selection depends on the number of receivers.

8.3 TRANSPORT SELECTION

There are variety to ways to transport messages between processes. This section discusses the use of the ring benchmark and the PIP attribute to make a selection. The process transport experiment examines the use of an independent process to transport a message from a sender process to a receiver process (Experiment 3) as compared to having the sender and receiver processes perform the task (Experiment 4). The first alternative is implemented by class ProcessTransport and the second alternative by class BufferedTransport. Both are subclasses of the LocalTransport class. The other message system parameters are the same, as shown in Table 8.1. The methods send and receive are overloaded to provide each alternative.

Results. Figure 8.1 shows that using a separate process to transport a message degrades the performance of the message system. The effect increases as the size of the message data increases.

Analysis. Adding a separate process to deliver messages introduces another process that must be scheduled. This therefore has the potential of increasing the time lost due to cache invalidation and context switching. If one of the application processes is context switched and the message delivery process is allocated to its processor, the cache will be invalidated. When the receiver and sender processes cooperate to deliver the message, however, as in the double-copy system of Experiment 4, they can both exploit the contents of their caches to improve message transmission times. With larger message sizes, more of the cache is invalidated.

8.3.1 Transport Selection Summary

For synchronous and bag-of-tasks PIPs, BufferedTransport is always chosen.

8.4 MESSAGE-HANDLING SELECTION

In this section, the circ/free synthetic benchmark and the type, CP, and message size attributes are used to construct MessageContainers. The abstract class MessageContainer is at the root of one of the message-handling class hierarchies. It defines the methods `put`, `get`, and `isEmpty`, which are overloaded by subclasses.

Typed messages are queued and processed by subclasses of TypedMC. This option is chosen only if types are used in the application; otherwise, the simpler implementation of NoTypeMessageContainer is chosen.

The abstract class TypedMC can have subclasses that allow asynchronous receives. All classes permitting asynchronous receives have the additional methods `ireceive`, `idone`, `iwait`, and `iprobe`, which allow nonblocking receives. These classes are only chosen when asynchronous receives are required.

The message size attribute is relevant only when the double-copy option is chosen in the DataTransfer class hierarchy. This is one of the rare occasions when there is a dependency between the selection of concrete classes of two different class hierarchies. Message sizes are then used to select between circular buffer and freelist implementation for message queues. The circ/free benchmark is used to select between the implementations. In contrast to the studies of Anderson on locking, which investigated lock contention, this work focuses on the effect of the message size on performance, taking into consideration the hardware cache. The two implementations of message queues are now discussed.

- **Circular buffer**. The `send` method adds a message to the head of the message queue. A send acquires the current index of the head of the queue, modulo the length of the queue from an index allocator. The index allocator atomically increments and returns the value of the head of the queue. The send operation acquires a different index every time it is invoked by a sender process and can update the queue in parallel. The critical section for the index allocator is extremely small (a few machine instructions).

The `receive` method takes messages from the tail. The tail pointer is incremented. If the head and tail of the queue are equal (this is rare), then a sender is blocked until they are no longer equal. This can be avoided by requiring the queue length and number of cooperating processors to be equal, and by disallowing asynchronous sends.

- **Freelist**. Alternatively, previous message queue entries are reused once the messages in them have been received. This method invalidates the cache less often than the circular buffer scheme but results in much more contention for acquiring a reused queue entry. The method employs a freelist. There is contention between accessing messages for inserting and deleting. This contention is very unlikely in a circular buffer and interference only occurs when the list is full.

The first alternative may continuously invalidate the hardware cache. In the first implementation, different memory is used by the kernel to buffer messages for each send operation. These new buffers must be brought into the hardware cache. In the second alternative, however, buffers are reused, increasing the chances of reusing an old buffer that may already be in the hardware cache. The larger the message, the greater the benefits of this scheme.*

The circ/free benchmark validates the analysis and is shown in Figure 8.8. The benchmark shows that for less than 400 bytes the cost of contention exceeds the hardware data cache reloading costs, making the circular buffer approach more attractive. These two implementation options exist for all subclasses of MessageContainers.

The actual type matching scheme is introduced at the leaves of the hierarchy that implement the `typeMatch` method. Options include hypercube and PVM type matching. For example, the HypercubeCirc class implements NX/2 style message types, asynchronous receives, and uses a circular buffer to implement its message queuing. HypercubeFree is similar except that it uses a freelist to buffer messages. To simplify the discussion of selection, only one type-matching scheme, that of the NX/2, is assumed.

Messages that are not typed are processed by subclasses of NoTypeMessageContainer. Subclasses NoTypeFree and NoTypeCirc implement freelist and circular buffers for the message queue, respectively. Concrete class ARFree implements asynchronous receives and uses a freelist for queuing messages, and

*The second alternative may cause excessive contention for queue locks. The first method is similar to that used by [GVV89, GLR83] on shared-memory multiprocessors. The customized implementation, however, does not require a lock for each entry since only one receiver and multiple senders are permitted per MessageContainer. Multiple receivers per queue would necessitate the use of a lock for each queue entry.

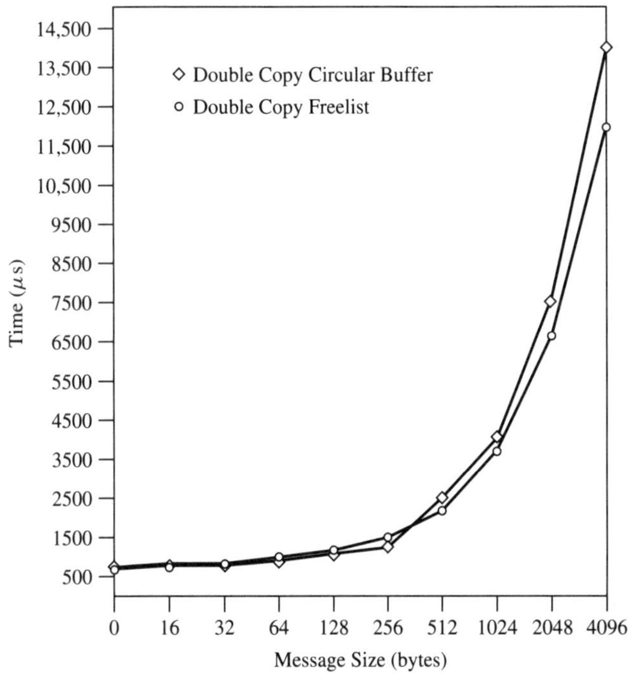

FIGURE 8.8 Round-trip time for circular buffer and freelist implementations on the Encore Multimax.

ARCirc implements asynchronous receives and implements a circular buffer for queuing messages.

8.4.1 MessageContainer Selection Summary

In summary, there are eight options for a subclass of MessageContainer. Each subclass either handles typed messages or it does not; it either handles asynchronous receives or it does not; and it implements message queuing using either a circular buffer or a freelist. To select an appropriate MessageContainer, one considers types, asynchronous receives, and then an implementation using a circular buffer or freelist. The choice between a circular buffer or freelist message-queuing implementation is only relevant when the double-copy data transfer scheme is chosen for the data transfer subframework specialization. If the double-copy data transfer mechanism is chosen, and if the message data size is larger than 400 bytes, then a freelist implementation is chosen. Otherwise, a circular buffer implementation is chosen. This is the only instance of a dependence between the various class hierarchies.

8.5 KERNEL PROTECTION

There are two different ways of implementing the message-passing system: inside the kernel or at user level. The ring message benchmark is used as the synthetic benchmark, and the PIP attribute is used. The kernel/user message-system placement experiment compares a kernel implementation (Experiment 1) against a user-level implementation (Experiment 5) while keeping other message system parameters the same, as shown in Table 8.1. Moving from user level to kernel level requires the interface classes to be compiled specially to generate proxy objects for the kernel interface classes [CIMR93, Rus91]. UserMessageSystem implements the message-passing system interface at user level. The class KernelMessageSystem implements the message-passing system interface through a kernel trap. Both are subclasses of class MessageSystemInterface.

Results. Figure 8.1 shows that kernel protection for the message system adds a fixed overhead to message latency that does not vary with the message data size.

Analysis. Putting the message system in the kernel adds approximately 144 μs to message latency, corresponding to the overhead of two kernel calls. Parameter checking and trap overhead remain constant as the message size increases.

8.5.1 Protection Selection Summary

The user-level message-passing system always outperforms the kernel version. The larger the message data size, however, the smaller the difference between the two implementations. The advantage of using a kernel-based message-passing system is additional protection between processes. If such protection is desired for debugging purposes, performance can be sacrificed for protection.

8.6 BASIC OVERHEADS

This chapter is primarily concerned with reducing the message latency overheads using application attributes. In this section, the cost of structuring the message-passing system as an object-oriented framework is examined. A summary of the breakdown of the round-trip time for a null message for Experiment 6 is shown in Table 8.2. The largest overhead is caused by the proxy call [CIMR93], which includes the time to trap into the kernel and copy arguments onto the kernel stack. Process identification overhead is high since process identifiers are not cached in memory. The bookkeeping time refers to the time the message system takes to set flags and any process idle or waiting time for spinlocks. The overhead of programming the message system in C++ corresponds to the virtual function call overhead, which was measured to be 11.25 percent of the message latency. It is

TABLE 8.2 Overhead for Null Message in μs

Number	Activity	Overhead	Total	Percentage
4	Proxy Calls	72	288	45
4	Process Identifications	30	120	29
12	Virtual Functions	6	72	11
4	Bookkeeping	40	160	25
	Total		640	100

independent of the message data size. Replacing the virtual function calls with C function calls halves the overhead from 72 μs to 36 μs. Thus, the additional cost for programming the message system in C++ is less than 6 percent. This demonstrates that the cost of the object-oriented structuring is low, particularly as the data set size increases.*

8.7 SELECTION PROCEDURE

The pseudocode for the shared-memory multiprocessor selection procedure is shown in Figure 8.9. It summarizes synthetic benchmark use in making appropriate implementation choices. The tool kit for the shared-memory multiprocessor is used, following the three rules described in Section 6.4. The class can be used directly, composed, or subclassed.

Most of the class hierarchies are constructed to be independently selectable, which means that optimization selection for one class hierarchy does not affect selections in another. The exception to this is the interaction between DataTransfer and MessageContainer. In Chapter 9, the selection procedures described in this chapter are used to construct optimized message-passing systems for real applications.

8.8 EASE OF CUSTOMIZATION

Typically, application writers select from existing options in the tool kit. It is, however, possible to extend the message-passing system tool kit with new optimizations. Extending the tool kit on shared-memory multiprocessors requires the creation of a new subclass. In Chapter 5 the class methods that are overloaded to create new subclasses are reviewed. The performance of a new subclass must be differentiated from the performance of the other subclasses using application attributes and synthetic benchmarks. For example, a new data transfer mechanism is added to the tool kit by subclassing the abstract class DataTransfer and overloading the `send` and `receive` methods. A synthetic benchmark and new attributes

*Not all of the functions shown in Figure 5.6 are virtual.

```
/* The five selection procedures used
 * on shared-memory architectures.
 * These apply to synchronous and bag-of-task PIPs.
 */
DataTransferSelection() {
        if(invalidation)
                SingleTransfer
        else if (multicast)
                DoubleTransfer
        else PointerTransfer
}
SynchronizationSelection() {

        N = numProcesses;
        if((CP with more than 2 processes) && (N => 8)) ArrayLock
                else TASLock
}
MessageContainerSelection() {
 // There are eight combinations.

        if(Types) subclass of TypedMC
        else subclass of NoTypeMessageContainer
        if(Async) subclass of AyncReceives or
                                        AsyncTMC
        For above four combinations, chose either
        freelist or circular buffer implementations
        if(DataTransfer == DoubleTransfer)
                if(Message Size > 400 bytes)
                        Free List Implementation
                else Circular Buffer Implementation
}
TransportSelection() {
        Always use BufferedTransport;
}
ProtectionSelection() {
        if(debugging is important)
                KernelMessageSystem;
        else UserMessageSystem;
}
```

FIGURE 8.9 Shared-memory selections.

are then used to differentiate this alternative from the three existing alternatives: PointerTransfer, DoubleTransfer, and SingleTransfer. Similarly, classes in the API, message-handling, synchronization, and transport subframeworks are subclassed for new optimizations.

8.9 SUMMARY

This chapter discusses how the message-passing framework is customized on a shared-memory multiprocessor, including how each of the subframeworks can be independently optimized for easy design and implementation. The ease of extending the tool kit with new optimizations is demonstated.

CHAPTER 9

Shared-Memory Multiprocessor: Application Results

This chapter describes customized message-passing systems for each of three parallel applications: (1) FFT, (2) Simplex, and (3) adaptive quadrature. The techniques described in the previous chapter are used to select the best message-passing system for each application. For comparison, this chapter presents the effects of data transfer on the performance of three applications on three experimental message-passing systems. These experiments confirm that the data transfer selections predict application performance. For the FFT and Simplex applications the results are compared to runs on the NX/2 operating system, as these applications were originally written for that system.

9.1 CUSTOMIZED MESSAGE PASSING FOR FFT

One of the attributes of the FFT application is invalidation. The ring and invalidation synthetic benchmarks must be used together to select the best customizations for the FFT. Together, they select the single-copy option SingleTransfer over the pointer version. This option avoids comprehensive cache line invalidation. The FFT application does not use types in its messages, which suggests the selection of a subclass of the more efficient NoTypeMessageContainer over other implementations, which have code to handle types. Subclass NoTypeFree or NoCircFree may be used.

The ring synthetic benchmark indicates that a subclass of Spinlock is a more efficient implementation than Semaphore for synchronization. Since there is no group communication, TASLocks are used. The use of BufferedTransport and UserMessageSystem is dictated by the ring benchmark.

To summarize, the following subclasses provide the best message-passing system for the FFT application: UserMessageSystem, NoTypeFree or NoTypeCirc, BufferedTransport, TASLock, and SingleTransfer. A detailed comparison of the FFT application running on three message-passing implementations that only differ in their data transfer mechanisms is presented next.

9.1.1 FFT Application Analysis

The FFT application illustrates how message systems behave as message sizes and numbers increase. Figure 9.1 shows the speedup versus the number of processors for each implementation of the FFT application for a fixed data size. For comparison purposes, the performance of the FFT on the Intel iPSC/2 under NX/2 is also displayed.

Results. The FFT speedup curves for the three variations in message-system transfer semantics are identical for one processor, indicating that there is essentially no overhead incurred as a consequence of modifying the FFT algorithm to accommodate the changes in transfer semantics. The pointer implementation performs worse than either of the other implementations when the number of processors is greater than four. Figure 9.1 shows that the single-copy implementation speeds up better than the other implementations, including the NX/2 implementation. The eight-processor case seems to indicate that the single-copy implementation continues to be a better implementation as the number of processors increases. The speedup curves of the application on the NX/2 and the double-copy shared-memory multiprocessor implementation are almost identical.

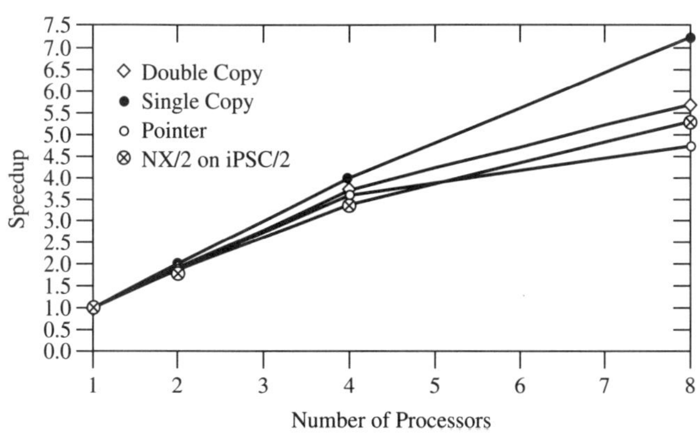

FIGURE 9.1 Speedup of 1024-point FFT.

Analysis. The pointer implementation's poor FFT behavior is predicted by the invalidation benchmark. It is 35 percent slower than the single-copy implementation. The data space for each processor is allocated as an integral multiple of 64K. Each processor is initialized with a copy of the data set, which is 16K in size, and is aligned on a 64K boundary. The algorithm on each processor receives messages containing pointers to other processors' data regions. The processor uses the same offsets into these data regions in its computations, causing comprehensive cache line invalidation. The measured difference in performance between the pointer and single-copy implementations is 335,432 μs. If a cache entry is invalidated, it will cause a read from memory when it is accessed. The cache access time is 25 ns, but memory access time is 320 ns [Cor86]. As the number of processors increases, the number of collisions will increase.

Because the processors are executing the same instructions concurrently, there is also a possibility that when the cache entry is reread, there will be memory module contention. In the pointer implementation, eight processors can access the same module in 2.56 μs. A single processor can read 4 bytes of data in a 4K message in 617 ns. If eight processors read all of the data in a message in a synchronized manner, contention will effectively quarter the performance of reading the message data.

Once the allocator was changed to return addresses that were not 64K aligned, the speedup of the pointer implementation increased from 4.68 times to 6.26 times for the eight-processor case. With this modification, the pointer version was 15 percent (instead of 35 percent) slower than the single-copy implementation.

One difference between the pointer implementation and the other implementations is that the index generation code has to differentiate between high and low indices. Factoring out the index generation code, additional overhead would increase the speed from 6.26 to 6.45. Factoring out this overhead (20,000 μs) and avoiding the cache line invalidation problem, the pointer implementation is still 72,000 μs or 11 percent slower than the single copy for eight processors. This remaining difference is most likely due to memory contention and interference in the cache between instruction and data access.

Both the single- and double-copy message systems rearrange the data by copying them to new locations, avoiding much of the cache line invalidation problems. The extra copying overhead in the double-copy implementation makes this implementation perform worse than the single copy.

The FFT NX/2 Control Experiments Results. Figure 9.1 shows that the speedup curve of the NX/2 implementation of the FFT is similar to the speedup of the double-copy customized implementation. Figure 9.2 shows that the proportion of time spent in the NX/2 message-passing system for the FFT application is almost the same as that spent in the double-copy message-passing system on the Encore for varying FFT data set sizes. This confirms earlier results that the overheads for processing a message of a given size using NX/2 and the double-copy customized message-passing systems are similar. For large data set sizes, the longer time spent

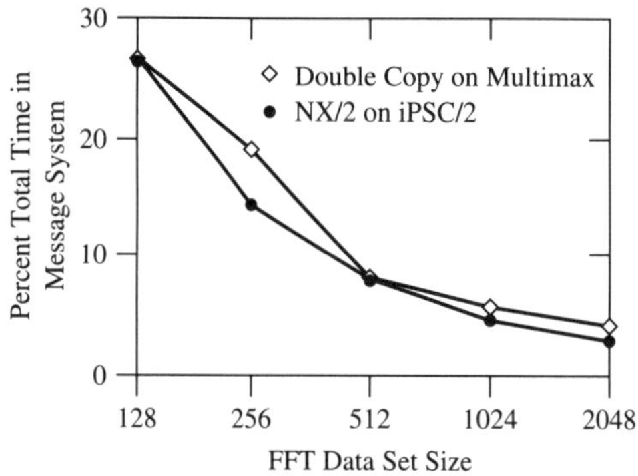

FIGURE 9.2 Variation of percentage of time in message system with increasing data size for an FFT running on four processors.

in the customized message-passing system can be attributed to the longer time to write to memory on the Encore Multimax.

FFT NX/2 Analysis. A detailed analysis of the FFT execution traces on the NX/2 reveal that there is variation [MII89] between the times of successive interprocessor communications. Although each processor executes identical application code, the data values differ, and the differing times to evaluate iteratively the trigonometric functions create a communications asynchrony. This application asynchrony results in some unavoidable message-passing overhead on both systems.

9.2 CUSTOMIZED MESSAGE PASSING FOR SIMPLEX

The Simplex application is considerably different from the FFT. There is no invalidation attribute as in the FFT, but there is a predominance of multicast and reductions using small messages in the Simplex application. The multicast benchmark dictates the use of the DoubleTransfer since there are a large number of read multicasts of small messages. As the number of processes increases, the use of DoubleTransfer becomes more important.

The Simplex application uses types, and thus the concrete subclass of MessageContainer that is used must implement types. Unlike the FFT application, no matter what the input data set size, the average message size for the Simplex application is small, primarily because of the predominance of small messages (16 bytes) that exchange pivot information. For the data set used in this section, the average message size is less than 400 bytes (see Table 3.2 in Section 3.2.1). Therefore, HypercubeCirc is used, which implements hypercube types and uses a circular buffer.

The ring benchmark suggests that a subclass of Spinlock should be used. Since the application uses multicast, if the number of processes given to the application is greater than or equal to eight, then an ArrayLock is used. If the number of processes is less than or equal to seven, TASLocks are used. The use of BufferedTransport is indicated by the ring benchmark. Since there is a predominance of small messages, the use of a UserMessageSystem would be beneficial to this application.

In summary, the analysis indicates that the best message-passing system for the Simplex application is UserMessageSystem, HypercubeCirc, BufferedTransport, DoubleTransfer, and some subclass of Spinlock that depends on the number of processes available to the application. This optimized message-passing system is quite different from the message-passing system that was best for the FFT application. A detailed comparison of the Simplex application running on three message-passing implementations that only differ in their data transfer mechanisms is presented next.

9.2.1 Simplex Application Analysis

The Simplex application has a nontrivial CP and permits a study of how message systems behave for bimodal message size distributions and data-dependent CPs.

Results. Figure 9.3 shows the speedup of the Simplex application on the various alternate message-passing systems and includes the NX/2 results. The speedup curves of all the message system implementations are similar, but the ordering of the performance of the implementations changes from that for the FFT. The single-copy implementation performs worse than both the pointer and double-copy implementations for the number of processors shown. For more than four processors, the double-copy implementation performs better than the pointer implementation. The NX/2 implementation performs better than any of the shared-memory implementations as the number of processors increases.

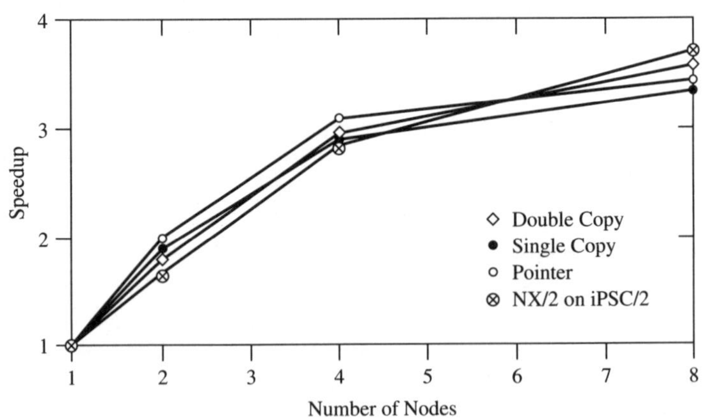

FIGURE 9.3 Speedup of Simplex.

Analysis. In the Simplex application, small messages dominate and the average message size is 171 bytes. Figure 3.2 shows that small messages predominate and the exact average is data set–size dependent. The fixed overhead for transmitting a message in Simplex is large compared with the variable overhead for copying message data. This has the effect of reducing the differences between the various shared-memory message-passing systems.

In the Simplex application, pivot distribution is multicast from one processor to the others. The single-copy message system is inefficient at multicast because each process receiving a message copies the message data. This causes read-access memory contention. The double-copy message system is more efficient than the single copy because the sender process copies the message data to be multicast from its cache into kernel buffers destined for other processes. These other processes copy the data from their individual kernel buffers and avoid memory contention. The multicast benchmark shows that for the eight-processor case multicast, using double-copy versus single-copy transfer semantics yields a 7 percent performance improvement for up to a 2K message.

The Simplex NX/2 Control Experiments Results. The behavior of the shared-memory implementations is similar to the NX/2 implementation. In both cases, the cause of sublinear speedup is communication overhead. Figure 9.4 shows that the amount of time spent in the message-passing system when the Simplex code executes under NX/2 is similar to that under the double-copy message-passing system.

Analysis. As the number of processors increases, the amount of time spent in the message-passing system increases. There are two reasons for this. First, the total computation is fixed and, as the number of processors increases, the percentage of the work assigned to each processor decreases. Second, the number of messages sent by all processors increases; most of these messages are small and represent the overhead to find a global minimum among a larger group of

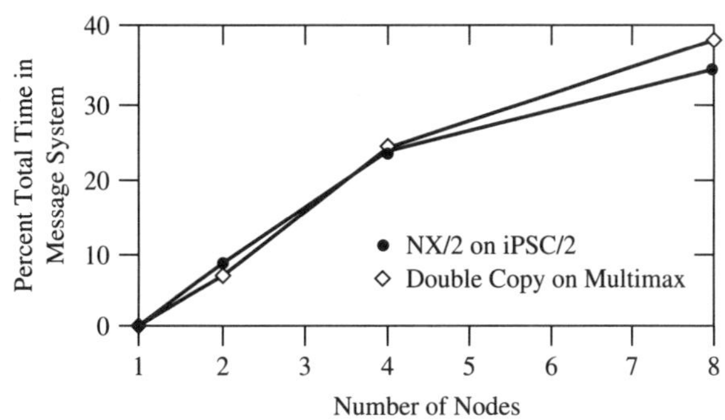

FIGURE 9.4 Time in the message system for the Simplex algorithm on NX/2 and customized message passing.

processors. Thus, in the case of the Simplex application, because of its large number of small messages, it may be desirable to use a message system in user space.

9.3 CUSTOMIZED MESSAGE PASSING FOR ADAPTIVE QUADRATURE

The parallel version of adaptive quadrature is written in the bag-of-tasks PIP. The program is structured to have a central administrator process that collects partial values from other processes. This example illustrates that the message-passing system can be customized for an application written with a PIP that is not synchronous. No comparisons are made with the NX/2, since a bag-of-tasks model is not a natural decomposition for the NX/2 operating system primitives.

As there are no multicasts or invalidation patterns, the PointerTransfer subclass of the class DataTransfer is used. Since the pointer version is used, either a circular buffer or a freelist will perform adequately as the implementation of the MessageContainer. Since types are not used in messages, the appropriate subclass of MessageContainer is either NoTypeCirc or NoTypeFree.

There are no multicasts, but the administrator has multiple senders. This pattern is similar to a reduction pattern [FJL$^+$88], but the message sends to the administrator are less predictable. Since the application uses reduction, if the number of processes given to the application is greater than or equal to eight, an ArrayLock is used. If the number of processes is less than or equal to seven, TASLocks are used. The BufferedTransport and UserMessageSystem are used as indicated by the ring benchmark. The ideal message-passing system is thus: UserMessageSystem, BufferedTransport, SingleTransfer, NoTypeCirc or NoTypeFree, and some subclass of Spinlock that depends on the number of processes available to the application. A detailed comparison of the adaptive quadrature application running on three message-passing implementations that only differ in their data transfer mechanisms is presented next.

9.3.1 Adaptive Quadrature Analysis

Results. The speedup curves for the three variations in message data transfer semantics are identical for one processor, indicating that there is no overhead for modifying the adaptive quadrature algorithm. Figure 9.5 shows that the pointer transfer mechanism performs the best, whatever the number of processes. The pointer version also scales best. The difference between the versions is a result of the data copying overhead, which differentiates between the pointer and the single transfer, and then between the single transfer and the double transfer.

Analysis. The adaptive quadrature is a simple application that has no invalidation patterns or multicasts. All the messages are small, and all processes send messages to the `administrator` process, which determines program termination.

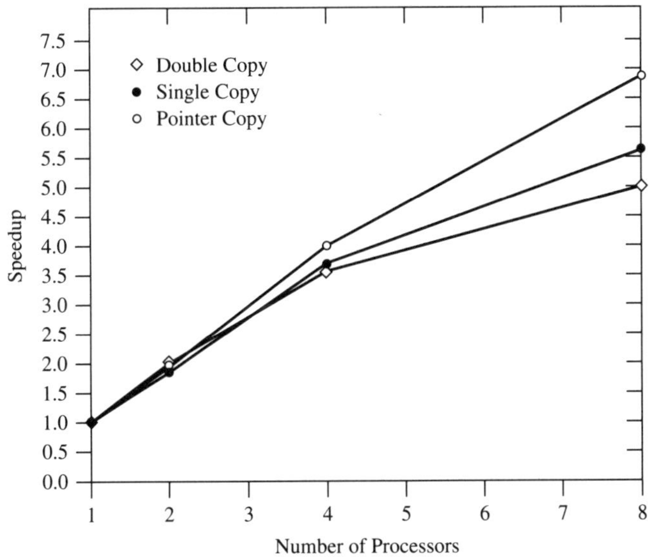

FIGURE 9.5 Speedup of adaptive quadrature.

9.4 SUMMARY

This section summarizes the best message-passing systems for the FFT, Simplex, and adaptive quadrature applications. Table 3.4 shows the various attributes of the applications and in particular shows the interesting features of the CPs of each of the applications. The attributes in these tables are used in this chapter to select the best available message-passing systems for the three applications.

The best set of concrete subclasses of the message-passing system for each application is shown in Table 9.1. Two customizations, BufferedTransport and UserMessageSystem, are common to all of the applications. Only the customizations that are different across applications are shown.

TABLE 9.1 Customized Message-Passing Systems for Applications on Shared-Memory Multiprocessor

Application	MessageContainer	DataTransfer	Synch
Benchmark	circ/free	Invalidation Multicast Ring	Ring Acquire/Release
FFT	NoTypeCirc or NoTypeFree	SingleTransfer	TASLock
Simplex ($p \leq 7$)	HypercubeCirc	DoubleTransfer	TASLock
Simplex ($p \geq 8$)	HypercubeCirc	DoubleTransfer	ArrayLock
Adaptive ($p \leq 7$) Quadrature	NoTypeCirc or NoTypeFree	PointerTransfer	TASLock
Adaptive ($p \geq 8$) Quadrature	NoTypeCirc or NoTypeFree	PointerTransfer	ArrayLock

CHAPTER 10

A Framework for Customized Scheduling

Most system designs separate and make independent the schedulers for distributed and parallel systems. The extensible scheduling framework is designed to encompass a large number of policies and mechanisms, making it general and efficient. Chapter 11 describes some of these algorithms and provides references to descriptions of many scheduling algorithms. The optimizations of the framework include gang scheduling support for applications that have a synchronous or bag-of-tasks PIP on both a bus-based, shared-memory multiprocessor and a distributed system.

Researchers [Ous82, FR92, FR90] have argued strongly for gang scheduling for fine-grained computations on shared-memory multiprocessors. They show that busy-waiting with gang scheduling is better than blocking for many parallel applications. When the processes of an application interact frequently, if all the processes of the applications are not run simultaneously, the rescheduling overhead increases. On a distributed system, a similar situation arises when gang processes wait for messages from descheduled processes. In such instances some application processes may spend a lot of time waiting in blocking receives. This chapter introduces gang scheduling for distributed systems to solve this problem. Gang scheduling minimizes the waiting time overhead for blocking receives. This chapter demonstrates that gang scheduling improves application performance on both shared-memory multiprocessors and distributed systems. Gang scheduling support decreases both application execution times and the variability of the execution runs.

The gang scheduling algorithm described in this book consists of two parts. First, applications should be dispatched simultaneously. Second, for applications run on a network of workstations, the gang scheduling approach requires that the application have exclusive access to the workstations for the duration of its execution. Gang scheduling resource allocation runs contrary to the view of workstations as dedicated resources for the tasks of the local user rather than dedicated to a remote task.

Sections 10.2, 10.3, 10.4, 10.5, 10.7, and 10.8 describe the design of the scheduling system and how it can be customized. Section 10.11 discusses the performance of various instances of the scheduling framework, and Section 10.12 discusses application performance results.

10.1 COMPONENTS OF THE SCHEDULING FRAMEWORK

The six major components in the scheduling framework are (1) Task, (2) LongTermScheduler, (3) ProgramLauncher, (4) ResourceMonitor, (5) ProcessContainer, and (6) Processor. In Sections 10.2, 10.3, 10.4, 10.5, and 10.7, each of these components is described. At the end of each of these sections the methods that have to be overloaded for each customization are reviewed. In Section 10.8, the framework for scheduling is described, showing how the components interact to perform scheduling. The relationships between the abstract classes must be maintained by the various new customizations of the scheduling system.

Two types of customizations are described: system specific and application specific. System-specific customizations are shared across applications and mediate the requirements of a specific type of application with those of the other types of applications. System-specific customizations are supported by LongTermScheduler, and application-specific customizations are supported by ProcessContainer, Task, ResourceMonitor, and ProgramLauncher. The LongTermScheduler helps organize application-specific scheduling by dispatching an application-specific Task to its appropriate set of concrete classes of ProcessContainer, ResourceMonitor, and ProgramLauncher. The role of the LongTermScheduler is the same as that of the ProtocolDispatcher class of the network I/O subframework, which dispatches network messages to the appropriate message-passing system instance. The Processor is customized once for a particular hardware architecture.

10.2 PROCESSES AND GANGS

A Task is a schedulable entity. Subclasses include Process and Gang. The class hierarchy for Tasks is shown in Figure 10.1. Central to the concurrency model are Process objects. A C++ function is bound to a Process using the initialization message. Subsequent messages may start, suspend, resume, or terminate the thread of control and the associated concurrent execution of the C++ function. The notion of a thread of control and the concept of a Process are distinct. The thread of control and the execution of the C++ function occur as a side effect of sending

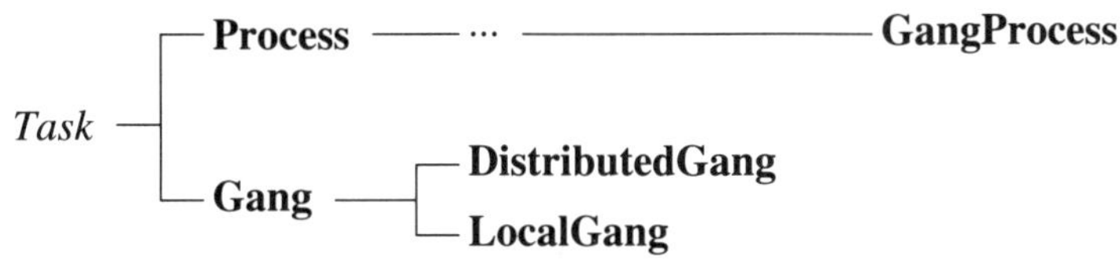

FIGURE 10.1 Process and Gang class hierarchies.

messages to the Process. A thread of control must have an associated Process, but a Process may not have a thread of control. For example, when a thread of control reaches the end of its C++ function, it ceases to exist. Its corresponding Process, however, will still respond to messages and it is used to release any resources, such as memory, that were associated with the execution of the C++ function.

Conceptually, the control flow that executes the C++ function bound to a process flows through application and system objects by invoking methods on these objects. The sequence of transformations that result from a thread of control flowing through objects is called a *process*. For the purposes of this book it is not necessary to distinguish between a process and a thread of control.

It is important for an operating system to have explicit control over which processes are running on which processors. Therefore, facilities are provided for both involutarily and voluntarily changing the execution of a process on a processor. For example, a process may be time sliced, may block on a semaphore, or may voluntarily relinquish the processor on which it is executing.

All of the methods associated with the Task class are used for scheduling. These methods are invoked by ProcessContainers, LongTermSchedulers, and ResourceMonitors. Task provides methods to access and change the SchedulerInfo and LongTermSchedulerInfo classes that are used to store short-term and long-term scheduling information about the Task. Concrete subclasses of Task will contain one instance of each of the SchedulerInfo and LongTermSchedulerInfo classes. A Process has methods to transfer control between Processes. A Process class has a pointer to the machine-dependent class to save and restore machine-dependent states during a context switch. Such states may include stack pointers and processor registers. A Process has method `block` to block the process.

Gangs schedule a group of GangProcesses, which is a subclass of Process. GangProcess performs all the regular duties of a process and also knows that it is a member of a gang and must therefore enter and leave a gang. This subclass is only chosen when gangs are being scheduled. Different customizations schedule gangs in different ways. For example, gangs may be scheduled on a network of workstations or on a shared-memory multiprocessor. A Gang has methods to `add` and `remove` members and to schedule its members. The methods of the Gang abstract class and its concrete subclasses are shown in Table 10.1. The method `conc`

TABLE 10.1 Gang Interface

Class::Method	add/remove	NumProcs/conc	scheduleMembers
▽ *Gang*	•	•	=0
▽ ▽ **DistGang**	▽	△	•
▽ ▽ **LocalGang**	▽	△	•

TABLE 10.2 Task Interface

Class::Method	dispatch	ready	remoteDispatch	block
Task	•	•	•	-
▽ **Process**	▽	▽	▽	•
▽ ▽ **GangProcess**	▽	▽	▽	▽

is used to specify the number of processors or nodes requested. Gangs can be multiprogrammed. Input parameters to the constructor specify whether the Gang requires exclusive access to machines. The Gang class has two primary subclasses: DistributedGang and LocalGang. A LocalGang is used for gang scheduling on a shared-memory multiprocessor. A DistributedGang is used for a gang that is divided among a number of workstations. All these Gangs can be run in dedicated mode or in multiprogrammed mode. In the dedicated mode, a processor is reserved for each process of the application. In the multiprogrammed mode, there may be fewer nodes or processors than application processes on a multiprocessor. In the case of a network of uniprocessors, the node can be multiprogrammed, and is then shared with other application processes. Moreover, more than one of the processes of the application can be on a particular processor or node.

DistributedGangs are used for gang scheduling on distributed systems. The `scheduleMembers` method performs synchronization between the processes of an application before running the processes of a gang. The GangProcess class informs the Gang when it ends so that the Gang can keep track of GangProcesses that are alive. The method `NumProcs` gives the number of nodes or processors that were actually allocated for the gang, and `Conc` is used to request a number of nodes. The interface protocols for the Task, Process, and Gang classes are shown in Tables 10.1 and 10.2. The use of most of these methods has been explained. Section 10.8 introduces and explains the remainder of the methods of the Task class and its subclasses.

10.3 LONG-TERM SCHEDULER

The LongTermScheduler controls the degree of multiprogramming in the system [PS85]. The degree of multiprogramming is specified as an input parameter to the constructor of the LongTermScheduler. All Tasks that are to run enter

TABLE 10.3 LongTermScheduler Interface

Class::Method	add/remove	commandLine
LongTermScheduler	•	•
▽ **RemoteExclusive**	▽	▽
▽ **UserExclusive**	▽	▽

the scheduling system through the dispatch queue of the LongTermScheduler. The LongTermScheduler decides whether a Task should be allowed to compete for local and global resources. Tasks enter the dispatch queue from the command line of the system shell, from the network, as the result of a call to the `remoteDispatch` method on a Task on some other node or from within an application process.

A Task enters the dispatch queue using the `add` method. A separate process takes processes off the dispatch queue by invoking the `remove` method, and the process consults the ResourceMonitor to determine on which node to dispatch the Task.

Table 10.3 shows two subclasses that implement different scheduling policies. Each Task records the size of a particular entity to schedule, whether the entity is remote, and whether it needs to be run in dedicated mode. This information is used to locate the best set of processors or nodes to run the application. One subclass, UserExclusive, does not allow remote processes to run on the local machine, making it a dedicated machine for the local user. Another subclass, RemoteExclusive, allows a remote job to acquire the workstation for its exclusive use for a short period of time. The two classes provide different types of control over the scheduling environment. The RemoteExclusive class is used for parallel applications, as it allows groups of workstations to be allocated to a single application.

New subclasses may be created with different policies for adding and removing Tasks from the LongTerm scheduler queues. The `add` and `remove` methods are overloaded to implement the requisite policy.

10.4 SHORT-TERM SCHEDULER

ProcessContainers are the short-term schedulers. The ProcessContainers export the methods `add`, `remove`, and `isEmpty`. The ProcessContainer subclass FIFOScheduler is used for first-in-first-out [Tan92] run to completion scheduling. LIFOScheduler is used for last-in-first-out scheduling. A deadline scheduler, Deadline, supports the additional method `setDeadline`, which allows one to set a soft deadline for all processes that are scheduled on this subclass. The RRScheduler class implements round-robin scheduling [Tan92]. The RRGangScheduler is a round-robin scheduler that interacts with Gangs to schedule them. The FIFOGangScheduler is used by the LocalGang to dispatch its processes. The short-term scheduler classes are shown in Figure 10.2.

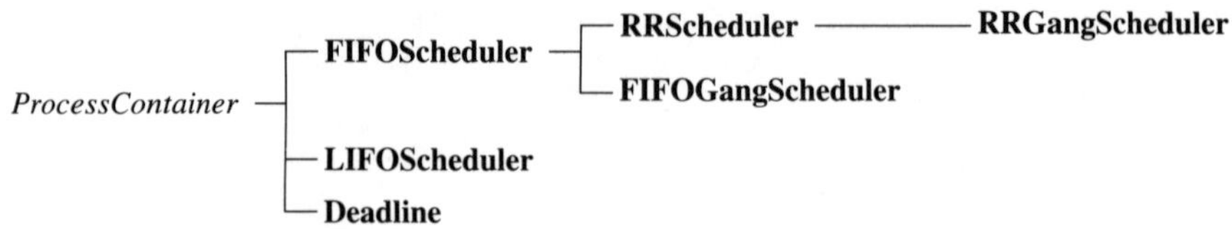

FIGURE 10.2 Short-term scheduler class hierarchies.

New subclasses may be created with different policies for adding and removing Tasks from the ProcessContainer scheduler queues. The `add` and `remove` methods are overloaded to implement the requisite policy. All of these classes can be used in a multiprocessor or a uniprocessor.

10.5 RESOURCE MONITORING

The ResourceMonitor class performs two functions: to collect local and global resource usage information, and to select the best set of sites for a task. Its methods, `updateSchedInfo` and `updateCPUInfo`, are invoked by the short-term scheduler classes and the CPU class. The individual subsystems are changed to update the ResourceMonitor. The short-term scheduler's information changes when its `add` and `remove` methods are invoked. These methods invoke the `updateSchedInfo` of ResourceMonitor to record these changes. The class ResourceMonitor exports the method `selectSite`. The LongTermScheduler invokes this method for every Task.

The ResourceMonitor class is abstract and has two concrete subclasses. The class PublishingResourceMonitor implements a publishing scheme, and the QueryResourceMonitor class implements a query scheme for resource monitoring. These schemes are discussed in [Stu88a].

In the query scheme, each time a task is scheduled, the most recent resource information is gathered from machines on the network. The steps for the query algorithm are as follows:

1. Query all members and select best subset.
2. Post list of members actually selected.

The publishing scheme uses locally cached resource information. The steps for publishing are as follows:

1. Search local performance cache.
2. Post list of members actually selected.

New resources can easily be monitored by the addition of new update methods and by overloading the method `selectSite`, which uses these metrics for site selection. A new selection algorithm must overload the method `selectSite`.

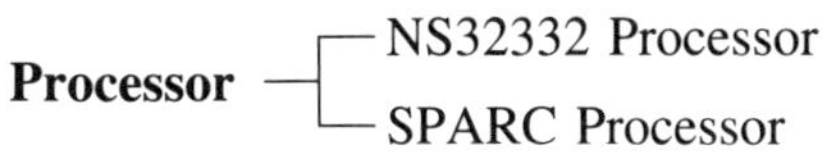

FIGURE 10.3 Process system class hierarchies.

10.6 PROCESSORS

Processors are objects that correspond to the CPU of the operating system. Each subclass represents the CPU of a particular processor. Subclasses include the SPARC processor and NS32332 processor, as shown in Figure 10.3. The Processor contains information such as the CPU indentification numbers (in a multiprocessor), the state of the various interrupts, and a pointer to the idle process that runs on the CPU when no other processes are running.

10.7 PROGRAM LAUNCHER

The ProgramLauncher class provides process migration facilities. It has one subclass, StaticLauncher, that implements static placement or initial placement.

The methods of ProgramLauncher allow one to launch a task by specifying a reference to the task (by invoking `launchref`) or by passing the task itself (by invoking `launchtask`).

10.8 A FRAMEWORK FOR SCHEDULING

This section describes the method invocation sequences for the important scheduling operations. Each concrete subclass of an abstract class must implement all the methods of the abstract class either through inheritance or refinement. Figure 10.4 shows the various abstract classes that represent the components of the scheduling framework and various method invocations between the instances of concrete subclasses of the abstract classes. The interactions of the various components across the network are shown in Figure 10.5.

Two levels of scheduling are supported. An application process or a group of application processes is first selected by a system-level scheduler and then by a processor-level scheduler. The presence of a queue in Figure 10.4 indicates places where a policy decision may be made as to which Task in the queue is processed next.

When a Task is to be run, it invokes the `dispatch` method on itself, which adds the Task to the dispatch queue of the LongTermScheduler on the local node. The LongTermScheduler invokes the `selectSite` method on the ResourceMonitor, passing appropriate resource usage requirements of the Task, and is returned a SchedulingVector, which describes where to schedule the Task. The LongTermScheduler uses the information in the SchedulingVector to invoke the `remoteDispatch` method to run a Task remotely, or to invoke the `ready` method on the Task if it is to be run locally. This branch is indicated by the arrow labeled 4 in Figure 10.4. The `remoteDispatch` method migrates the Task to the appropriate machine(s). It uses the ProgramLauncher for task migration.

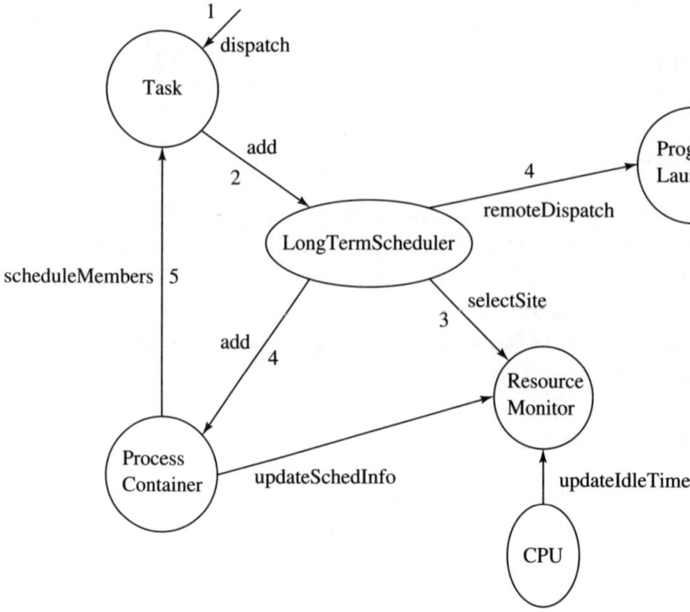

FIGURE 10.4 Control flow for scheduling.

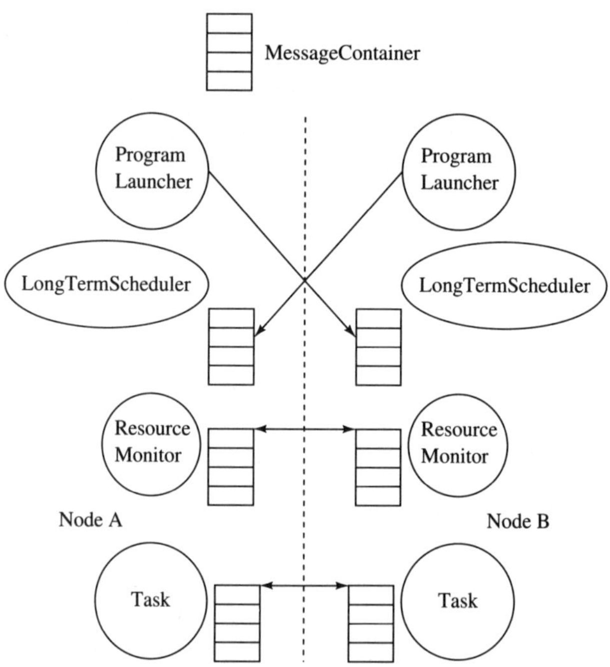

FIGURE 10.5 Network interactions.

The Task and the SchedulingVector are passed to the ProcessContainer, and the ProcessContainer then attempts to schedule the Task. Once a task is in the ProcessContainer, it waits for a local processor or processor set to run it. It will then invoke the `schedulerMembers` method on the Task. As processors execute the `remove` method on the ProcessContainer, they are collected and asked to run the processes from the Gang. The code sketch for scheduling is shown here.

```
On local machine:
-----------------
1.dispatch
2.findOptimal*
3.load program
4.if(local)ready,(optional added sync)
else remoteDispatch

On the remote machine:
----------------------
1.create remoteGang
2.dispatch
3.findOptimal*
4.if (remoteGang not loaded)
load program
5.if(local)ready,(optional added sync)
else remoteDispatch
```

The methods `updateSchedInfo` and `updateIdleTime` are called by the short-term schedulers, and by the Processor classes to maintain the local resource usage information.* Figure 10.5 depicts the remote interactions between classes on two separate machines. The arrows show three types of communication: one for process migration, one for resource information dissemination, and one for fine-grained synchronization for initial process execution. The arrows show the direction in which messages are sent. Once a Task enters the short-term scheduler, it stays there until it is suspended or it runs to completion. When a Task terminates, the data structures used for its scheduling are freed. Figure 10.6 is an entity relationship diagram that shows the relationship between instances of the classes on one node. In particular, on each node there is exactly one LongTermScheduler. Multiple Tasks may be in the system at one time and there may be more than one ResourceMonitor, ProcessContainer, and ProgramLauncher, reflecting the requirement that they each be application specific. A ProcessContainer is only affiliated with one Processor.†

*Other parts of the system, such as the memory system and the file system, can be modified to find out information about physical memory and disk usage. Such modifications are simple extensions to the design presented here.

†Alternate organizations in which a CPU may have several different ProcessContainers on a multiprocessor are not considered, although other systems do provide such organizations.

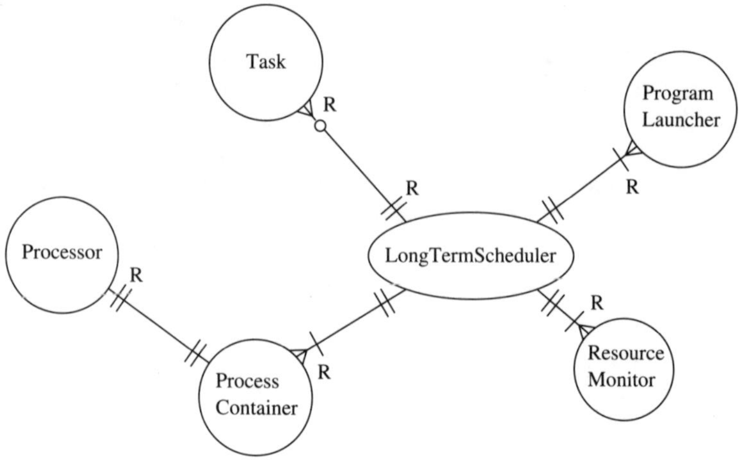

FIGURE 10.6 Entity relationship diagram of the scheduling framework.

10.9 OBJECT FLOW DIAGRAM OF THE PROCESS MANAGEMENT SYSTEM

This section traces how a process is moved between the various process containers and processors in the system. The movement of the process using an object flow diagram [IC92b], which is a variant of the data flow graph, is described. The object flow diagram depicts how a particular object, in this case an instance of the class Process, is passed between various system objects. Figure 10.7 shows the movement of an instance of class Process from creation to blocking and, finally, to deletion. The diagram also identifies the state of a process when it is in different ProcessContainers. For example, a Process is in the **blocked** state when it is in a semaphore's ProcessContainer. The following transitions are shown in Figure 10.7.

1. The `ready` method is invoked on the Process, which puts the process on the SystemScheduler.
2. The Process is taken off the SystemScheduler in FIFO order (or some other discipline) and the `restore` method is invoked on it. The process is now said to be **running** on a Processor.
3. A Process may become blocked; that is, it invokes the `P` method on a Semaphore, invokes the `relinquishProcessor` method on itself, or puts itself on a specialized ProcessContainer and invokes the `block` method on itself.

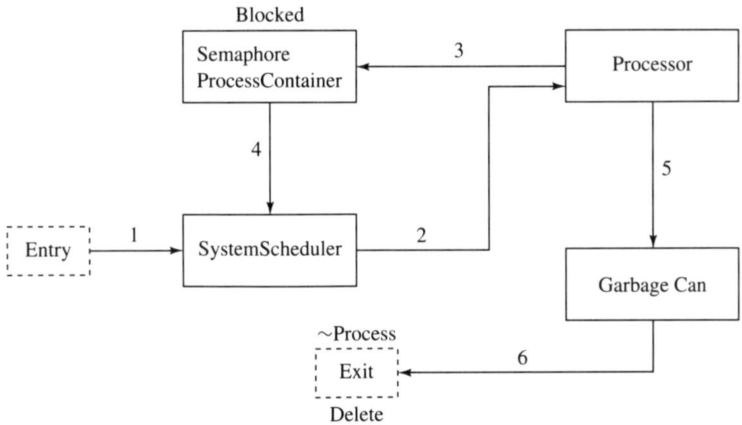

FIGURE 10.7 Object flow diagram of the process management system.

4. While the Process is blocked, if another process invokes the `V` method on the Semaphore that this process is waiting for, and it is the next Process to be chosen from the ProcessContainer, it is put on the SystemScheduler.
5. If a Process invokes the `die` method on itself, it is put into the `GarbageCan` ProcessContainer.
6. A WasteManagerProcess will remove this zombie Process from the garbage can and invoke the **delete** operator on it.

10.10 SELECTING CUSTOMIZATIONS

The scheduling system may be customized in a variety of ways. In addition to application-specific customizations there are two other types of system-specific customizations supported by the scheduling framework. In total, there are three types of customizations.

1. Per-workstation
2. Per-application
3. System configuration time

The system configuration customization is determined by the hardware platform. For example, the context switching code has machine dependencies that must be implemented through the process class. Such selection is shown in Figure 10.8. Each workstation may be configured by the owner of the workstation. In the scheduling framework, the owner of an individual workstation makes a selection as to what type of long-term scheduler and short-term scheduler to use.

Each application programmer can select the type of resource monitoring and, in particular, how accurate the resource information must be. The application

```
/*
 * The scheduling selection mechanism depends upon
 * whether or not gangs are allows in the system
 * There are three types of customizations. They are
 * workstation specific, per-application and hardware specific.
 */

 /* Workstation */

LTSSelection() {
        if(remoteJobAllowed) RemoteExclusive
                else UserExclusive
}

STSSelection () {
        if(FIFO) FIFOScheduler;
        else if(LIFO) LIFOScheduler;
        else if (RR) RRScheduler;
        else if(Deadline scheduling) Deadline;
}

/* per application */

ResourceMonitorSelection(){
        If(extreme accuracy required) Query
        else Publishing
}

ProgramLauncherSelection() {
        if(lauchingRef) Lauchref;
        else (launchTask) launchTask;
}

TaskSelection() {
        if(gangs in application)
                if MultiProcessors LocalGang and GangProcess
                else DistributedSystem DistGang and GangProcess
        else Process
}
/* system configuration or hardware specific */

ProcessorSelection() {
        if(NS32332)
                NS32332Processor
        else if (SPARC) SPARCProcessor
}
```

FIGURE 10.8 Selecting a customized scheduler.

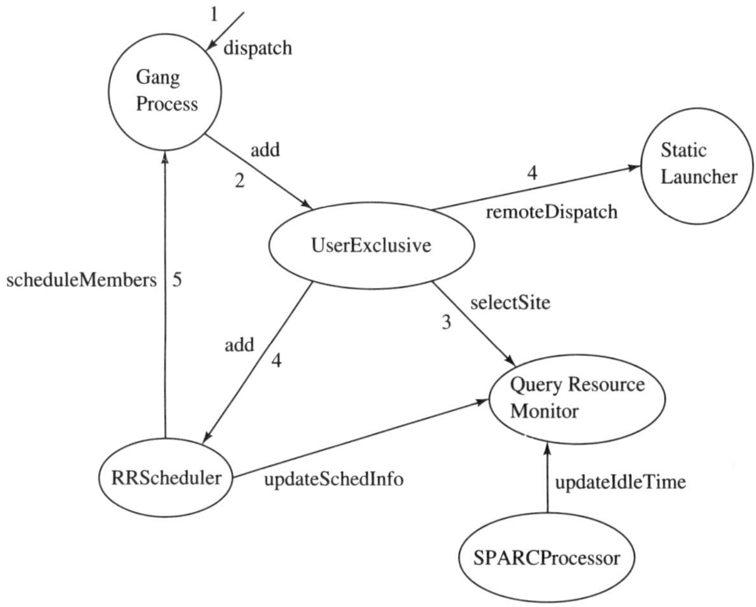

FIGURE 10.9 Instance of scheduling framework.

programmer can also choose between the type of program launching and the types of tasks used in the application. These selections are summarized in Figure 10.8.

A sample instance of the scheduling framework is shown in Figure 10.9. The instance of the framework shows user-exclusive access to workstations, short-term scheduler set to RRScheduler. The system was ported to a network of SPARC workstations and, hence, the process classes are SPARC specific. The application has chosen the query resource monitor, a gang process, and the static program launcher. This instance of the scheduler was used to run the FFT, Simplex, and Cholesky applications on a network of SPARCStations connected by an Ethernet (see Chapter 7).

10.11 IMPLEMENTATION PERFORMANCE

In this section, the performance results of running a LocalGang with a LocalExclusive on a shared-memory multiprocessor, and a DistributedGang with a RemoteExclusive on a distributed system, are presented. Where application-specific data are important, results were obtained for a parallel version of the FFT application. The experiments were conducted when the network was lightly loaded. The results represent the basic costs of the scheduling framework.

TABLE 10.4 Gang Scheduling Parameter Costs in ms

Number of Gang Members	$n = 2$	$n = 4$	$n = 6$	$n = 8$
A. Distributed System				
Create gang and add to list	2.5	2.6	2.6	2.8
B. Shared-Memory Multiprocessor				
Create gang and add to list	78	85	90	98

There are two parts to the performance model for scheduling gangs. The first part entails gang membership management;* its performance is shown in Table 10.4. Section B of the table shows the slight variation as the number of members increases, in the time to create a gang and add members to it on the shared-memory multiprocessor. The cost to add members to the gang increases linearly; this is the cost to sequentially access the gang member list structure. Section A of the table shows faster times for the distributed system with the same number of members. This is a result of the distributed system's faster processor and unithreaded memory allocator.

The second part of the performance model entails the time spent in the various classes of the scheduling framework. The time to schedule a gang is

$$\text{Scheduling time} = (HOPS + 1) * (T_{LTS} + T_{RM}) + HOPS * T_{PL} + T_{STS}$$

HOPS is the number of times the process is moved between nodes. The subscript *LTS* is for LongTermScheduler, *RM* for ResourceMonitor, *PL* for ProgramLauncher, and *STS* for short-term scheduler. This model is evaluated on a shared-memory multiprocessor and a distributed system.

10.11.1 Multiprocessor Gang Scheduling: Performance Results

This section evaluates the performance of gang scheduling on a shared-memory multiprocessor. T_{STS} is the most important parameter for scheduling a LocalGang. The dispatcher will not schedule the LocalGang unless a multiprocessor is found that will accommodate it. Processors are self-scheduling and look for processes to run from their ready queues. These processors are collected by changing the pointer to the system ready queue into a special FIFOGangScheduler. When the requisite number has been collected, the gang processes are added to the FIFOGangScheduler and run on the collected processors one by one.

The values of the parameters are $T_{LTS} = 876\ \mu s$; $T_{PL} = 0\ \mu s$ (no process relocation); and $T_{RM} = 120\ \mu s$. The two parameters of interest for short-term

*In this case, the term *gang membership* is the same as *group membership* as defined in other systems such as Amoeba.

scheduling are

1. The time to schedule a gang and collect N processors
2. The time to dispatch N processes on N processors

Rows 1, 2, and 3 in Table 10.5 present the values for these two parameters in the absence of any multiprogrammed workload. This table also shows that the overhead for scheduling the gang does not change with the number of gang members. There is, however, a variable component for collecting the N processors for the gang; it increases linearly with the number of gang members. The time necessary to run processes that are ready is greater than the corresponding uniprocessor dispatch time (2 ms). The performance is similar to that of Mach [Bla90].

The performance of collecting a gang of processes in a time-shared, multiprogrammed environment is highly dependent on the multiprogramming workload and time-slice, unless preemption is permitted. The theoretical time to collect a gang of size p, with N processors in the system and a time-slice of TS seconds, is given by the functions *First* (time to collect the first processor) and *Collect* (time to collect the remainder). *First* is $TS/(2 \times N)$ if the time-slicing interrupts of the processes are distributed uniformly and independently between zero seconds and TS seconds. The first processor runs the process that collects the processors, reducing the problem to collecting $p - 1$ out of $N - 1$ processors. Each of the $p - 1$ processors needed for the collection can be chosen out of the next $p - 1$ processors that are time-sliced. Assuming the remaining $N - 1$ processor time-slice interrupts are independent of one another, each collected processor contributes a waiting time of $TS/[2 \times (N - 1)]$ to the collection time. Therefore, $Collect(TS, N, p) = [TS \times (p - 1)]/[2 \times (N - 1)]$. Figure 10.10 shows the expected and measured times for collecting processes as a function of p, with a time-slice of 10 ms, averaged over several experiments. $Collect(TS, N, p)$ predicts the measurements fairly accurately for small numbers of processors. Each

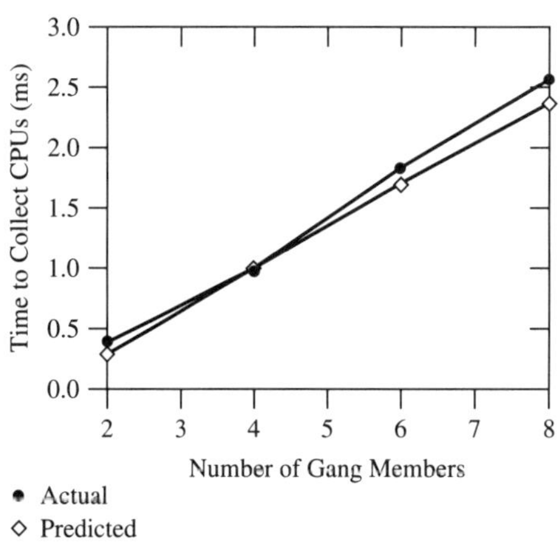

FIGURE 10.10 Time to collect processors under multiprogrammed workloads.

TABLE 10.5 Time to Collect Processors in the Absence of Multiprogramming in ms

Number of Gang Members	$n = 2$	$n = 4$	$n = 6$	$n = 8$
1. Schedule gang and collect CPUs	4.0	4.2	4.4	5.0
2. Ready to running (min)	3.0	3.1	3.8	4.3
3. Ready to running (max)	3.4	3.5	4.6	5.0

time-slice interrupt incurs a slight overhead that is not accounted for by the estimated collection time. As the number of processes increases, the sum of these overheads increases linearly. These numbers are greater than those reported in rows 1, 2, and 3 of Table 10.5 because the measurements were taken in a multiprogrammed environment.

10.11.2 Distributed Gang Scheduling: Performance Results

This section explains the performance of distributed gang scheduling. The node where the DistributedGang is originally created is the originating node. The originating node becomes a centralized scheduler.

The values of the parameters of the performance model are $T_{STS} = 1.40\ ms^*$; $T_{LTS} = 140\ \mu s$; and $T_{PL} = 500\ \mu s$ (this result is application-size dependent). The size of the file is 98,304 bytes. The cost of the QueryResourceMonitor and PublishResourceMonitor algorithms is shown in Table 10.6. The results show a tradeoff between using the most recent results and using cached information. The cost of the querying mechanism increases as the number of machines increases. The publishing algorithm scales better, although the effects of updating the cache are not evident from the experiments. The costs of the query mechanism are dominated by the costs of collecting machines across the network, which increase with the number of machines.

*This number is high due to an interaction between the proxy interface and the virtual memory system.

TABLE 10.6 Query and Publishing Costs in ms

Number of Members	1	2	4	8
QueryResourceMonitor				
1. MultiRR	2.45	2.9	4.7	9
2. Multicast + Bookkeeping	1.0	1.0	1.0	1
3. Total	3.45	3.9	5.6	10
PublishResourceMonitor				
1. Search Local Cache	.1	.1	.1	.2
2. Multicast + Bookkeeping	1.0	1.0	1.0	1.0
3. Total	1.1	1.1	1.1	1.2

There are circumstances under which one type of resource allocation is more desirable than another. For example, for scalability studies of parallel applications it is more beneficial to use the query algorithm since it provides the most up-to-date information, even though it is more expensive to invoke than publishing. For an extremely large number of processes the cost of the query algorithm increases, and beyond a certain number of nodes it might be more beneficial to use the publishing algorithm. For process relocation of regular or long-lived processes, a publishing algorithm is as good as the query algorithm but is a lot cheaper to invoke.

10.12 APPLICATION PERFORMANCE

In this section, effects of gang scheduling on applications are discussed. The purpose of the experiment is to demonstrate that a judicious selection of machines results in better performance than using no heuristic at all. To investigate the effectiveness of gang scheduling, the FFT application was run on four processors or nodes with a data set of 1024 points.

On the distributed system, there were eight nodes; four were kept idle while compute-bound programs were run on the other four. The uncoordinated scheme does not take resource scheduling into account and randomly distributes the processes from the LongTerm scheduler. For synchronous applications, having even one process run on a heavily loaded system can affect the speedup of an application, as all other processes must wait for the descheduled process. The time-slice was set to 10 ms. Table 10.7 shows that distributed gang scheduling can improve the performance of an application by as much as 40 percent. The execution time of an application can vary by as much as 30 percent without gang scheduling, and gang scheduling can reduce this to 5.5 percent.

On the shared-memory multiprocessor there were 16 processors; again, four processes were gang scheduled. Apart from the gang, regular non-gang applications were run independently on the system. The jobs were compute intensive. These were run on the system before the gang was scheduled. The time-slice was set to 100 ms. Table 10.7 demonstrates the benefits of gang scheduling for a parallel version of the FFT application. It shows that without gang scheduling the average execution times are about 75 percent higher. The variance changes, however, from 14 percent of the execution time without gang scheduling to 4 percent of the execution time with gang scheduling.

TABLE 10.7 FFT Performance With and Without Gang Scheduling in ms

Scheduling	Gang	Uncoordinated
Distributed System	72 ± 4	101 ± 30
Shared Memory	1223 ± 50	2136 ± 300

The difference between coordinated and uncoordinated scheduling seems to be quite pronounced on the shared-memory multiprocessor. This is primarily due a shared central queue that was used on the shared-memory multiprocessor for this experiment. As a result, processes often get relocated to new processors after a context switch. This results in much cache invalidation since a cache must be reloaded with the new process's data when the process runs on another processor. On a distributed system, such relocation would correspond to dynamic process migration. Dynamic process migration is not, however, part of the model, and only static placement is considered. Thus, there is less of a difference in the absolute time between the two scheduling schemes on a distributed system. The variance of the results is also different because there is a chance that all four processes get relocated to the idle workstations or to all the heavily loaded workstations. On the shared-memory multiprocessor, the environment for each run is approximately the same for the uncoordinated scheme because of the central queue. Thus, from run to run, the behavior does not vary much.

10.13 SUMMARY

The contributions of this chapter are a design of a customizable scheduling system that can be tailored to the needs of applications, and an instance of this customizable scheduling system that implements the novel concept of distributed gang scheduling.

The results of the experiments show that gang scheduling can be implemented on both a bus-based, shared-memory multiprocessor and a distributed system. On both systems this technique considerably improves the performance of parallel application execution times and the variability of the execution runs. The gang management routines are much more expensive on the shared-memory multiprocessor. It is interesting to note, however, that even though much network communication is involved in the distributed system, apart from the costs associated with the ProgramLauncher, the costs are similar between the two platforms in absolute times. This reflects the high cost of contention and memory latencies on the shared-memory multiprocessor. This chapter demonstrates that a technique that was originally intended for a shared-memory multiprocessor can be efficiently implemented on a distributed system. The portability of the implementation is enhanced by separating the hardware-dependent parts into abstractions such as Processor.

CHAPTER 11

Discussion

Most operating systems and system software designs encourage fixed interfaces and fixed implementations for system services. There are two reasons for this. First, it was thought that there would never be a need for extensible interfaces. A single, fixed interface is simple, and easy to remember for most users. Second, it was thought that there would never be a need for multiple implementations of the same interface. Since small, simple operating systems are hard to design, implement, and test, it was thought that designing multiple implementations of a single interface would be an impossible task. Over time, however, there has been a proliferation of operating systems with different interfaces and implementations. Generic operating systems, such as UNIX, did not keep pace with the requirements of new applications and new hardware architectures. Many of these operating systems are specialized to handle a class of applications or are specific to a hardware architecture. These specialized operating systems have subsystems that are tuned to the functionality and performance requirements of different applications or are designed for the new architectures. These specialized subsystems may be viewed as problem-oriented as described by Cheriton [Che86a]. Cheriton defines a problem-oriented shared memory as a (distributed) shared memory that is specialized to the particular problem or application it is supporting. Cheriton discusses two primitives that are essential for implementing memory: fetch and store. Applications customize the fetchand store operations to implement particular problem-oriented semantics. In problem-oriented shared-memory systems, maintaining the consistency of shared memory is important. Cheriton provides a variety of examples of problem-oriented shared memory from distributed systems, including name service, time service, global scheduling, and file service.

While it is possible to specialize an entire operating system, most research has focused on a small number of subsystems of an operating system. In particular, there have been a large number of specialized file systems, schedulers (scheduling algorithms in particular), communication protocols, and distributed shared-memory implementations. Operating systems that used these new subsystems either were designed from scratch or were major modifications to existing operating systems. There was little design or implementation relationship between these various operating systems, resulting in many worker-months to design, implement, and test a new operating system. In addition, it was difficult to make performance comparisons between the various implementations because there are often hidden implementation costs that are not factored into the comparison. In this book, a new methodology for designing multiple implementations of the various subsystems of an operating system is described. This new methodology is object-oriented frameworks. The design of the message-passing, process, and scheduling subsystems of an operating system is described as an example of this technique.

The purpose of this chapter is to discuss how and why a variety of special-purpose message-passing and scheduling systems have been developed. This chapter first highlights the necessity of designing operating systems that support multiple interfaces and implementations. Several approaches to designing customized operating systems are then discussed. Finally, object-oriented frameworks are introduced as a solution to designing customized operating systems.

11.1 MESSAGE PASSING

Simple interfaces and models are considered to be so important for communication between computers that an international standards committee, the International Organization for Standardization (known as ISO), proposed a reference model for designing and implementing network protocols. This model is called the Open Systems Interconnect (OSI) [Zim80].

The OSI protocol suite is a layered architecture called a *reference model.* It consists of seven layers. The OSI model is concerned with the interconnection between layers and not with the internal functions that are performed by the layers. There are two types of interfaces between layers: One set of interfaces exists between layers on a single node and another set exists between layers on two different nodes. The OSI layers are shown in Figure 11.1. The solid arrows indicate interfaces that are defined on a per-node basis and the dashed arrows show interfaces between nodes. No similar reference models were defined for shared-

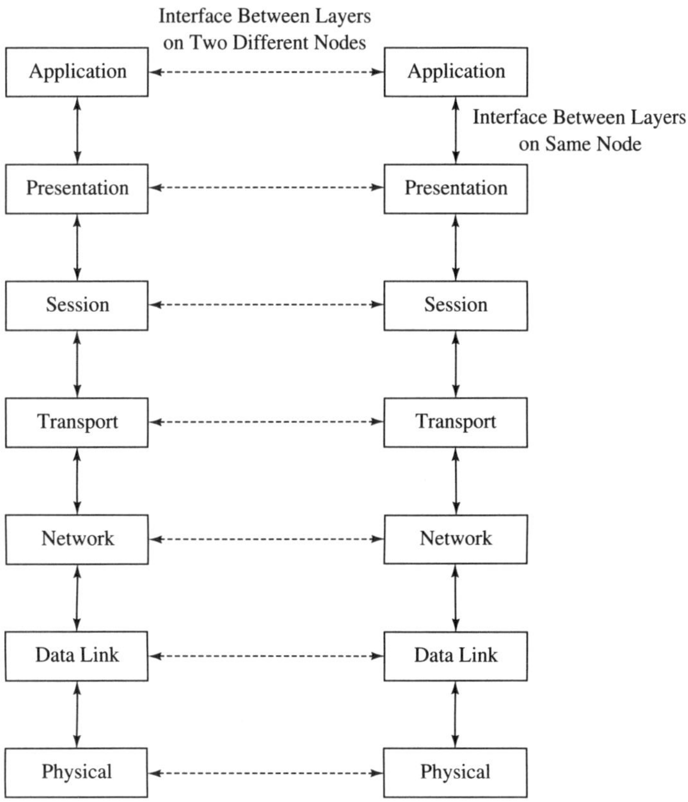

FIGURE 11.1 The layers of the ISO OSI protocol suite.

memory architectures because these architectures have not been widely available until recently and only recently have researchers shown interest in implementing message-passing system software on shared-memory multiprocessors. This makes it easy to port applications written for a distributed system onto a shared-memory architecture.

Despite the efforts of the ISO standards committee, several layered designs appeared primarily because the OSI layered model was too "heavyweight": It had too many layers to be efficient for many situations [Mul89]. For example, many protocols that are used solely for supporting remote procedure calls only have three layers [BN84]. These new protocol designs encouraged simplicity and each design was tailored to a particular hardware architecture, environment, or application. There are still some designs, however, such as IBM's SNA, that also have seven layers, but each layer has a different function from the layers of the OSI reference model. A number of specialized protocols are now reviewed. These protocols have differing designs, interfaces, and implementations.

Message Passing on Distributed Systems. V [Che88a] is a distributed operating system that has specialized synchronous interprocess communication primitives and an implementation that is optimized for client-server programs used for implementing systems services. It uses the VMTP [Che88b, Che86b] protocol for implementing the message-passing primitives on a local area network.

Amoeba [TvRvS+90] is a distributed operating system that provides its own request-response protocol. The Amoeba primitives were also designed for efficient RPC or request-response communication. Amoeba uses the Flip protocol for its request-response communication [KRST93] and provides special support for ordered and reliable multicast [KT91]. The V and Amoeba primitives and protocols were originally designed for client-server programs on distributed systems. Both systems have, however, been used to run parallel applications on distributed systems.

On the V distributed operating system, Stumm and Cheriton [Che88a] explore a parallel program structure called the Multi-Satellite Star, in which a central satellite holds tasks and individual processes ask the central satellite for tasks to work on. They conclude that a satellite structure scales well and performs well with respect to scheduling, communication overhead, and fault tolerance.

Orca [BKT92] is a language for programming parallel applications based on the shared data object model. Orca uses Amoeba [TvRvS+90] as its underlying distributed operating system. It relies on the Amoeba reliable broadcast protocol for group communication. In Amoeba and V, a parallel application must conform to a particular structure, such as the Multi-Satellite Star used in the V operating system. Neither Amoeba nor V can be modified to suit the needs of an application.

Mach [Ras86] provides a request-response style of communication that was originally intended for a shared-memory multiprocessor [YTR+87] and porting to a local area network [Dra90]. The network protocol can be implemented in a separate server process. Recent proposals have suggested moving network protocols to the user level in Mach [MB93]. The Chorus [RAA+88] operating system also supports asynchronous communication and RPC facilities. It also has support for group communication. The primitives of both systems are primarily intended for writing distributed applications or systems services.

UNIX [Bac86] provides communication facilities through its socket, stream, and pipe interface. It is possible to choose a specific protocol from those installed in the operating system for socket communication. Most of the UNIX protocols (such as TCP) and related interfaces are used for system services, such as file services. They are also targeted for applications running on the Internet. It is difficult, however, to extend UNIX with new protocols.

Message-passing libraries such as PVM [Sun90], Express [Cor88], and PICL [GHPW91] are used to provide functionality on top of operating systems. These libraries overcome the interface and implementation deficiences of the underlying operating system. Libraries such as PVM implement their own message-passing on UNIX to bypass the overhead of the native UNIX implementations that use protocols such as TCP. These libraries add some degree of flexibility to the message-passing programming interface on general-purpose operating systems such as UNIX.

NX/2 [Pie86] is an operating system designed for a distributed-memory multicomputer. Its message-passing primitives were designed explicitly for parallel applications written using synchronous and asynchronous communication. The message-passing system on the CM-5 [Cor91, Cor92] computer was also designed for parallel applications and has special support for applications written using active messages.

Group Communication Primitives and Implementations. Parallel and distributed programs are often programmed with collective or group communication primitives. Multicast is an important group communication primitive that has various implementations [CZ85, KTHB89] on distributed systems. Just as algorithms were developed for point-to-point communication, many specialized algorithms have been designed for collective communication routines. Different algorithms provide different types of reliability and ordering guarantees. Some algorithms also consider node fault tolerance.

One algorithm, employed by the V system, allows for a best-efforts send; there are no ordering or reliability guarantees. In a second algorithm, employed by PVM, there are $N - 1$ point-to-point sends and $N - 1$ replies. This requires $2 \times (N - 1)$ network messages. Reliability is guaranteed, and it is assumed that the applications maintain their own message ordering. In a third algorithm, also employed by the V system, an application sends a message and waits for the number of replies it wants. When hardware-assisted multicast is used, N network messages are generated. The multicast takes one network message, and there are $N - 1$ replies. Reliability must be implemented by the user; no help is provided by the system. The Amoeba multicast supports the ordered and reliable [KT91, KTHB89] delivery of messages in the face of node failures. This multicast algorithm employs a central coordinator or sequencer that serializes messages. For small messages the following protocol is used. The multicaster sends a point-to-point message to the sequencer. The sequencer packages the message, adds a sequence number S to it, and then multicasts the message to the group. The sequencer keeps a list of all outgoing messages. If a receiver gets a message out of order, it asks the sequencer for the missing message. No explicit acknowledgments are sent back from the receivers. Receivers are expected to multicast messages regularly and piggyback acknowledgments on their regular multicast messages. The protocol detects network message loss using time-outs. The sequencer and the receiver kernels have timers that expire during periods of communication inactivity and resynchronize the sequencer with the receivers.

For large messages, the initial message is multicast and the sequencer then sends out a separate sequence number to match the message. Ordering and reliability are guaranteed. This protocol is similar to that described by Chang and Maxemchuck [CM84].

Other multicast protocols for ordered and reliable delivery include [BSS91, BJ87, MS91, MSMA90]. In particular, the ISIS [BSS91] protocols assume a reliable network protocol. A variety of other collective communication primitives are described in [FJL+88]. For example, there are primitives such as `vm_shift` to shift data around a circular ring of processes, and `vm_combine` to combine data from a set of processes [FJL+88].

Message Passing on Shared Memory. On shared-memory multiprocessors there are several message-passing systems intended primarily for applications written in a particular style. Demos [BHM77] and Mach [Ras86] are examples of operating systems that implement message-passing primitives on top of a shared-memory multiprocessor. These primitives were written to structure system services. Bershad [BALL91] shows a fast user-level, interaddress space communication scheme for shared-memory multiprocessors, also intended for writing system services.

Leblanc [LeB86] and Lin et al. [LS90] present message-passing systems on shared-memory multiprocessors that are used for programming parallel applications rather than system services. Their work shows that some parallel applications perform better when coded using message-passing techniques, rather than shared variables on a shared-memory multiprocessor.

11.2 SCHEDULING AND PROCESS MANAGEMENT

Popular reference models do not exist for many other parts of the operating system. In particular, there are no reference models for processes and scheduling. Most operating systems employ a simple model of processes, and they seldom vary radically from each other. There have been numerous studies on scheduling policies for uniprocessor and parallel systems. Most operating systems, however, employ a single scheduling algorithm. There have been several attempts to classify and organize the various scheduling algorithms. Rushitzka et al. [RF77] provide a classification of scheduling algorithms that formalizes the notion of priority. This formalization makes the implementation of multiple scheduling policies easy. Casavant et al. [CK88] provide a hierarchical classification of a variety of different algorithms for scheduling in distributed systems. A survey of scheduling on parallel systems is given in [Fei94].

One type of scheduling, gang scheduling, is examined in this book. Briefly, gang scheduling is the simultaneous scheduling of all the processes of an application on a set of processors. Although gang scheduling has been implemented on shared-memory multiprocessors, it has not been implemented on distributed systems. In this section, gang scheduling on shared-memory multiprocessors and general scheduling techniques on distributed systems are reviewed. Most scheduling systems are designed for a particular style of application programming. As a result, most existing scheduling systems are not extensible.

Scheduling on Shared-Memory Multiprocessors. The performance of a parallel application on shared-memory multiprocessors is sensitive to the scheduling mechanisms and policies of the operating system [Bla90, Ous82]. The Medusa operating system implements co-scheduling [Ous82], a technique that tries to schedule the processes of an application to run at the same time. The Alliant scheduler [Jac86] supports a fixed number of scheduler classes. Groups of processes are assigned to a scheduler class and each group within a class is run simultaneously. In the process control approach, applications must negotiate with a processor allocation server to determine how many processors can be used [TG89]. Together the server and the application determine the level of application concurrency.

Distributed Scheduling. Scheduling is an extremely important issue in distributed systems as well. Condor [LLM88] and Marionette [SA89] schedule application processes on distributed systems by locating idle workstations. These systems are implemented on top of the UNIX operating system. Condor schedules a single process (not a group) and ensures the completion of an application's computation in a fault-tolerant manner. Marionette uses a master-slave model for parallel distributed computation. Some library packages, such as Express, allow programs to be loaded and then started. This provides minimal support for tightly coupled co-scheduling of applications. Once started, program performance depends on the UNIX scheduler of each workstation. Recent simulation studies [ES93] have evaluated the effects of co-scheduling on a network of workstations and have found that it can improve the performance of parallel applications. The V [Che88a, The86] distributed operating system has facilities for preemptable remote execution of individual processes but not groups of processes. The V program manager maintains a cache of information about the resources of machines that can be used for remote execution. Stumm has studied the dissemination of resource usage information in [Stu88a].

Several distributed-memory architectures have operating systems that support gang scheduling. The CM-5 [LAD$^+$92] provides gang scheduling within partitions. Batch mode partitions provide for dedicated access to a partition until the application finishes. Interactive partitions allow partitions to be time-sliced between applications. In this mode a central control processor manages the coordinated context switching of the nodes in the partition. A single message is sent to all the nodes, which then simultaneously switch to a new process. The control processor has a UNIX process that represents the parallel application. When the UNIX process on the control processor is scheduled, the other processes of the application are scheduled, on the nodes of the partition. Partitions are created by a system administrator.

In the Meiko CS-2 [BCM94], partitions are also created by the system administrator. A partition manager coordinates interactive gang scheduling. The partition manager is composed of a set of demons, one on each node. When a time quantum is up on the root process, the partition manager gets an alarm. The root process then broadcasts a message to all the demon processes on the other nodes, and all collectively pick the next application to run. The algorithm used is the matrix algorithm of Ousterhout [Ous82].

11.3 OPERATING SYSTEM CUSTOMIZATION TECHNIQUES

The use of layered designs and virtual machines has been discussed for designing multiple implementations of operating systems. In this section, several generic mechanisms for creating multiple implementations of systems are considered, including modular systems, reflection, microkernel-based designs, object-based designs, object-oriented designs and dynamic code synthesis. These generic techniques can be used to construct both message-passing and scheduling subsystems. Techniques and mechanisms that have been used specifically for a message-passing subsystem or scheduling subsystem are then considered.

Modular Systems. Modular design techniques for operating systems were first proposed by Dykstra [Dyk68] in his THE operating system. Venus [Lis72] was a layered operating system similar in spirit to THE. In THE, the operating system implementation was modular, with a process associated with each module or layer. There could be different implementations of each layer. In such an organization, however, the cost of communication between layers is very high, as process or protection boundaries must be crossed on each interaction between layers. Haberman [HFC72] refined Dykstra's ideas and suggested the notion of a family of operating systems. Each member of a family is designed to suit the needs of a class of applications. In Haberman's design, virtual machines are layered on top of each other. New families are created by implementing new virtual machines. Haberman's proposed structure was similar to that of Dykstra except that the hierarchy of layers was among functions. It is the system design that is hierarchical, not its implementation. For example, such a design allows layers to be collapsed or combined in an implementation, leading to better performance. Haberman further points out that there is a distinction between levels and modules. Modules may be interleaved in such a way as to span levels. The concept of virtual machines has found its way into commercial products such as the IBM VM system designed for the IBM 370 machine [SD74]. These designs favor fixed interfaces but allow multiple implementations.

Reflection. Reflection is a technique that has recently received enormous attention in the programming language community [Smi82]. A reflective program is one that can reason about itself. A fully reflective procedural architecture is one in which a process can access and manipulate a fully explicit, causally connected representation of its own state, where causally connected means that any changes made to a process' self-representation are immediately reflected in its actual state and behavior. The reflection paradigm was introduced into object-oriented systems by Maes [Mae87] in a language called 3-KRS. Each object is partitioned into a domain-specific referent and a metaobject. The metaobject contains information describing its referent as a computational entity in itself. Manipulation of an object's metaobject can affect the way computation for its referent object is carried out. The ability to introduce temporary, localized changes to an object's semantics without changing the object itself accounts for a great deal of reflection's power.

Apertos [Yok92] is an operating system that uses reflection to design a customizable operating system. In Apertos, object-level and metaobject-level programming are separated. The domain-specific algorithms are implanted in an object, and operating system-specific information is controlled through the metaobject. A metaobject is a virtual processor on which an object runs. For example, how an object might communicate with another object is implemented in the metaobject. To insure greater flexibility, Apertos uses a group of metaobjects, also known as a metaspace, to collaboratively control the execution of an object. The system functions required by an object are provided by its metaspace. Figure 11.2 depicts how the objects and metaobjects are related to each other. It shows that an object's functionality, such as network communication, is provided by a metaspace. This architecture and technique allow the network communication to be changed for an individual object by the metaobject. One aspect of reflection that has yet

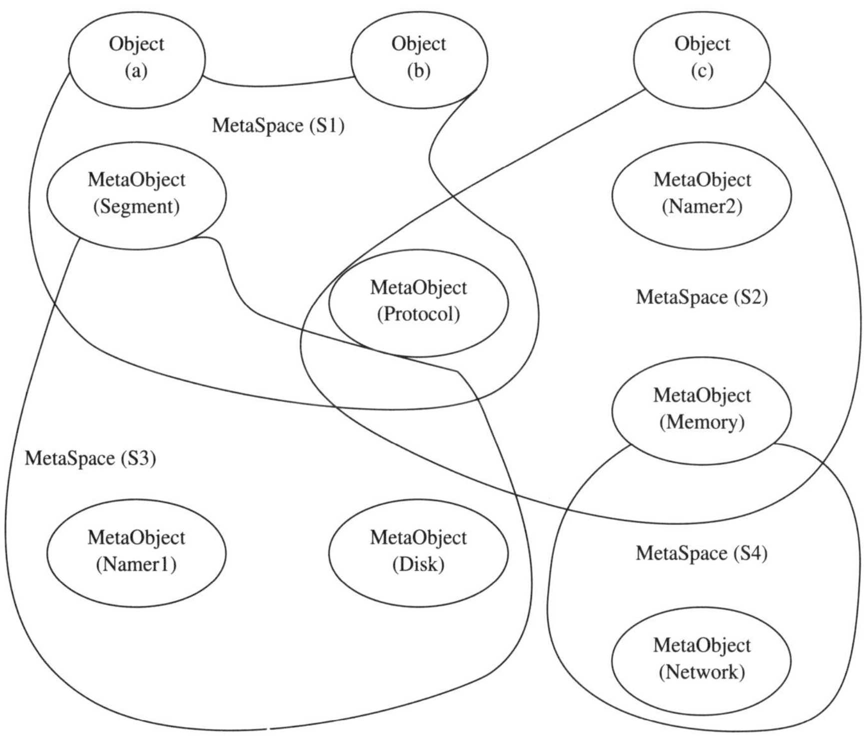

FIGURE 11.2 The Apertos reflective operating system.

to be fully tested is how it will perform. Reflection can be used to change both interfaces and implementations.

Object-Based Systems. In object-based systems, objects are used to provide encapsulation. Examples of such systems include [DLA88, ea74, RAA+88]. In some sense, server-based designs can also be considered object based, where a server is a large-grained object. In this regard the Mach and Chorus operating systems are object based. In object-based systems, objects reference other objects in the system through a reference or capability to the object. The reference can define what permissions the invoking object has with respect to the object on which it is operating. These references can be as simple as direct pointers to other objects, in effect providing no protection, or as complex as capabilities in full capability-based systems [KL87, MB80]. Object-based systems allow both multiple implementations and interfaces but favor multiple implementations hidden by a single interface.

Object-Oriented Systems. SOS [SGH+89] is an object-oriented operating system that was designed to help in the construction of distributed object–based applications. SOS designers focused on techniques for structuring applications using fragmented objects. As such, SOS has focused more on services for distributed object management than the internal structuring of an operating system. It extends the object concept to distributed or fragmented objects. Communication between the fragments of a distributed object is implemented through an application interface and an invocation protocols interface. The invocation protocols are intended to be extensible. In [SGH+89] four invocation protocols were implemented: (1) RPC, (2) multicast, (3) synchronous, and (4) asynchronous. A special communicator object implemented the transport layer. SOS, however, lacked a notion of object-oriented frameworks that makes the design and implementation extensible. The techniques presented in this book could be used to design object-oriented systems such as SOS.

Spring [HPM93, HK93] is an object-oriented operating system developed at Sun Microsystems Laboratories. It is based on a microkernel concept. Spring programmers use an interface definition language (IDL) to code interfaces for system services. This IDL conforms to the OMG's CORBA [Gro93] model. An IDL compiler generates the code for the client and server stubs so that a client and a server can communicate. In addition, the servers in Spring are made from constituent objects that can be combined in a variety of ways to form new but similar services. The approach used in Spring is similar in that objects are composed to form new services. Spring does not, however, use object-oriented frameworks to organize objects. Object-oriented systems allow both multiple interfaces and implementations.

Microkernels. In an attempt to make kernel debugging easier and to allow a kernel to be easily extended, microkernel structuring became popular. Traditional operating systems are monolithic; all systems services reside in the kernel in the same address space. When an application requests an operating system service, the request call traps into the operating system, the system service routines are invoked, and the call returns to the application. In a microkernel architecture a small kernel handles basic functionality, such as low-level process management, scheduling, low-level input/output, interprocess communication, and some minimal memory management. All other system services are implemented outside the kernel in user-level processes. When an application requests a system service it traps into the kernel and the flow of control moves to the appropriate user-level server. The requisite routines are invoked and the results are passed to the application through the kernel.

Figure 11.3 shows what a monolithic microkernel looks like. All operating system services are implemented in one kernel address space. The monolithic kernel provides file, network communication, and naming services. Figure 11.4 shows a microkernel version of the same operating system. In this diagram, much of the functionality in a traditional kernel is provided in user-level servers outside the microkernel. In the figure file, network communication and naming services are provided outside the kernel. Each service may be independently developed, debugged, and subsequently modified. The Mach scheduler [Bla90] allows scheduling policy servers to be built. New scheduling policies are instituted by implementing and then installing a new server.

A major advantage of this approach is that servers can be developed and debugged like an ordinary application rather than an operating system kernel.

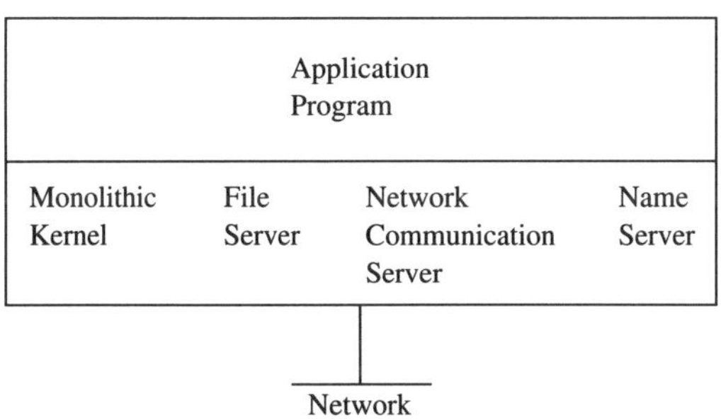

FIGURE 11.3 A monolithic kernel architecture where all the operating system functionality is provided in one address space.

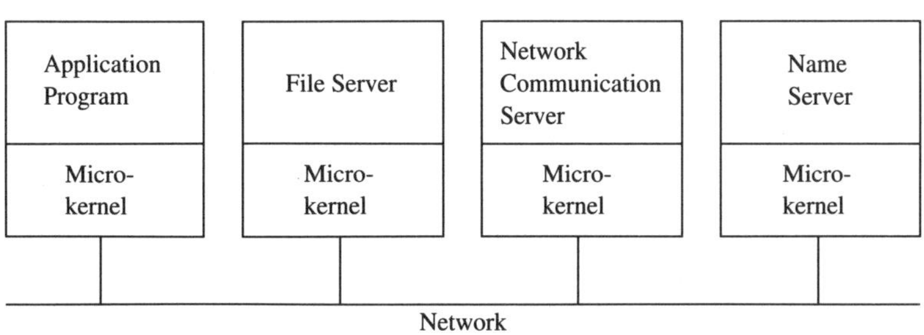

FIGURE 11.4 A microkernel architecture where much of the operating system functionality is provided through several user-level processes.

Microkernel structuring techniques were pioneered by the Mach and Chorus operating systems. In Mach, servers implement filing services, network communication, and paging among other facilities traditionally implemented in the kernel. The operating system kernel implements address spaces, cross-address-space message passing, interrupt handling, and kernel threads. To install a new server one need only modify an existing server and reinstall it, without rebooting or changing the microkernel itself. The microkernel design is orthogonal to object-oriented operating system design. It is possible to use object-oriented frameworks to design microkernels. The microkernel eases the task of creating multiple implementations of system services. Although multiple interfaces for a single system service are possible, this requires providing the application with knowledge of the various interfaces, making the introduction of new interfaces more difficult.

Dynamic Code Synthesis. An interesting experiment in dynamically modifiable systems is Pu's Synthesis kernel [PMI88, MP89, PM91]. The Synthesis kernel dynamically synthesizes code using three methods: (1) factoring invariants, which bypasses redundant computations (similar to constant folding); (2) collapsing layers, which eliminates unnecessary procedure calls; and (3) context switches, both vertically for layered modules and horizontally for pipelined threads. Finally, the executable data structures method shortens data structure traversal time when the data structure is always traversed the same way. In Synthesis, alternatives are compiled as the operating system runs. Dynamic code synthesis techniques have been used for multiple implementations.

11.4 CUSTOMIZING MESSAGE PASSING

This section reviews customization techniques that have been used mostly in message-passing systems. Almost all of the customization work for message-passing has been in distributed systems; very little work has been done in customized message passing on shared-memory architectures.

Protocol Graphs. One interesting new design approach is the *x*-kernel/avoca. The *x*-kernel/avoca [HP91, HPAO89, O'M90] system allows the generation of multiple network protocols. The *x*-kernel supports a wide variety of existing network protocols, such as UDP, TCP, and Sun RPC.

The *x*-kernel provides three standard entities from which to construct arbitrary network protocols: (1) protocols, (2) sessions, and (3) messages. These entities are composed together like modules or layers to generate new network protocols. The *x*-kernel permits the generation of efficient network protocols by eliminating unnecessary layers in constructing the network protocol, by using a process-per-message model, and by using fbufs or zero-copy buffers [DP93]. In the *x*-kernel process-per-message model, when a message does not encounter contention for resources, it is possible to send or receive a message with no process switches. The *x*-kernel project is concerned with building arbitrary network protocols and is less concerned with application-specific optimizations. More important, the approach uses module-based customization rather than inheritance-based customization for communication. Little attempt has been made to experiment with the methodology on a wide variety of platforms such as a shared-memory architecture.

The *x*-kernel uses a top-down approach to designing dynamic network architectures. Reuse is achieved primarily through composing existing microprotocols. The result of the composition is a protocol graph. The protocol graph for the Internet FTP protocol is shown in Figure 11.5. In contrast to the typical layered design of the OSI protocol suite, the *x*-kernel can describe designs based on arbitrary graphs. In the *x*-kernel methodology, code reuse is obtained by reusing existing microprotocols. For example, the Sprite RPC protocol can be implemented by reusing the IP and Ethernet microprotocols.

Streams. The design of the *x*-kernel is similar to the System V Stream architecture. System V Stream emphasizes modular components that possess uniform interfaces. Although streams were originally developed for terminal drivers they were later extended for local IPC through multiplexor drivers and STREAM pipes [Rit84].

Protocol Compilers. The advent of user-level device drivers for network I/O has led to projects on protocol compilers by Felten (PDL) [Fel93] and Islam et al. [I+95]. These approaches essentially ignore the layers proposed by the ISO standard, and generate a single layer that goes from the application onto the network interface or some other low-level interface. The Real Time Asynchronous Grammar (RTAG) developed by Anderson makes it easy to design complex software protocols and efficient automated implementation. RTAG was used primarily to develop protocols that run inside an operating system kernel and are shared by all applications that wish to communicate through the network.

RTAG is based on a context-free grammar notation in which ordinary symbols correspond to messages sent and received. RTAG also has mechanisms

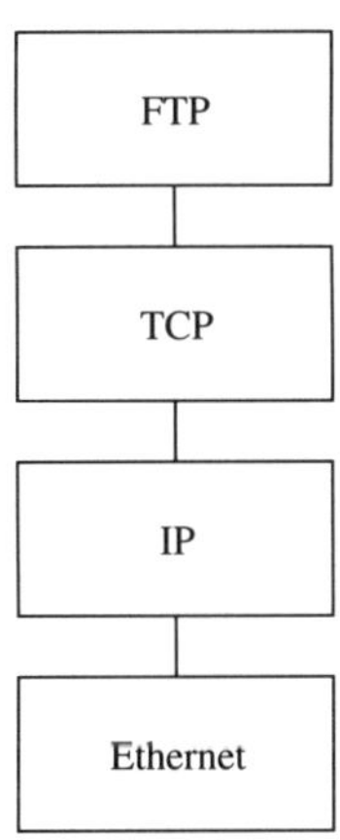

FIGURE 11.5 Protocol graph for internet protocol implementing FTP.

for specifying concurrent protocol activities and real-time constraints. It differs from traditional finite-state machine (FSM) approaches in that it directly supports encapsulation and abstraction in protocol design and specification by allowing protocols to be decomposed into subprotocols. This is similar to the approach used for the *x*-kernel. The language used in RTAG is more powerful than the one employed by the *x*-kernel; the subprotocols may be instantiated dynamically and concurrently.

Most formal description techniques (FDT) are oriented toward verification and performance analysis, and are often based on FSMs. Pure FSMs are amenable to automated protocol verification but can represent only simple or idealized protocols. They are often augmented with a high-level language (HLL) to express real-world properties of protocols. RTAG has been used to design TCP and TP-4 Internet protocols.

Felten describes a language-based approach, PDL, that automatically designs protocols. PDL uses a context-free grammar to describe the communication in an application. The intent of PDL is to describe and implement per-application protocols. Felten's work concentrates mainly on buffering, and addresses the following design choices.

- Which messages will be buffered and which will not
- Where messages will be buffered in memory (for example, should the sender or receiver buffer the message)

He shows that these two design options permit the design of tailored protocols for five applications. Compilers, however, typically do not take interapplication relationships or data-dependent behavior into account in the message-passing system optimizations. Additionally, tool kits are more appropriate for experimentation than compilers because they are easier to modify. Protocol compilers typically assume unique interfaces for applications using the communication systems services.

Message-Passing Libraries. A library may be subroutine based or object oriented. No matter how the library is constructed there are several differences between a library and an object-oriented framework. When using an object-oriented library, one selects a class from the library, creates an instance, and uses it. Occasionally the library is subclassed to specialize it. The designer becomes proficient with the system by learning a catalog of classes. The library imposes very few constraints on the classes selected. On the other hand, programming using frameworks requires study of the collaborations and responsibilities of several classes. New subclasses of framework classes are created, or one chooses from and modifies classes from sample libraries. The classes are connected to form a part on the system. The user must adopt the collaborative model adopted by the designer of the framework. Libraries can provide both new interfaces and new implementations.

Compiling to Message-Passing Libraries. Some parallel program compilers insert calls in the parallel program code to the primitives of generic message-passing libraries. Examples include Fortran D [HKT91a, HKT91b], CM-Fortran [Cor89], and C* [For90]. Some compilers also make use of efficient collective communication routines if they exist in the supporting library. These compilers differ from the work presented here.

Ad Hoc. Astra is an asynchronous RPC mechanism that allows the selection, at bind time, of low latency or high throughput. The application programmer must explicitly make this choice. Astra supports two important and distinct uses of RPC. First, there can be many intermittent calls between a client and a server—such calls require low latency. Second, there can be many RPC calls from one client to a particular server, or there can be a bulk data transfer between a client and a server. This requires high throughput. Since Astra only supports two types of communication policies, the design is ad hoc.

11.5 DISTRIBUTED SHARED-MEMORY SYSTEMS

Although the design of distributed shared-memory systems is not considered in this book, they are mentioned because they are an important alternative for processes to communicate in a distributed system, and significant work has been done to design systems that support multiple implementations of distributed shared-memory systems. Distributed shared-memory systems support a virtual address space that spans a network of computers. The existence of multiple implementations of distributed shared memory is based primarily on the fact that variables can be shared with different consistency semantics. Each type of consistency can have a different implementation.

Munin [CBZ91] is an example of a system that uses multiple consistency protocols. It supports both multiple interfaces and implementations. No single consistency protocol has proved best for all applications. Variables in a program can be shared differently, and this sharing can change dynamically as the program runs. In Munin, sharing patterns are specified using programmer annotations. Before the program runs, a parser statically interprets user annotations for the Munin system and selects the best consistency protocol for that sharing pattern. The implementation of multiple protocols is divided into two parts: high-level sharing pattern annotations, and low-level protocol parameters. The high-level annotations are specified as part of a shared variable declaration. These annotations correspond to the expected sharing pattern of the variable. The low-level protocol parameters control specific aspects of the individual protocols, such as whether an object may be replicated or whether to use invalidation or update to maintain consistency. In the Munin prototype, the simple annotations were useful in improving the performance of several parallel applications. From a programming perspective, the authors report that annotations were not difficult to use.

11.6 CUSTOMIZING SCHEDULING SYSTEMS

There are far fewer customized scheduling systems even though there has been much theoretical work on scheduling algorithms [SST93, FR92, ES93]. In particular, there have been few techniques to allow multiple policies to be implemented and evaluated. Sevcik [Sev89] performed a simulation study on characterizing the parallelism of an application and used the results to schedule the tasks of an application. Sevcik's simulation study considered the following parallel applications attributes.

- Average parallelism
- Average parallelism and variance of parallelism
- Average, variance, minimum, and maximum parallelism

The response time was used as the metric to differentiate among the three options. Light loads made little difference between various strategies. Heavy loads performed better when more information was used.

Although a large number of different scheduling algorithms exist, few operating systems employ more than one policy or have the ability to use different policies. Very few extensible techniques have been designed that are unique to scheduling.

Shahayog [DTJ89] is a test bed for experimenting with dynamic load-sharing policies without preemptive job transfer. It provides an interactive interface for testing various load-sharing strategies. Based on user specifications it creates independent job streams at different nodes in the system.

Other techniques, such as scheduler activations [ABLL92] and split-level scheduling [GA91], provide kernel mechanisms for designing user-level schedulers that can be customized. These mechanisms define a protocol between the kernel and a user-level threads package.

Customizing the process structure itself is not a concept that is supported in most systems. An exception is the Apertos [Yok92] operating system, which uses reflection to change the model of processes.

11.7 OBJECT-ORIENTED FRAMEWORKS

One important customization technique is object-oriented frameworks—the topic of this book. Object-oriented frameworks have typically been used to design application software. Two of the most popular frameworks have been designed and implemented for user interfaces. These are the Model/View/Controller framework [KP88] for building user interfaces for Smalltalk-80 applications, and the Unidraw framework for building graphical editors [VL89]. They have not been used to design operating system software. One of the primary goals of this book is to demonstrate the usefulness of this customization technique in designing systems software.

The work here extends previous work on object-oriented frameworks in three ways. First, the frameworks are constructed to allow easy per-application customizations. Second, customizations are implemented for improving application performance as well as providing new functionality to applications. Third, object-oriented frameworks are specifically applied to the design of message-passing and scheduling systems.

11.8 SUMMARY

Most operating systems encourage unique interfaces and implementations. The demands of new applications and hardware architecture, however, have led to a proliferation of new operating systems with new interfaces and implementations. As a result, it has been hard to standardize either interfaces or implementations. For example, the OSI reference model, which was intended to promote standards for network protocols, is rarely implemented; instead, a variety of specialized network protocols have been developed. In order to reduce the design and development costs, a variety of operating systems customization techniques have been developed. Table 11.1 summarizes some of the customization techniques and some of the systems that support these techniques. The general techniques are listed above the specialized techniques for message passing.

Object-oriented frameworks are proposed as an efficient alternative for designing extensible operating systems. An operating system that is designed using object-oriented frameworks can have its interface and implementation extended.

TABLE 11.1 A Summary of Techniques Used for Designing Customized Systems Software

Technique	System
Layers	System V Stream, THE, and Venus
Modules and Levels	Haberman's System
Virtual Machine	Haberman's System and IBM VM 370
Microkernel	MACH, Chorus, and V
Object Based	Clouds
Object Oriented	SOS
Dynamic Code Synthesis	Synthesis
Protocol Graph	*x*-kernel
Reflection, Metaobjects and Metahierarchy	Apertos
Compiler/CFG	RTAG, PDL, and Morpheus

CHAPTER 12

Conclusions

In this chapter the main features of the book are summarized and avenues for future work are discussed. The primary goal of this book is to describe a methodology for improving the performance of parallel and distributed applications using application-specific message-passing and scheduling systems. These systems were designed using object-oriented frameworks.

This book describes techniques for generating optimized message-passing and scheduling systems on a distributed system and a shared-memory multiprocessor for several different types of parallel and distributed applications. To generate these optimizations, application attributes are identified and then used to minimize operating system overheads, such as message latency. Using these attributes a tool kit of implementations is constructed. To generate an optimization for an application, its attributes are used to select from the tool kit of implementations.

To maximize application performance, one attribute—communication pattern—is particularly useful. Communication patterns are used to generate global optimizations to reduce the message-passing overheads. For example, communication patterns are used to reduce the number of acknowledgment packets in the message-passing system of a distributed system. Since communication patterns vary from application to application, message-passing system optimizations are application specific. The use of communication patterns in generating optimizations for application-specific message-passing systems on a distributed system and on a shared-memory multiprocessor is a major contribution of this book.

On the distributed system, the Fast Fourier Transform ran 29 percent faster on an optimized message-passing system than on PVM, a popular message-passing library that runs on UNIX. On a shared-memory multiprocessor, the Fast Fourier Transform performs 35 percent better on an optimized message-passing system than on an unoptimized alternative. On both the distributed system and the shared-memory multiprocessor, applications that use an optimized message-passing system scale better than unoptimized alternatives.

Just as a message-passing system is customized, the scheduling system is also customized on a per-application basis. This book demonstrates that optimized scheduling improve the performance of parallel applications. It makes two specific contributions in scheduling: (1) it describes a customizable software architecture for scheduling based on object-oriented frameworks, and (2) it generalizes the model of gang scheduling on both shared-memory multiprocessors and distributed systems. In particular, the implementation of gang scheduling on a distributed system, distributed gang scheduling, is novel. The implementation of distributed gang scheduling allows a system to coordinate the scheduling of processes of a parallel application on a network of workstations. This technique also provides dedicated access to workstations for the parallel processes of an application. Gang scheduling improves the execution time and variability of these execution times for parallel applications.

As a practical concern, as there are a large number of possible optimizations, object-oriented frameworks are employed to organize the implementations and to facilitate the choice of an implementation. Object-oriented frameworks allow the easy porting of the system software code, easy incremental development of optimizations, and easy experimentation.

The extensibility of a system is judged by the amount of work needed to create a new optimization. A new optimization can be added to the message-passing system with as few as 10 lines of new code. The elegance of the tool kit approach is that as the number of sample implementations in the tool kit increases, it becomes easier to optimize the systems software for a new application by using existing optimizations.

One of the traditional concerns with object-oriented systems is that they perform poorly. This book shows that the overhead of using virtual functions is 6 percent for the bus-based, shared-memory multiprocessor and 2 percent for the distributed system for a null message using an optimized message-passing system. As the message data set size increases, this overhead becomes smaller still. Therefore, the overhead of the object-oriented framework structure of the message-passing system is negligible.

It was demonstrated that the message-passing system can be ported easily to different architectures. As a further test of the portability of the system, it has been moved to the Intel iPSC/2 architecture with ease. More information about the comparison of the message-passing software on various architectures appears in [IMC93].

The research presented in this book can be extended in a variety of ways. Some of the techniques employed could be used on machines with reliable networks, such as the Intel Delta or Paragon. On reliable networks, it would be possible to improve the performance of the message-passing system by using application attributes to reduce the contention on the network, particularly for collective communication routines.

The pattern-based approach can be used on other types of applications. For example, multimedia applications could benefit from this approach. Media such as voice have properties that could be exploited to generate efficient message-passing systems.

The designs of the message-passing and scheduling frameworks stabilized after they were ported to several architectures and were customized for a variety of applications. It would be interesting to see how the system would adapt to applications written in quite different styles, such as those written using active messages. Additionally, it would be interesting to examine how the application characterization changes to accommodate irregular parallel applications where the communication patterns are not easily determined statically.

Irregular parallel applications suggest the need for a dynamically customizable system that can adapt itself at runtime to the needs of an application. This would entail recognizing the communication pattern of an application while it is running and then making the selection of the appropriate optimization at runtime. Although recognizing arbitrary patterns at runtime is undecidable, good heuristics likely exist for recognizing commonly occurring patterns.

Another avenue of further research involves understanding the interplay between application-level and system-level optimizations. For example, it is possible to design a system that allows one to examine a variety of application-level partitioning strategies and, for each strategy, to investigate the optimized communication strategy for that partitioning. This technique would produce a better estimate of the best execution time of a particular application on an architecture. The work of this book could therefore be incorporated with application-level restructurings presented in [KGGK94].

Another alternative is to use a language-based approach, which was hinted at in Chapter 3. A compiler would be used to generate the appropriate optimizations for applications. This will require recognizing appropriate communication patterns automatically by examining program code that is written using simple primitives, such as `send`s and `receive`s. For an implementation on a distributed system, the communication patterns would then be analyzed to find implicit acknowledgments automatically.

APPENDIX A

Comparison of Platforms

Table A.1 shows a comparison of the performance parameters of the hardware architectures and systems used in this book; Table A.2 compares the interconnection networks. These numbers are from manufacturers' specifications. The distributed system platform consists of a group of SPARCStationII's connected by an Ethernet. The bus-based, shared-memory multiprocessor is the Encore Multimax 320.

TABLE A.1 Comparison of Systems

System	Processor	Clock Rate	MIPS	Cache	OS	Coding
Multimax	NS32332	15 MHZ	2	64K	Custom	C++
SPARCStationII	SPARC	40 MHZ	28	64K (virtual)	Custom	C++
SPARCStationII	SPARC	40 MHZ	28	64K (virtual)	PVM/UNIX	C

TABLE A.2 Comparison of Interconnection Networks

System	Network	Topology	Mbits/sec	Reliable?	Routing
Multimax	Nanobus	Bus	800	Yes	Connectionless
SPARCStationII	Ethernet	Bus	10	No	Connectionless

A.1 ENCORE MULTIMAX

The Encore Multimax 320 is a shared-memory multiprocessor [Cor86]. NS32081 coprocessors provide floating point processing. Each processor accesses memory through a 64K write-through cache and a 100 Mbytes/sec bus. Cache accesses do not invoke processor wait states for main memory access and do not impose any nanobus (the processor/memory bus) traffic. The cache is thus much faster than the main memory. Maintaining locality of reference to data in the cache is an essential part of achieving high performance [HL90].

Each cache has 16-byte cache lines, and each line is divided into 4-byte entries. A read from the cache fetches 8 bytes from memory into the cache line. For two consecutive reads, the second read will access cached data. A write to the cache stores 4 bytes back into memory in the write-through. The cache RAM has an access time of 25 ns. It takes 320 ns to fetch 8 bytes to or from memory to accommodate an uncached read; if consecutive reads are to different memory banks, then the eight-way interleaved memory allows the transfer of 8 bytes every 80 ns, in the absence of bus contention. An uncached write takes 120 ns because it first reads 8 bytes of data and then changes 4 bytes of data.

A.2 SUN SPARCSTATION II

The SPARCStation II is a 40 MHz machine that has a 64K virtual write-through cache and 16 MB of physical memory. A maximum of eight machines were used for the experiments reported in this book.

Each machine is configured with an Am7990 LAN controller for IEEE-802.3/Ethernet. The LAN controller provides for 128 send and receive buffers. It may be polled or interrupt driven. The minimum packet size is 60 bytes and the maximum packet size is 1514 bytes. The driver has facilities for multicast, which is used extensively for group communication. The Ethernet has a maximum bandwidth of 10 megabits per second.

APPENDIX B

Programming Model: An Example

This appendix illustrates how to write a message-passing application using an object-oriented interface. The sample application shows how to set up two asymmetric processes: a client and a server. The code for the client is shown in Figure B.3.2, and the code for the server is shown in Figure B.2.3. The client-server application uses the RRMessage class (shown in Figure B.1.1 with its superclass Message, which was defined in Chapter 5). In this example, the server process creates a NoTypeCirc message container and gives it the character string name "Server". The NoTypeCirc automatically registers itself with the DistributedNameServer. The server process then creates an RRMessage, which allows request-response style message passing, specifying in the constructor of the class the maximum size, in bytes, of the data to be handled by this class. A pointer to a user buffer for messages leaving and entering the application is set, and the server process states that it does not want the application buffer destroyed when the RRMessage is deleted. The RRMessage supports the request-response CP. The server process then uses the method `NoTypeCirc` to set NoTypeCirc, from which messages will be received, and then invokes the rrReceive method on RRMessage and blocks, waiting for a message to arrive.

The client application asks the DistributedNameServer for a NoTypeCirc for the name "Server". It creates an RRMessage object with the same arguments to its constructor as the server process. It then sets the destination to the

```
class Message {
public:
  Message(char* initData,int initSize,int delData=1); /* default is to delete
related data */
  Message(int delData=1); /* default is to delete related data */
  ~Message();

  void setReceiveContainer(MessageContainer *);/* set receiver container */
  void setDestination(ContainerRepresentative *);/* set destination field */
  void setUserData(char *data,int size); /* set pointer to data area */
  long size(); /* size of message */
  void* data(); /* pointer to data area of msg */
  void send(); /* send the message */
  void receive(); /* send the message */
};

class RRMessage : public Message {
public:
  RRMessage(char* initData,int initSize,int delData=1); /* default is to delete
related data */
          RRMessage();
          void rr(); // client calls this function

          void reply(); // server calls this function


          void rrReceive(); // server calls this function

          void setReplyContainer(MessageContainer*); // to set reply container


};
```

FIGURE B.1 The Message and RRMessage class public method interfaces.

NoTypeCirc it received from the DistributedNameServer. Since it wants a reply, it creates its own private NoTypeCirc for receiving the reply message. This NoTypeCirc is not registered with the name service since it uses zero as an argument to its constructor. The `setReplyContainer` method is used to set this private NoTypeCirc for receiving reply messages. The application data buffer is initialized and then sent using the method `rr`. The message moves into the message-passing system framework and is received by the server process. The

```
clientProcess( int, char ** )
{
   DistributedNameServer * DNS = NameServer→
lookup("DistributedNameServer", DistributedNameServerClass);
    ContainerRepresentative * Server = DNS → lookup ("Server",
ContainerRepresentativeClass);
   MessageContainer * reccon = new NoTypeCirc (0);
    char * buf = new char[1024];
    RRMessage rmsg(buf,1024,0);
    rmsg.setReplyContainer(reccon);
    rmsg.setDestination(Server);
    strcpy(buf,"Request-Response demo");
    rmsg.setUserData (char*)buf,strlen (buf) + 1);
    rmsg.rr();/* block until reply is in buffer*/
}
```

FIGURE B.2 Request-response: Client process.

```
serverProcess(int, char **)
{
        MessageContainer * mcon = new NoTypeCirc ("Server");
        char * buf = new char[1024];
        RRMessage msg(buf,1024,0);
        while(1) {
                msg.setReceiveContainer(mcon);
                msg.setUserData((char*)buf,1024);
                msg.rrReceive();/* wait for message*/
                strcpy(buf,"thanks");
                msg.setUserData((char*)buf,strlen(buf) +1);
                msg.reply(); /*Send reply to the client*/
        }
        return 0;
}
```

FIGURE B.3 Request-response: Server process.

server modifies the buffer and sends it back using the `reply` method. The client call to the `rr` method returns with the data buffer overwritten with the reply message from the server. The server does not need to explicitly locate a ContainerRepresentative to communicate with the client since the reference to the remote NoTypeCirc is transparently managed by the message-passing system.

B.1 GANGS

This section describes how to program distributed Gangs.

```
enum LTSTYPE{ Multi,RemoteExclusive };
class DistGang {
  DistGang( LTSTYPE, unsigned int waittime );
        ~DistGang();
// Applications programmer invokes these methods.

         virtual int dispatch();
         virtual void add(char *newMember);
         virtual void conc(int machNum);

// only the kernel scheduler calls this method
         virtual void scheduleMembers();
};
```

Using the DistGang interface, a user specifies which application program to run and the number of requested processors. For a distributed gang, a processor is the same as a machine or workstations. Workstations are selected automatically given the preferences and requirements of the user. Gangs may be run in exclusive mode (preferred by scientists running parallel numerical applications) or in a partition of workstations that is multiprogrammed between a variety of users. A programmer specifies the name of the program to run.

The applications are SPMD (single program, multiple data stream) programs and the maximum number of processors that they will need during their execution is known a priori. Depending on availability, the *Choices* execution environment may or may not choose to grant the requested number of processors. The return value from dispatch specifies the number of actual processors granted; if it does not, a processor will be multiprogrammed with two or more of the application's processes.

The following is a code fragment for programming a gang on a distributed system. It requests that the program be run on two idle processors. If fewer than two idle processors are found at runtime, then one node is multiprogrammed with the two application processes.

```
DistGang* g =  new DistGang(RemoteExclusive,TIME_OUT);
               // exclusive use of idle processors
               // and timeout service request
g->conc(2);    // number of nodes requested

g->add("FFTProgram");

int granted = g->dispatch();
               // gang now joins the long term scheduler
```

Glossary of Terms

Abstract class A class that only specifies an interface and is not meant to be instantiated. By subclassing an abstract class one can achieve interface sharing.

Application programming interface The interface presented to application programmers by an operating system for accessing system services.

Application-specific software Software that can be designed to suit the needs of applications.

Blast protocols A class of network protocols in which a large message is packetized into smaller packets and, instead of acknowledging each individual network packet, the entire set of packets is acknowledged.

Bus-based, shared-memory multiprocessor A multiprocessor in which a single globally addressable memory is accessed through a bus.

Class A template for building similar objects [Nie89]. A class specifies the instance variables and operations common to all objects belonging to that class.

Data abstraction is supported by classes since they describe the structure and behavior of a set of objects [GR83, Str91]. Classes allow programmers to extend the set of built-in types provided by the programming language. Classes differ from traditional user-defined type mechanisms because they support the notion of subtypes [Nie89]. A class is a subtype of a second class if instances of the first class can be used where instances of the second class are expected.

Class hierarchies Class hierarchies consist of abstract classes, often at the root of the hierarchy, and concrete subclasses, often at the leaves. In class hierarchies, abstract classes are shown in italics and concrete classes are shown in bold. In this book, all class names appear in sans serif font and all method names appear in `teletype` font. C++ class definitions are used to describe in more detail the public member functions of individual classes.

Collective communication A style of communication in which a group of processes communicates as part of a single primitive. Typically, this form of communication is atomic; either all participating processes communicate successfully or they fail.

Concrete class A subclass of an abstract class that implements the operations specified by a superclass. By subclassing a concrete class one can achieve both interface and code sharing. In practice, many classes both specify an interface for subclasses and provide an implementation of that interface. A concrete class must have an implementation for all methods either through inheritance or its own implementation (overloading). In C++ the virtual functions of a parent class are overloaded.

Connection management On distributed systems, the implementation of a message-passing protocol requires the use of connection management and error handling because the underlying network hardware is unreliable. Connection management and error handling techniques affect the performance of parallel and distributed applications running on distributed systems.

Data encapsulation Data encapsulation requires two features. First, state changes on objects must occur through the invocation of operations only. Second, systems are decomposed into objects insulated from other objects.

In C++ [Str91], invoking an operation on an object is equivalent to calling a member function (or method) on that object. Public member functions define an object's interface protocol.

Direct memory access (DMA) Allows I/O on a bus to access memory without interfering with the CPU.

Direct virtual memory access (DVMA) Allows I/O on a bus to access virtual memory addresses without interfering with the CPU.

Distributed applications Distributed applications are often written for fault tolerance, availability, and resource sharing. The recent increase in the number of distributed systems, however, has made the design of high-performance distributed applications important. System services are important distributed applications. Examples include file servers, name servers, and distributed scheduling facilities. Other types of distributed applications include those that support collaborative work and distributed databases. Several computer architectures support parallel and distributed applications.

Distributed-memory multicomputer A parallel system that has physically separate memories and a reliable communication network. Communication is through message passing. Examples include Intel's iPSC/2 and Paragon machines, and IBM's SP2.

New scalable shared-memory architectures have physically distributed memories and point-to-point communication networks for which the hardware provides a single shared address space. Communication on these architectures is through shared variables.

Distributed system A group of computers, including workstations, connected by a local area network (LAN), such as an Ethernet [Tan92]. Distributed systems are often called *loosely connected* because of the high latency of their interconnect. They often support many independent users working on different problems. Each node of a distributed system has a physically separate memory. The network is unreliable; that is, messages can be lost in transit. Such systems implement software measures to guarantee the reliable delivery of data. Communication on a distributed system is usually through message passing.

Ethernet A popular LAN technology that has a 10 Mbit/sec bandwidth. It has a CSMA/CD bus.

Gang scheduling A resource allocation technique that improves the performance of parallel applications. Gang scheduling and co-scheduling attempt to schedule the processes of an application on the various nodes of a computer at approximately the same time.

Group management Must be known before a group of processes can participate in group communication.

There are two types of group management algorithms: static and dynamic. In a static group, membership of the group is known at the time the group is created. In a dynamic group, members enter and leave the group while the application is executing. There are two types of dynamic groups: groups in which exact membership information is not necessary, and groups in which exact membership information is required.

Interconnection network The underlying network that connects machines. Common network topologies include buses, hypercubes, and meshes.

Interface and code sharing Classes have member functions or methods that define their interface. Classes can belong to a class hierarchy and share structural and behavioral descriptions through inheritance. Within a hierarchy, a subclass or derived class can inherit methods and data from one or more base classes or superclasses.

Internet protocol (IP) The Internet standard protocol that enables the sending of datagrams between hosts on interconnected networks. It provides a connectionless, best-effort delivery service. The IP and ICMP control protocols are the building blocks for other protocols such as TCP and UDP.

Message passing A style of interprocess communication in which processes send discrete messages to one another. These processes typically do not share memory.

Parallel and distributed applications are structured as processes that communicate to exchange data and synchronize. Message-passing systems enable the processes of parallel and distributed applications to communicate.

In the message-passing paradigm, the programmer must explicitly insert instructions in the application to move the data (for example, by using a `send` call) to another process and accept data (for example, by using a `receive` call) from another process. The `send` and `receive` calls are implemented by a message-passing system.

When two processes communicate, one process invokes the `send` operation on the channel or port, and the other process invokes a `receive` operation on the same channel or port. Messages that are sent but not yet received are put in the message queue associated with that port or channel.

MPI A message-passing interface under consideration for standardization.

Multicast A type of collective communication in which more than one process sends a message to a group of processes.

Node Basic computing block of a multicomputer or a distributed system. Typically, a node refers to a processor with a memory system and a mechanism for communicating.

Nonblocking An operation that does not block the execution of the process using it.

Object An object consists of state data and a set of operations on those data.

Object-based programming A programming model supporting data abstraction.

Object-oriented framework A set of cooperating classes that make up a reusable design for a specific class of software. For example, frameworks can be geared toward operating systems, graphical editors, or programming languages. A framework may make use of tool kit libraries.

Object-oriented frameworks add another dimension to the design of object-oriented software by describing how classes and objects interact. An object-oriented framework is an architectural design for object-oriented systems. By simplifying the construction of the customized system software support for applications, it enables the creation of efficient application-specific software.

Object-oriented programming A programming model supported by data abstraction, polymorphism, and inheritance. The following programming techniques are used to create object-oriented frameworks: data encapsulation, data abstraction, polymorphism, and interface and code sharing.

Object-oriented programming language A language that supports data abstraction, polymorphism, and inheritance. Examples include C++, Smalltalk, and Self.

Packet A quantity of data sent over the network.

Parallel applications Applications whose processes are fairly tightly synchronized and work together to perform a task. The main decomposition for performance.

Parallel program The main purpose of writing a parallel program is to reduce the execution time of an application. Parallel applications have been used to solve many scientific and numerical problems, such as the wave and Laplace equations.

There are a variety of models for expressing parallelism in an application, some of which have been influenced by computer architectures. In particular, Flynn's taxonomy of computer architecture has led to several popular models.

Parallel system Typically, a set of CPUs connected by a special-purpose interconnection network. Parallel systems are often called *tightly connected* because there is a low-latency interconnect between CPUs. Parallel systems are used primarily to increase the performance of individual applications, with the operating system providing dedicated resources to the application.

Parallel virtual machine (PVM) A message-passing library for writing parallel programs on networks of workstations.

Polymorphism Polymorphic base class interfaces allow objects to be manipulated uniformly, although they can be instances of either the base class or any derived class [Jor90]. In object-oriented languages, dynamic binding mechanisms support polymorphism. In C++, the virtual function mechanism supports dynamic binding of methods and hence supports polymorphism. The actual method invoked depends on the instance of the derived class that is being used. New derived classes can be defined and easily incorporated into a system since existing software expects the interface of the base class.

Ports The endpoints of communication in message-passing systems.

Process An address space, I/O state, and one or more threads.

Protection If the logically separate processes involved in message passing are in separate protection domains, then the message-passing system allows information to pass from one protection domain to another. The implementation of the message-passing system must ensure that protection violations do not occur as messages pass from one protection domain to another. Protection can be sacrificed to gain performance when communication occurs between processes of the same application. Performance improvements can be obtained by implementing the message-passing system at user level.

Protocols To move a message between processes, a protocol must be obeyed between the sending and the receiving processes. It is the job of the message-passing system to implement this protocol on behalf of application processes. Message-passing protocols can be implemented on a shared-memory multiprocessor, a distributed-memory multicomputer, or a distributed system.

Remote procedure call (RPC) Many distributed applications require request-response style message passing. Request-response style message passing is often used to support the language level mechanism known as remote procedure call [BN84].

Semaphore A data type for controlling concurrency. A semaphore is initialized to an integer value. Two operations, P and V, may be applied to it. P increments the semaphore's value by one, and V blocks its caller until the semaphore's value is greater than zero, then decrements the semaphore.

Shared memory A style of communication in which two processes exchange information through mutually accessible memory.

Speedup Speedup as used in this book is defined as follows:

$$\text{Speedup} = \frac{T(1)}{T(N)}.$$

In this definition, the speedup for N processors is the ratio of the time to execute the same application code on one processor, T(1), divided by the time spent on N processors, $T(N)$.

Tool kit libraries A library made from predefined classes that can be used to design an application. Unlike frameworks, they do not encode design decisions.

Transmission control protocol (TCP) Part of the Internet protocol suite. Delivers messages reliably and in sequence.

User datagram protocol (UDP) Part of the Internet protocol suite. A simple protocol that allows delivery of messages over low-level protocols such as IP. It can duplicate or lose messages.

Bibliography

[ABLL92] T. Anderson, Brian Bershad, Edward Lazowska, and Henry Levy. Scheduler Activations: Effective Kernel Support for the User Level Management of Parallelism. *ACM Transactions on Computing Systems*, 10(2):53–79, February 1992.

[Agh86] Gul Agha. *ACTORS: A Model of Concurrent Computation in Distributed Systems*. MIT Press, Cambridge, Mass., 1986.

[AHP92] G. Agha, C. Houck, and R. Panwar. Distributed Execution of Actor Systems. In D. Gelernter, T. Gross, A. Nicolau, and D. Padua, editors, *Languages and Compilers for Parallel Computing*, pages 1–17. Springer-Verlag, 1992. Lecture Notes in Computer Science 589.

[AL81] T. Anderson and P. A. Lee. *Fault Tolerance, Principles and Practice*. Prentice Hall International, 1981.

[And90] Thomas E. Anderson. The Performance of Spin Lock Alternatives for Shared-Memory Multiprocessors. *IEEE Transactions on Parallel and Distributed Systems*, 1(1):6–16, January 1990.

[And91a] Thomas E. Anderson. Operating System Support for High Performance Multiprocessing. Technical Report 91-08-10, University of Washington, Seattle, Wash., August 1991.

[And91b] Gregory R. Andrews. Paradigms for Process Interaction in Distributed Programs. *ACM Computing Surveys*, 23(1):49–90, March 1991.

[ASU87] Alfred Aho, Ravi Sethi, and Jeffrey Ullman. *Compilers, Principles, Techniques and Tools*. Addison Wesley, Reading, Mass., 1987.

[Bac86] Maurice J. Bach. *The Design of the UNIX Operating System*. Prentice Hall, Englewood Cliffs, N.J., 1986.

[BALL91] Brian Bershad, T. Anderson, Edward Lazowska, and Henry Levy. User Level Interprocess Communication for Shared Memory Multiprocessors. *ACM Transactions on Computing Systems*, 9(2):175–198, May 1991.

[BCM94] E. Barton, J. Cownie, and M. McLaren. Message Passing on the Meiko CS-2. *Parallel Computing*, 20(4), 1994.

[BHM77] Forest Baskett, J. H. Howard, and John T. Montague. Task Communication in DEMOS. *ACM Operating Systems Review*, pages 23–31, November 1977.

[BJ87] Kenneth P. Birman and Thomas A. Joseph. Exploiting Virtual Synchrony in Distributed Systems. In *Proceedings of the 11th ACM Symposium on Operating Systems Principles*, pages 123–138, Austin, Tex., November 1987. ACM.

[BKT92] Henri Bal, Frans Kaashoek, and Andrew Tanenbaum. Orca: A Language for Parallel Programming of Distributed Systems. *IEEE Transactions on Software Engineering*, pages 190–205, March 1992.

[Bla90] David Black. Scheduling Support for Concurrency and Parallelism in the Mach Operating System. *IEEE Computer*, pages 35–43, 1990.

[BN84] Andrew D. Birell and Bruce J. Nelson. Implementing Remote Procedure Calls. In *ACM Transactions on Computer Systems*, February 1984.

[BPG+94] Mike Barnett, David Payne, Satya Gupta, Lance Shuller, Robert van de Geijn, and Jerell Watts. Interprocessor Collective Communication Library. In *Proceedings of SHPCC'94*, 1994.

[BSS91] Kenneth Birman, Andre Schiper, and Pat Stephenson. Lightweight Causal and Atomic Group Multicast. *ACM Transactions on Computer Systems*, 9(3):272–314, August 1991.

[CBZ91] John B. Carter, John K. Bennett, and Willy Zwaenepoel. Implementation and Performance of Munin. *Proceedings of the 13th ACM Symposium on Operating Systems Principles*, 25(5):152–164, October 1991.

[CG90] Nicholas Carriero and David Gelernter. *How to Write Parallel Programs*. MIT Press, Cambridge, Mass., 1990.

[Che86a] David Cheriton. Problem Oriented Shared Memory: A Decentralised Approach to Distributed System Design. In *6th International Conference on Distributed Computing Systems*, 1986.

[Che86b] David R. Cheriton. VMTP: A Transport Protocol for the Next Generation of Communication Systems. In *SICOMM'86 Conference*, Stowe, Vt., August 1986. ACM.

[Che88a] David Cheriton. The V Distributed System. *Communications of the ACM*, pages 314–334, 1988.

[Che88b] David R. Cheriton. VMTP: Versatile Message Transaction Protocol. In *RFC: 1045*, February 1988.

[CI92] Roy H. Campbell and Nayeem Islam. A Technique for Documenting the Framework of an Object-Oriented System. In *Proceedings Second International Workshop on Object-Orientation in Operating Systems*, Paris, France, September 1992.

[CI93a] Roy Campbell and Nayeem Islam. *Choices*: A Parallel Object-Oriented Operating System. In Gul Agha, Peter Wegner, and Akinori Yonezawa, editors, *Research Directions in Concurrent Object-Oriented Programming*. MIT Press, Cambridge, Mass., 1993.

[CI93b] Roy H. Campbell and Nayeem Islam. A Technique for Documenting the Framework of an Object-Oriented System. *Computing Systems*, 6(4), 1993.

[CIM92] Roy H. Campbell, Nayeem Islam, and Peter Madany. *Choices*, Frameworks and Refinement. *Computing Systems*, 5(3), 1992.

[CIMR93] Roy Campbell, Nayeem Islam, Peter Madany, and David Raila. Designing and Implementing *Choices*: an Object-Oriented System in C++, pages 117–126, 1993.

[CK88] Casavant and Kuhl. A Taxonomy of Scheduling in General-purpose Distributed Computing Systems. In *IEEE Transactions on Software Engineering*, pages 141–154, February 1988.

[Clo86] Paul Close. The iPSC/2 Node Architecture. In *Proceedings 3rd International Conference on Hypercube Concurrent Computers and Applications*, January 1986.

[CM84] J. M. Chang and N. F. Maxemchuck. Reliable Broadcast Protocols. In *ACM Transactions on Computer Systems*, volume 2, pages 251–273, August 1984.

[Com89] Intel Scientific Computers. *Intel-iPSC/2 Concurrent Programming*, volumes 1 and 2. Intel, Beaverton, Ore., 1989.

[Cor86] Encore Computer Corp. *Multimax Technical Summary*. Encore, Marlborough, Mass., 1986.

[Cor88] Parasoft Corporation. *Express Version 1.0: A Communication Environment for Parallel Computers*. Parasoft, 1988.

[Cor89] Thinking Machines Corporation. *CM Fortran Reference Manual, Version 5.2*. Thinking Machines Corporation, 1989.

[Cor91] Thinking Machines Corporation. *CM-5 Technical Summary*. Thinking Machines Corporation, 1991.

[Cor92] Thinking Machines Corporation. *CMMD 2.0 Reference Manual*. Thinking Machines Corporation, 1992.

[CR86] Roy Campbell and Brian Randell. Error Recovery in Asynchronous Systems. In *IEEE Transactions on Software Engineering*, pages 811–826, August 1986.

[CZ85] David Cheriton and Willy Zwaenepoel. Distributed Process Groups in the V Kernel. In *ACM Transactions on Computing Systems*, 3(2):77–107, May 1985.

[Deu89] L. Peter Deutsch. Design Reuse and Frameworks in the Smalltalk-80 Programming System. In Ted J. Biggerstaff and Alan J. Perlis, editors, *Software Reusability*, volume II, pages 55–71. ACM Press, Reading, Mass., 1989.

[DLA88] P. Dasgupta, R. J. LeBlanc, and W. F. Appelbe. The Clouds Distributed Operating System: Functional Description, Implementation Details and Related Work. In *Proceedings of the 8th International Conference on Distributed Computing Systems*, pages 2–9. IEEE, June 1988.

[DP93] Peter Druschel and Larry L. Petersen. Fbufs: A High-Bandwidth Cross-Domain Transfer Facility. In *Proceedings of the 14th ACM Symposium on Operating Systems Principles*, pages 189–202, Asheville, N.C., December 1993. ACM.

[Dra90] Richard Draves. A Revised IPC Interface. *USENIX MACH Workshop Proceedings*, pages 101–121, 1990.

[DSS90] Sean M. Dorward, Ravi Sethi, and Jonathan E. Shopiro. Adding New Code to a Running C++ Program. In *Proceedings of the USENIX* C++ *Conference*, pages 279–292, San Francisco, Calif., April 1990.

[DTJ89] Piyush Dikshit, Satish Tripathi, and Pankaj Jalote. SHAHAYOG: A Test Bed for Evaluating Dynamic Load-sharing Policies. *Software Practice and Experience*, 19(5), May 1989.

[Dyk68] Edsger W. Dykstra. The Structure of THE Multiprogramming System. *Communications of the ACM*, pages 341–346, May 1968.

[ea74] William Wulf et al. HYDRA: The Kernel of a Multiprocessor Operating System. *Communications of the ACM*, pages 337–345, 1974.

[ES93] Kemal Efe and Margaret Schaar. Performance of Co-Scheduling on a Network of Workstations. In *Proceedings of 13th International Conference on Distributed Computing Systems*, 1993.

[Fei94] Dror G. Feitelson. A Survey of Scheduling in Multiprogrammed Parallel Systems. Technical Report RC-19790, IBM T. J. Watson Research Center, Yorktown Heights, N.Y., December 1994.

[Fel93] Edward W. Felten. *Protocol Compilation: High-Performance Communication for Parallel Programs*. Ph.D. thesis, University of Washington, Seattle, Wash., September 1993.

[FJL+88] Geoffrey Fox, Mark Johnson, Gregory Lyzenga, Steve Otto, John Salmon, and David Walker. *Solving Problems on Concurrent Processors*, volume 1. Prentice Hall, Engelwood Cliffs, N.J., 1988.

[For90] High Performance Fortran Forum. *C* Programming Guide (Version 6.0)*. August 1990.

[FR90] Dror Feitelson and Larry Rudolph. Distributed Hierarchical Control for Parallel Processing. *IEEE Computer*, 1990.

[FR92] Dror Feitelson and Larry Rudolph. Gang Scheduling Performance Benefits for Fine-Grain Synchronization. *Journal of Parallel and Distributed Computing*, 1992.

[GA91] Ramesh Govindan and David Anderson. Scheduling and IPC Mechanisms for Continuous Media. In *Proceedings of the 13th ACM Symposium on Operating Systems Principles*, pages 68–80, Pacific Grove, Calif., October 1991. ACM.

[GHPW91] Al Geist, Michael Heath, B. W. Peyton, and P. H. Worley. A User's Guide to PICL, a Portable Instrumented Communication Library. Technical Report ORNL-TM-11616, Oak Ridge National Laboratory, Oak Ridge, Tenn., 1991.

[Gir88] Gintaras R. Gircys. *Understanding and Using COFF*. O'Reilly and Associates, Inc., Newton, Mass., 1988.

[GL89] Charles Golub and Van Loan. *Matrix Computations*. Johns Hopkins University Press, Baltimore, Md., 1989.

[GLR83] Gottlieb, Lubachevsky, and Rudolph. Basic Techniques for the Efficient Coordination of Very Large Numbers of Cooperating Sequential Processors. In *ACM Transactions on Programming Languages and Systems*, pages 164–189. April 1983. ACM.

[Gos91] A. Goscinski. *Distributed Operating Systems: The Logical Design*. Addison-Wesley, Sydney, Australia, 1991.

[GR83] Adele Goldberg and David Robson. *Smalltalk-80: The Language and Its Implementation*. Addison-Wesley, Reading, Mass., 1983.

[Gro93] Object Management Group. *Common Object Request Broker Architecture and Specification*. OMG Document, 1993.

[GVV89] Jeffrey Goodman, Mary Vernon, and Philip Voest. Efficient Synchronization Primitives for Large-Scale Cache-Coherent Multiprocessors. In *Third International Conference on Architectural Support for Programming Languages and Operating Systems*, pages 64–73. April 1989. ACM.

[HE91] Michael Heath and J. A. Etheridge. Visualizing the Performance of Parallel Programs. Technical Report TM-11813, Oak Ridge National Laboratory, Oak Ridge, Tenn., May 1991.

[HFC72] A. N. Haberman, L. Flon, and L. Cooprider. Modularization and Hierarchy in a Family of Operating Systems. *Communications of the ACM*, 15(12), 1972.

[HK93] Graham Hamilton and Panagiotis Kougiiouris. The Spring Nucleus: A microkernel for Objects. In *Proceedings of Summer 1993 USENIX*, Cincinnati, Ohio, June 1993. USENIX.

[HKT91a] S. Hiranandani, Ken Kennedy, and Chau-Wen Tseng. *Compiler Support for Machine-Independent Parallel Programming in Fortran D*. Elsevier, Amsterdam, 1991.

[HKT91b] Seema Hiranandani, Ken Kennedy, and Chau-Wen Tseng. Compiler Optimizations for Fortran D on MIMD Distributed-Memory Machine. In *Proceedings of Supercomputing 1991 Conference*, pages 86–100, 1991.

[HL90] Mark Hill and James Larus. Cache Considerations for Multiprocessor Programmers. In *Communications of the ACM*, pages 97–102, 1990.

[HP91] Norman Hutchinson and Larry Peterson. The *x*-kernel: An Architecture for Implementing Network Protocols. In *IEEE Transactions on Software Engineering*, 17(1):64–75, January 1991.

[HPAO89] Norman Hutchinson, Larry Peterson, Mark Abbott, and Sean O'Malley. RPC in the *x*-kernel: Evaluating New Design Techniques. In *Proceedings of the 12th ACM Symposium on Operating Systems Principles*, 23(5):91–101, December 1989.

[HPM93] Graham Hamilton, Michael Powell, and James Mitchell. Subcontract: A Flexible Base for Distributed Programming. In *Proceedings of the 14th ACM Symposium on Operating Systems Principles*, pages 69–79, Asheville, N.C., December 1993. ACM.

[HQ91] Hatcher and Quin. *Data-Parallel Programming on MIMD Computers*. MIT Press, Cambridge, Mass., 1991.

[I+95] Nayeem Islam et al. Communication Compilation for Unreliable Networks. Technical Report UIUCDCS-11616, University of Illinois at Urbana-Champaign, Urbana, Ill., 1995.

[IC92a] Nayeem Islam and Roy H. Campbell. Design Considerations for Shared Memory Multiprocessor Message Systems. In *IEEE Transactions on Parallel and Distributed Systems*, pages 702–711, November 1992.

[IC92b] Nayeem Islam and Roy H. Campbell. Reusable Data Flow Diagrams. Technical Report UIUCDCS-R-92-1770, University of Illinois at Urbana-Champaign, Urbana, Ill., November 1992.

[IL90] John A. Interrante and Mark A. Linton. Run-time Access to Type Information in C++. In *Proceedings of the USENIX C++ Conference*, pages 233–240, San Francisco, Calif., April 1990.

[IMC93] Nayeem Islam, Robert E. McGrath, and Roy Campbell. Parallel Distributed Application Performance and Message Passing: A Case Study. In *Symposium on Experiences with Distributed and Multiprocessor Systems IV*, pages 73–88, San Diego, Calif., September 1993.

[Inc90] Sun Microsytems Inc. *Network Programming Guide*. Sun Microsystems Inc., Mountain View, Calif., 1990.

[Isl90] Nayeem Islam. The XView User Interface Toolkit Object Model. In *EUUG (European USENIX)*, pages 139–150, Munich, Germany, April 1990.

[Jac86] Herb Jacobs. A User-tunable Multiple Processor Scheduler. In *1986 Winter USENIX Conference Proceedings*, pages 183–191, January 1986.

[Jor90] David Jordan. Implementation Benefits of C++ Language Mechanisms. *Communications of the ACM*, 33(9):61–67, September 1990.

[JZ93] David Johnson and Willy Zwaenepoel. The Peregrine High Performance RPC System. In *Software Practice and Experience*, pages 201–221, John Wiley, New York, 1993.

[KGGK94] Vipin Kumar, Ananth Grama, Anshul Gupta, and George Karypis. *Introduction to Parallel Computing*. Benjamin/Cummins Publishing Company, Reading, Mass., 1994.

[KL87] R. Kain and L. Landwehr. On Access Checking in Capability-Based Systems. In *IEEE Transactions on Software Engineering*, pages 202–207, February 1987.

[KP88] Glen E. Krasner and Stephen T. Pope. A Cookbook for Using the Model-View-Controller Paradigm in Smalltalk-80. *Journal of Object-Oriented Programming*, pages 26–49, 1988.

[KRST93] M. Frans Kaashoek, Robert Van Renesse, Hans Van Staveren, and Andrew Tanenbaum. FLIP: An Internetwork Protocol for Supporting Distributed Systems. In *ACM Transactions on Computer Systems*, volume 11, pages 73–106, February 1993.

[KT91] M. Frans Kaashoek and Andrew Tanenbaum. Group Communication in the Amoeba Distributed Operating System. In *Proceedings of the 1991 International Conference on Distributed Computing Systems*, pages 222–230, 1991. IEEE.

[KTHB89] M. Frans Kaashoek, Andrew Tanenbaum, S. Flynn Hummel, and H. E. Bal. An Efficient Reliable Broadcast Protocol. In *Operating Systems Review*, pages 5–20, October 1989. IEEE.

[LAD$^+$92] Mark Leiserson, Z. S. Abuhamdeh, D. C. Douglas, C. R. Feynman, M. N. Ganmukhi, J. V. Hill, W. D. Hillis, B. C. Kuszmaul, M. A. St. Pierre, D. S. Wells, M. C. Wong, S-W Yang, and R. Zak. The Network Architecture of the Connection Machine CM-5. In *4th Symposium on Parallel Architectures and Algorithms*, pages 272–285, June 1992. IEEE.

[LeB86] T. J. LeBlanc. Shared Memory Versus Message Passing in a Tightly Coupled Multiprocessor: A Case Study. In *Proceedings of the 1986 International Conference on Parallel Processing*, pages 463–466, 1986. ACM and IEEE.

[Lis72] Barbara Liskov. The Design of the Venus Operating System. *Communications of the ACM*, pages 144–149, March 1972.

[LLM88] Michael Litzkow, Miron Livny, and Matt Mutka. Condor: A Hunter of Idle Workstations. In *Proceedings of the 8th International Conference on Distributed Computing Systems*, pages 104–111, 1988. IEEE.

[Lop91] Keith Lopere. Mach 3 Kernel Principles. *OSF*, 1991.

[LS90] Calvin Lin and Lawrence Snyder. A Comparison of Programming Models for Shared Memory Multiprocessors. In *Proceedings of the 1990 International Conference on Parallel Processing*, pages 163–170, August 1990.

[Mae87] Pattie Maes. Concepts and Experiments in Computational Reflection. In *Proceedings of OOPSLA '87*, pages 147–155, Orlando, Fla., October 1987.

[MB80] G. Myers and B. Buckinham. A Hardware Implementation of Capability-Based Addressing. In *Operating Systems Review*, pages 13–25, October 1980.

[MB91] Jeffrey Mogul and Anita Borg. The Effect of Context Switches on Cache Performance. In *Fourth International Conference on Architectural Support for Programming Languages and Operating Systems*, pages 75–84, 1991. ACM.

[MB93] Chris Maeda and Brian Bershad. Protocol Service Decomposition for High-Performance Networking. In *Proceedings of the 14th ACM Symposium on Operating Systems Principles*, pages 244–255, Asheville, N.C., December 1993. ACM.

[MCS91] John M. Mellor-Crummey and Michael L. Scott. Algorithms for Scalable Synchronization in Shared-Memory Multiprocessors. In *ACM Transactions on Computer Systems*, 9(1):21–65, February 1991.

[Mey92] Scott Meyers. *Effective C++*. Addison-Wesley Publishing Company, Reading, Mass., 1992.

[MII89] H. Miyata, T. Isonishi, and A. Iwase. Fast Fourier Transformation Using Cellular Array Processor. In *Parallel Processing Symposium JSPP 1989*, pages 297–304, February 1989.

[MIKC92] Peter Madany, Nayeem Islam, Panayotis Kougiouris, and Roy H. Campbell. Practical Examples of Reification and Reflection in C++. In *International Workshop on Reflection and Meta-Level Architecture*, pages 76–81, November 1992.

[Moh84] Joseph Mohan. *Performance of Parallel Programs: Models and Analyses*. Ph.D. thesis, Carnegie Mellon University, Philadelphia, Pa., July 1984.

[MP89] Henry Massalin and Calton Pu. Threads and Input/Output in the Synthesis Kernel. In *Proceedings of the 12th ACM Symposium on Operating Systems Principles*, pages 191–201, Litchfield Park, Ariz., December 1989. ACM.

[MS91] Hector Garcia Molina and Anne M. Spauster. Ordered and Reliable Multicast Communication. *ACM Transactions on Computer Systems*, 9(3):272–314, August 1991.

[MSMA90] P. Melliar-Smith, Louise Moser, and Vivek Agrawala. Broadcast Protocols for Distributed Systems. In *IEEE Transactions on Parallel and Distributed Systems*, 1(1):17–25, January 1990.

[Mul89] Sape Mullender. Interprocess Communication. In Sape Mullender, editor, *Distributed Systems*, pages 37–64. ACM Press, Reading, Mass., 1989.

[Nie89] Oscar Nierstrasz. A Survey of Object-Oriented Concepts. In Won Kim and Frederick H. Lochovsky, editors, *Object-Oriented Concepts, Databases, and Applications*, pages 3–22. Addison-Wesley, Reading, Mass., 1989.

[O'M90] Sean O'Malley. *Avoca: An Environment for Programming with Protocols*. Ph.D. thesis, University of Arizona, September 1990.

[Ous82] John K. Ousterhout. Scheduling Techniques for Concurrent Systems. In *Third International Conference on Distributed Computing Systems*, pages 22–30, July 1982.

[Pie86] Paul Pierce. The NX/2 Operating System. In *Proceedings 3rd International Conference on Hypercube Concurrent Computers and Applications*, January 1986.

[PM91] Calton Pu and Henry Massalin. Quaject Composition in the Synthesis Kernel. In *Proceedings First International Workshop on Object-Orientation in Operating Systems*, pages 29–34, 1991.

[PMI88] Calton Pu, Henry Massalin, and John Ioannidis. The Synthesis Kernel. *Computing Systems*, 1(1):12–32, 1988.

[Pre87] Roger Pressman. *Software Engineering*. McGraw Hill, New York, N.Y., 1987.

[PS85] James L. Peterson and Abraham Silberschatz. *Operating System Concepts*. Addison-Wesley, Reading, Mass., 1985.

[PV81] Franco Preparata and Jean Vuillemin. The Cube-Connected Cycles: A Versatile Network for Parallel Computation. *Communications of the ACM*, pages 300–309, May 1981.

[RAA+88] M. Rozier, V. Abrossimov, F. Armand, I. Boule, M. Gien, M. Guillemont, F. Herrmann, C. Kaiser, S. Lanlois, P. Leònard, and W. Neuhauser. CHORUS Distributed Operating Systems. *Computing Systems*, 1(4), 1988.

[Ras86] Richard Rashid. Threads of a New System. *UNIX Review*, 1986.

[RF77] Manfred Rushitzka and R. S. Fabry. A Unifying Approach to Scheduling. *Communications of the ACM*, 20(7):469–477, 1977.

[Rit84] Dennis Ritchie. A Stream Input-Output System. *AT&T Bell Laboratories Technical Journal*, 63:311–324, October 1984.

[RMC90] Vincent F. Russo, Peter W. Madany, and Roy H. Campbell. C++ and Operating Systems Performance: A Case Study. In *Proceedings of the USENIX C++ Conference*, pages 103–114, San Francisco, Calif., April 1990.

[Rus91] Vincent F. Russo. *An Object-Oriented Operating System*. Ph.D. thesis, University of Illinois at Urbana-Champaign, Urbana, Ill., January 1991.

[SA89] Mark Sullivan and David Anderson. Marionette: a System for Parallel Distributed Programming. In *Proceedings of the 9th International Conference on Distributed Computing Systems*, pages 181–188, 1989. IEEE.

[SD74] S. E. Madnick and J. J. Donovan. Virtual Machine/370. In *Operating Systems*, pages 549–563. McGraw-Hill, New York, N.Y., 1974.

[Sev89] Kenneth Sevcik. Characterizations of Parallelism in Applications and Their Use in Scheduling. *International Conference on Measurement and Modeling of Computer Systems*, pages 171–180, 1989.

[SGH+89] March Shapiro, Yvon Gourhant, Sabine Habert, Laurence Mosseri, Michel Ruffin, and Celine Valot. SOS: An Object-Oriented Operating System—Assessment and Perspectives. *Computing Systems*, 2(4), 1989.

[Smi82] Brian C. Smith. *Reflection and Semantics in a Procedural Langauge*. Ph.D. thesis, Massachusetts Institute of Technology, Cambridge, Mass., January 1982.

[SST93] Sanjeev Setia, Mark Squillante, and Satish Tripathi. Processor Scheduling on Multiprogrammed Distributed Memory Parallel Comptuers. In *Proceedings of the 1993 ACM Sigmetrics Conference*, 1993.

[Str91] Bjarne Stroustrup. *The C++ Programming Language*. Addison-Wesley, Reading, Mass., 1991.

[Stu88a] Michael Stumm. The Design and Implementation of a Decentralized Scheduling Facility for a Workstation Cluster. In *Proceedings of the 2nd IEEE Conference on Computer Workstations*, pages 12–22, 1988.

[Stu88b] Craig B. Stunkel. Linear Optimization via Message-Based Parallel Processing. In *Proceedings of 1988 International Conference on Parallel Processing*, pages 264–271, August 1988.

[Sun90] V. S. Sunderam. PVM: A Framework for Parallel Distributed Computing. *Concurrency Practice and Experience*, 2(4):315–339, December 1990.

[TA91] S. Y. Tzou and David Anderson. A Performance Evaluation of the Dash Message Passing System. In *Software Practice and Experience*, pages 1631–1644. John Wiley, New York, N.Y., 1991.

[Tan92] Andrew Tanenbaum. *Modern Operating Systems*. Prentice Hall, Englewood Cliffs, N.J., 1992.

[TG89] A. Tucker and A. Gupta. Process Control and Scheduling Issues for Multiprogrammed Shared Memory Multiprocessors. In *Proceedings of the 12th ACM Symposium on Operating System Principles*, pages 159–166, 1989. ACM.

[The86] Marvin Theimer. *Preemptable Remote Execution Facilities for Loosely Coupled Distributed Systems*. Ph.D. thesis, Stanford University, Palo Alto, Calif., June 1986.

[TvRvS+90] Andrew S. Tanenbaum, Robert van Renesse, Hans van Staveren, Gregory J. Sharp, Sape J. Mullender, Jack Jansen, and Guido van Rossum. Experiences with the Amoeba Distributed Operating System. *Communications of the ACM*, 33(12), December 1990.

[VL87] George Varghese and Tony Lauck. Hashed and Hierarchical Timing Wheels: Data Structures for the Efficient Implementation of a Timer Facility. In *Proceedings of the 11th ACM Symposium on Operating Systems Principles*, pages 25–38, Austin, TX, November 1987. ACM.

[VL89] John M. Vlissides and Mark Linton. Unidraw: A Framework for Building Domain-Specific Graphical Editors. In *User Interface Software Technologies*, pages 81–94, 1989. ACM SIGGRAPH/SIGCHI.

[Weg87] Peter Wegner. Dimensions of Object-Based Language Design. In *Proceedings of OOPSLA '87*, pages 168–183, Orlando, Fla., October 1987.

[Yok92] Yasuhiko Yokote. The Apertos Reflective Operating System: The Concept and Its Implementation. In *Proceedings of the 1992 Conference on Object-Oriented Programming Systems, Languages and Applications*, pages 414–434, October 1992.

[YT87] Yasuhiko Yokote and Mario Tokoro. Concurrent Programming in ConcurrentSmalltalk. In Akinori Yonezawa and Mario Tokoro, editors, *Object-Oriented Concurrent Programming*, pages 129–158. MIT Press, Cambridge, Mass., 1987.

[YTR+87] Michael Young, Avadis Tevanian, Richard Rashid, David Golub, Jeffrey Eppinger, Jonathan Chew, William Bolosky, David Black, and Robert Baron. The Duality of Memory and Communication in the Implementation of a Multiprocessor Operating System. In *Proceedings of the 11th ACM Symposium on Operating Systems Principles*, pages 63–76, Austin, Tex., November 1987. ACM.

[Zim80] H. Zimmerman. OSI Reference Model—The ISO Model of Architecture for Open Systems Interconnection. In *IEEE Transactions on Communications*, pages 425–432, April 1980.

Index

ABOUT THE AUTHOR

Nayeem Islam is a research staff member at the IBM T. J. Watson Research Center. He leads a project on the design and implementation of an adaptable object-oriented operating system. Portions of the operating system will ship as part of IBM's product line.

He was one of the principle designers and implementors of Choices, an operating system built using object-oriented frameworks. This work has influenced many other research projects, such as the Spring operating system from Sun Microsystems as well as commercial projects at companies such as IBM and Microsoft. In particular, the technology has been used to build the AS/400 operating system and Microsystem OLE foundation classes. Prior to his work on operating systems, he was a project leader at Sun Microsystems where he led the design and implementation of an object-oriented graphical user interface tool kit. He made major contributions to the design and implementations of the Xt Intrinsics tool kit version four. The code and documentation for this product are used worldwide.